Lost Attractions of SILVER SPRINGS

Lost Attractions of SILVER SPRINGS

TIM HOLLIS

THE History PRESS

Published by The History Press
Charleston, SC
www.historypress.com

Cover images: author's collection.

First published 2018

Manufactured in the United States

ISBN 9781467139564

Library of Congress Control Number: 2018936073

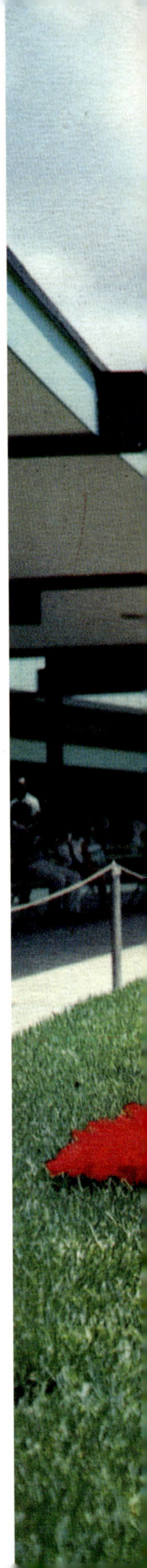

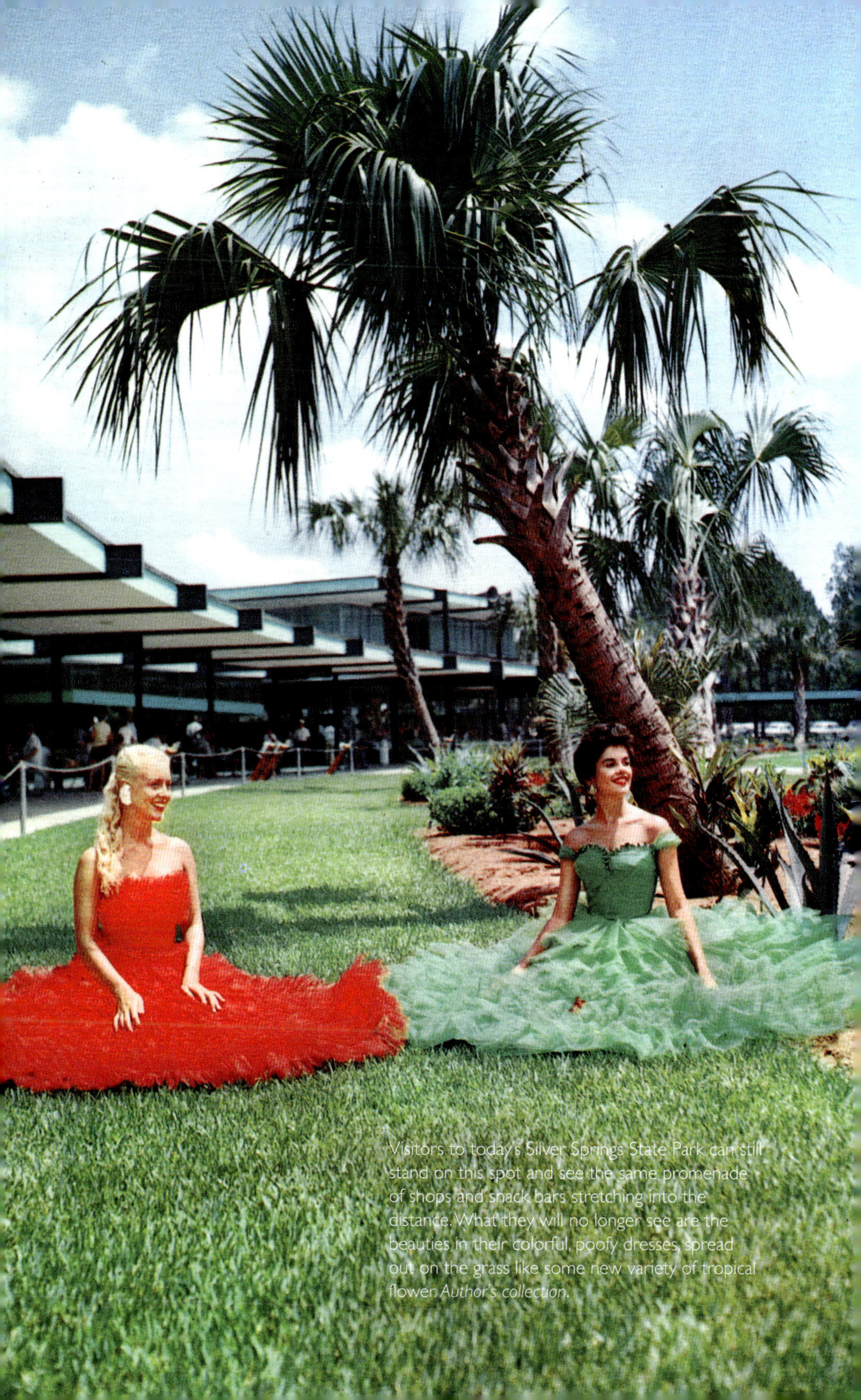

Visitors to today's Silver Springs State Park can still stand on this spot and see the same promenade of shops and snack bars stretching into the distance. What they will no longer see are the beauties in their colorful, poofy dresses spread out on the grass like some new variety of tropical flower. *Author's collection.*

CONTENTS

ACKNOWLEDGEMENTS

Some very helpful people were kind enough to share their information, memories and memorabilia during this book's assembly process: Rob Bradshaw, with probably the state's largest collection of Ocala Caverns artifacts; Chuck Keith, longtime denizen of Six Gun Territory; Craig Littauer, David Smith, Rayne Summers and Mickey Summers of Silver Springs State Park; Herby Moore, formerly of the Silver Springs Wax Museum; another wax museum enthusiast, Mark Pedro, with a special interest in the Prince of Peace Memorial; my dear friend Delee Perry, whose family has been involved in the area's tourism since the 1930s; and Brian Rucker, who started as a kid tourist and evolved into a scholar on the subject.

In addition, since some of this book was based on research conducted for my earlier treatments of the subject, I must reiterate my thanks to those who supplied material more than a decade ago: Ken Breslauer, Ricou Browning, Kitty Carr Carpenter, David Cook, Neal Frisbie, Ginger Stanley Hallowell, Bill Ray, Page Robinson, Steve Specht and Val Valentine.

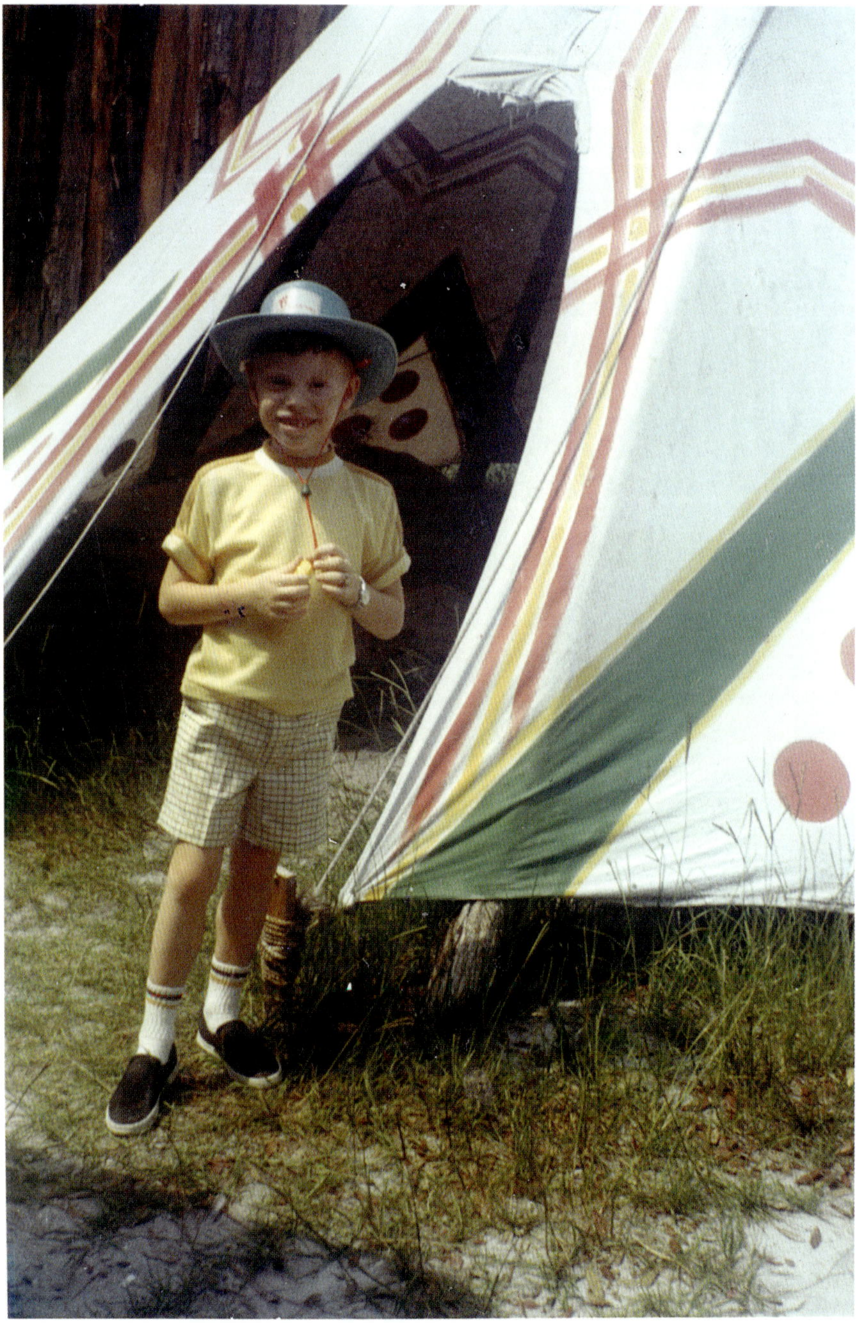

As with most of his previous books, the author began the preliminary research for this one many decades ago. Here he is at age seven with a souvenir cowboy hat keeping his wig warm in a wigwam at Six Gun Territory in 1970. *Author's collection.*

INTRODUCTION

Since there may be those readers who have not encountered the concept in past books, perhaps it would be best to begin here by explaining the title. Just what is a "lost attraction" of Silver Springs, anyway? Well, it is very simple. A lost attraction can be any type of tourism-related business—roadside attraction, motel, restaurant or other—that no longer exists. Casually flipping through the pages, one might conceivably run across an image and comment, "Hey, that place is still there!" That would bring us to the secondary definition: a business that has changed radically over the years and no longer resembles its depiction in vintage photos and postcards, even though technically it may still be operating (sometimes even under the same name, as with the Sun Plaza Motel).

This book is not intended to be a history of Silver Springs or the many tourist attractions that grew up around it in the hope of siphoning some overflow dollars. That story can be found in other books, including some by yours truly and others by some of my distinguished colleagues. Our purpose here is to concentrate on "things that ain't there no more," to use some typically blunt southern terminology. But, before diving headfirst into the springs and the collection of eye-popping color images that follow, perhaps it would be good to give a short background concerning the days preceding the earliest of those images.

Silver Springs made its first ripples as a tourist attraction in the years immediately following the Civil War as the destination at the end of steamboat trips down the Ocklawaha River. Surviving documentation makes it sound as if the journey to get to the springs warranted more attention than the springs themselves. This was the case in particular for those well-bred tourists from up north, to whom *anything* in the South seemed charmingly barbaric.

By the 1880s, Silver Springs was popular enough to boast its own hotel on the shore. But things began to change when a local businessman named Ed Carmichael bought Silver Springs and started his own fleet of boats powered by internal combustion engines, which certainly made the trip down the river faster, if less romantic. He had soon put the Ocklawaha steamboat lines out of business, but the effects of World War I had, in turn, put Carmichael's own boats into dry dock by 1919. It appeared that Silver Springs' popularity had run its course, and it once again sat in the middle of a dense forest, known only to a few local residents. (Carmichael, for his part, will be making a surprise guest appearance for us in the final chapter of this book.)

The biggest turning point in Silver Springs' history came about in 1924. That was when another Ocala businessman, William Carl Ray, started taking a second look at what was not being done with such a beautiful spot. Ray's son Bill explained what was on his pop's mind: "When my dad was a young man, he would visit Silver Springs, and he'd say, 'If people just knew about this place, they'd want to come and see it.' So, when he was older he wanted to lease the property—about eighty acres around the head of the spring. [Later, the attraction took in some four thousand acres.] Well, every time Dad thought he had a deal with Mr. Carmichael, the price would change. So finally, after one of their meetings, Dad left and parked his car where no one could see it and watched."

What Carl Ray saw as a result of his espionage confirmed his suspicions. Another businessman, W.C. "Shorty" Davidson, arrived and began dickering with Carmichael as well. This explained the mysteriously fluctuating price, and Ray immediately made it a point to have a private meeting with Davidson. He convinced his rival that as long as Carmichael was able to keep them bidding against each other, neither of them was ever going to get anywhere. Ray proposed that they join forces to acquire and operate Silver Springs, and that is exactly what happened. The attraction would be a venture of the firm of Ray and Davidson for the next four decades.

That is where things stood as the pages that follow got underway. We will be seeing how the Silver Springs park itself has changed through the years and how it took on a number of add-on attractions that boasted everything from snakes to baby deer to antique automobiles to the entire life of Christ. So popular was Silver Springs as a tourist draw that other attractions glommed onto the highways that led to it, including the legendary Six Gun Territory, the ever-changing Ocala Caverns and the barely remembered Silver Springs U-Drive-It Railroad—not to mention scores of motels and restaurants just waiting for those out-of-town visitors and their open wallets.

And now that you have been thoroughly versed in the prehistory, let's get in the car and head out State Highway 40. See who can be the first to spot the Silver Springs entrance up ahead on the right!

CHAPTER ONE

Silver Springs' Lost World

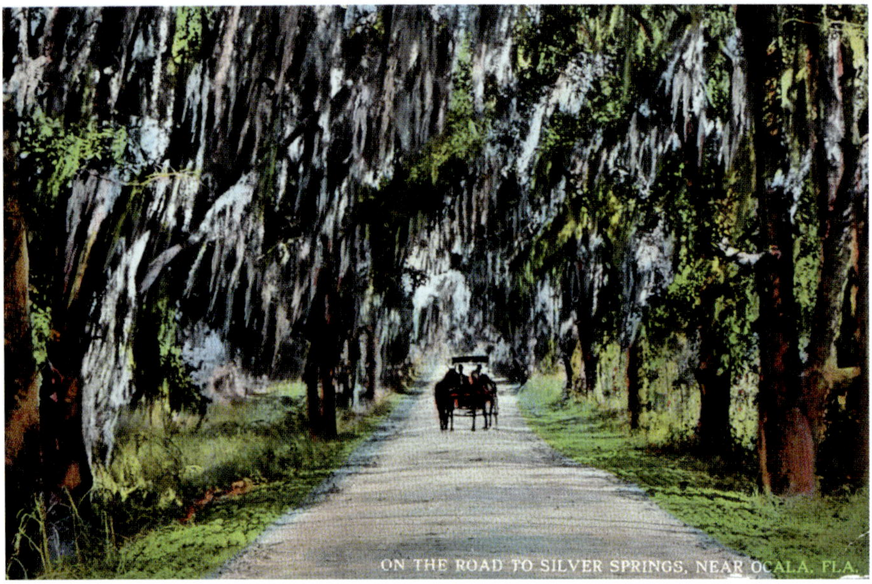

Even in the pre-automobile era, early Florida tourists were visiting Silver Springs. Most of them arrived by boat, but there were a few hardy souls who traveled a dirt road east of Ocala to where Silver Springs' natural, undeveloped beauty sat in the middle of the subtropical jungle. *Delee Perry collection.*

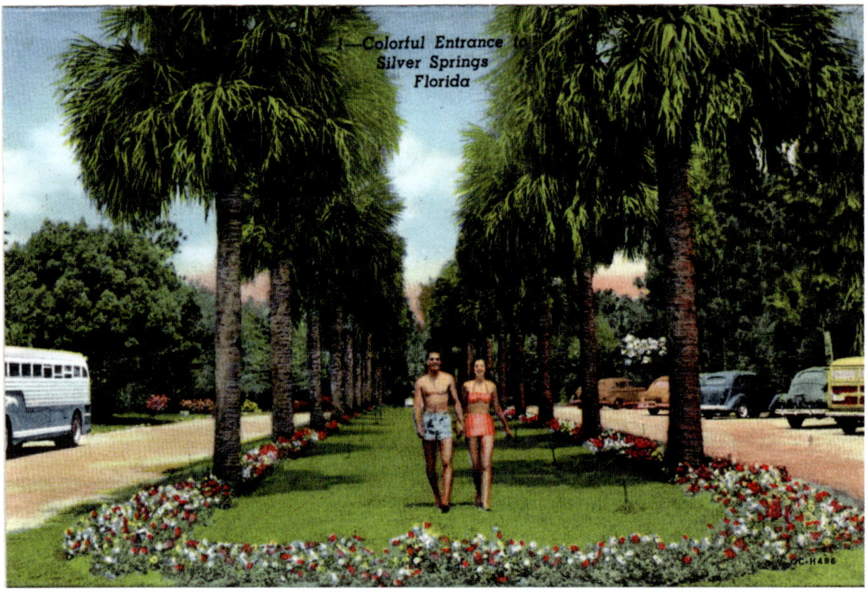

When that dirt road eventually became State Highway 40, Silver Springs finally developed into a true roadside attraction. This was the sight that greeted visitors at the original entrance. *Author's collection.*

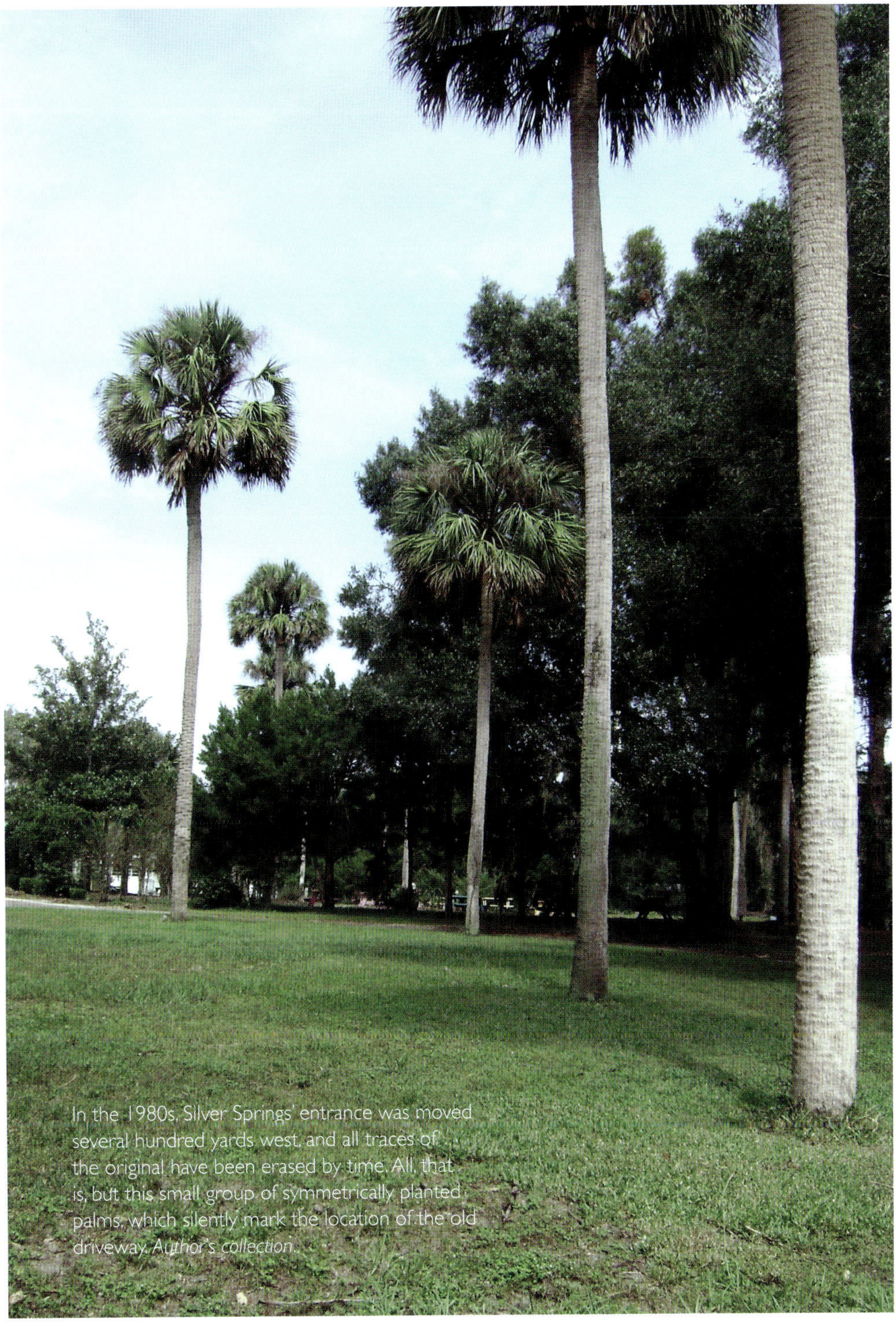

In the 1980s, Silver Springs' entrance was moved several hundred yards west, and all traces of the original have been erased by time. All, that is, but this small group of symmetrically planted palms, which silently mark the location of the old driveway. *Author's collection.*

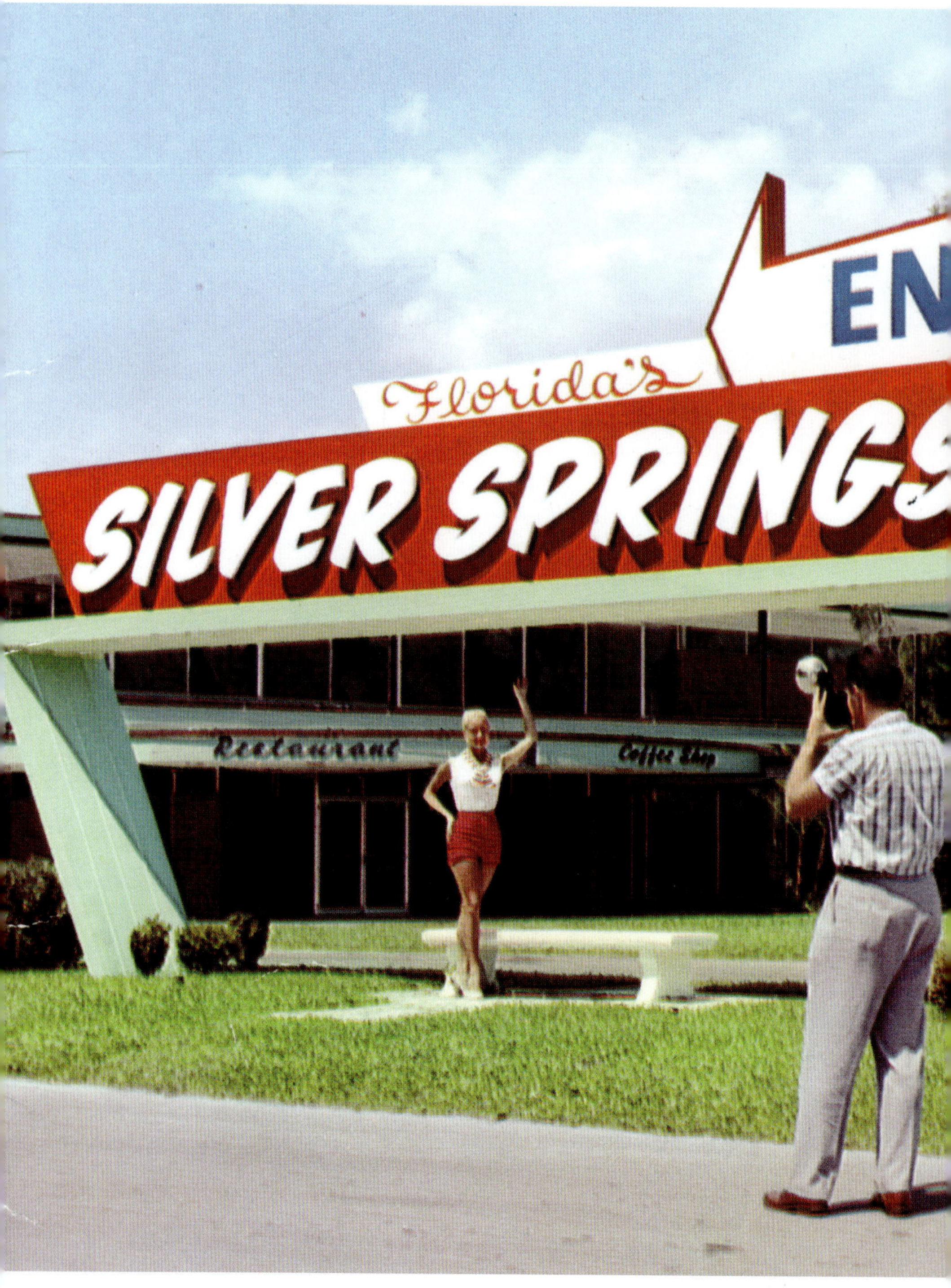
EN
Florida's
SILVER SPRINGS
Restaurant
Coffee Shop

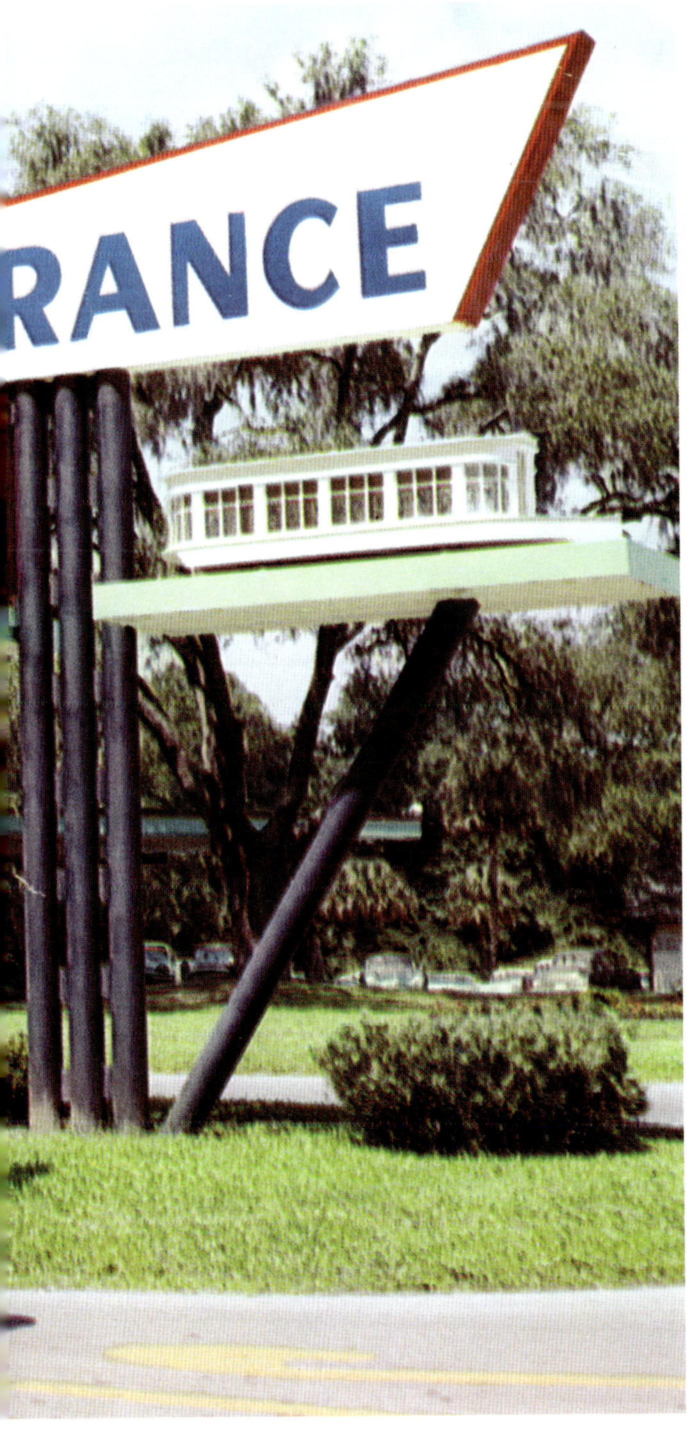

In the 1950s, the Silver Springs entranceway gained this geometric marvel of a sign. Behind the waving lady can be glimpsed the somewhat Art Deco cafeteria building; nothing visible remains of this entrance, but the old cafeteria structure still stands in dangerously decrepit condition. *Author's collection.*

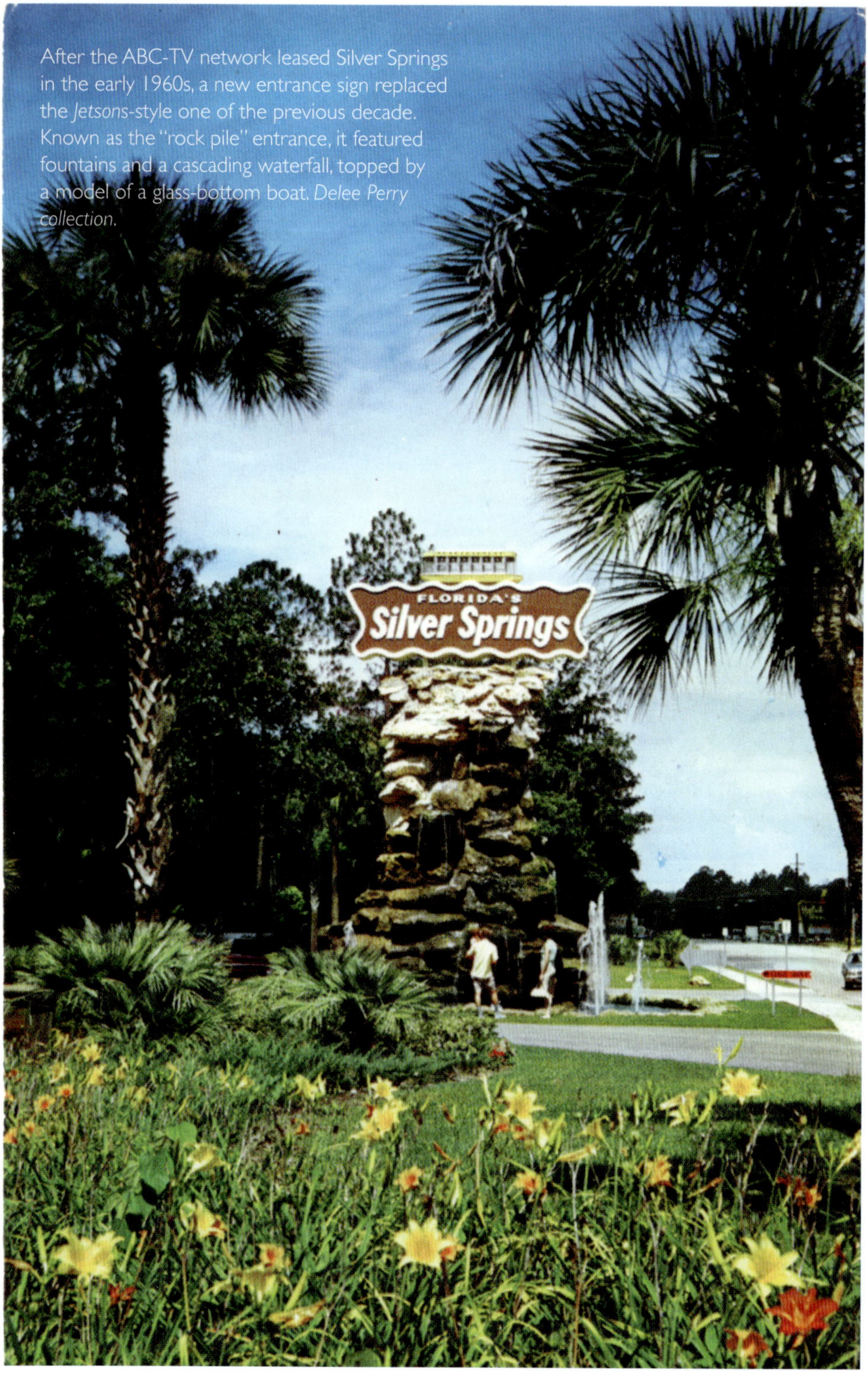

After the ABC-TV network leased Silver Springs in the early 1960s, a new entrance sign replaced the *Jetsons*-style one of the previous decade. Known as the "rock pile" entrance, it featured fountains and a cascading waterfall, topped by a model of a glass-bottom boat. *Delee Perry collection.*

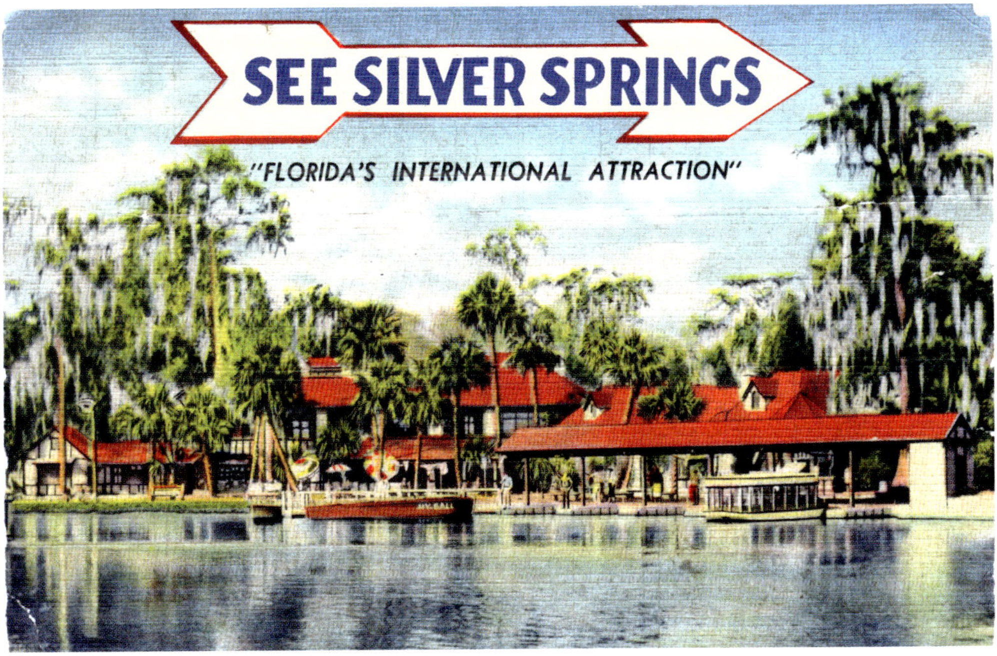

We now travel back to 1935, when this postcard folder was produced. The emblem at the top is one of the countless "silver arrows" that lined the U.S. highways of the South, pointing tourists in the right direction. *Author's collection.*

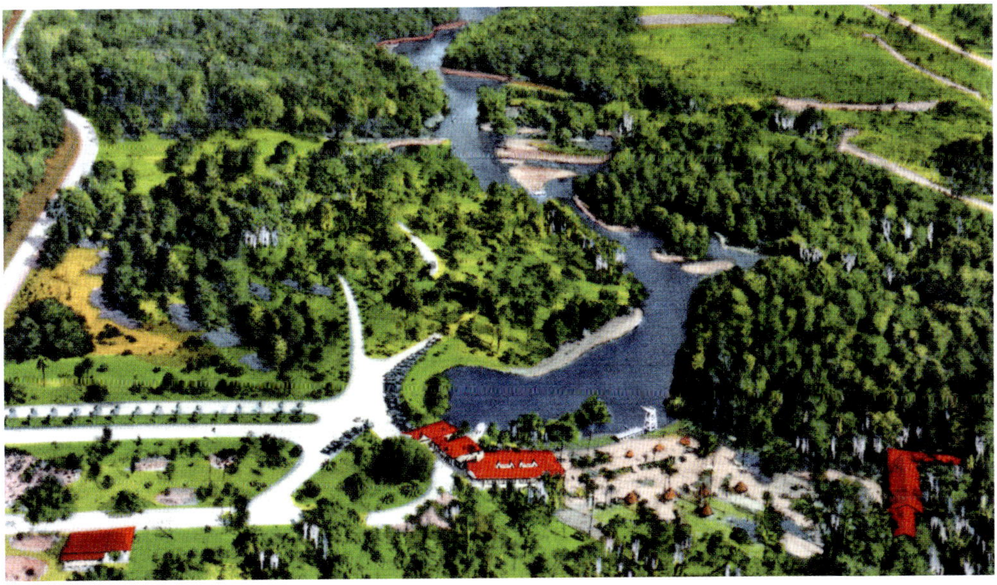

All one has to do is compare this 1930s aerial view of the entire Silver Springs property to a current Google view to see just how much of it has become a "lost attraction." The springs and the river they form are pretty much the only things that remain recognizable. *Author's collection.*

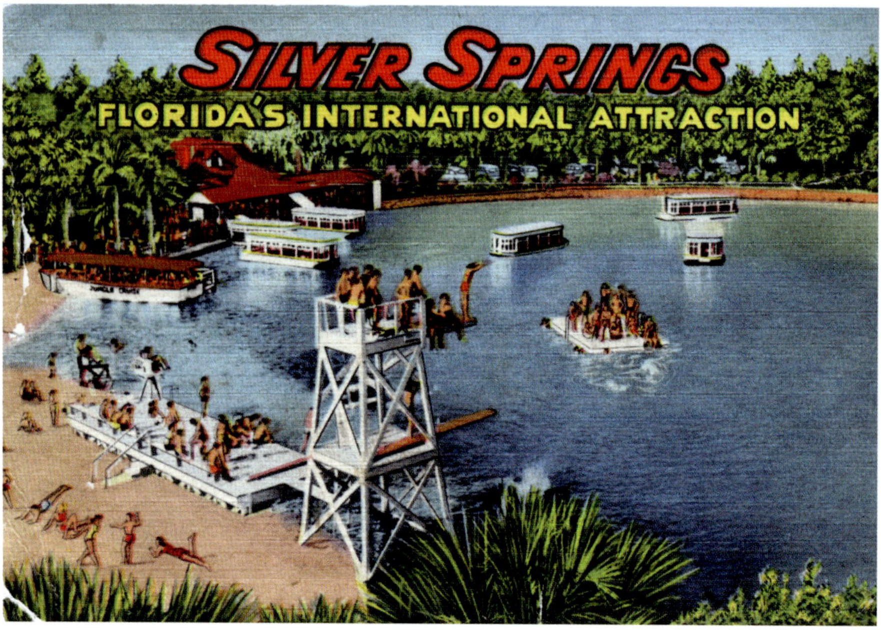

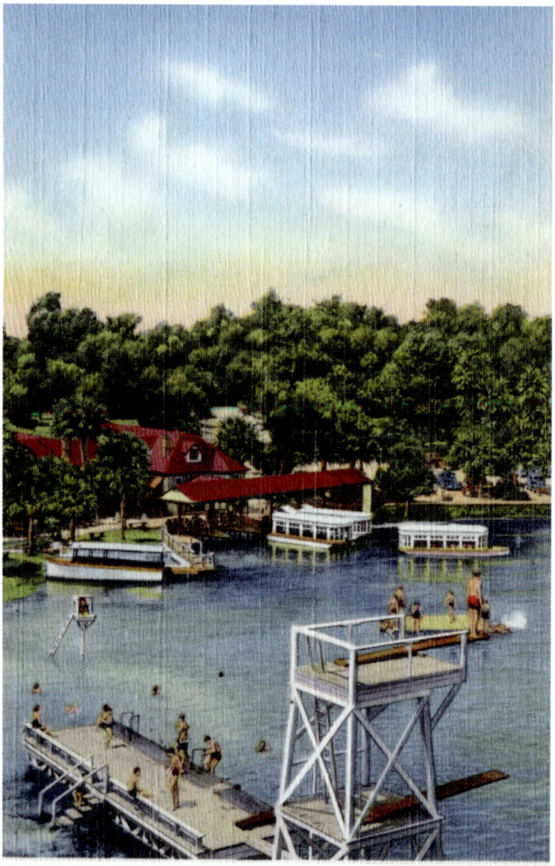

There was an amazing amount of activity in the water at the time of these 1940s postcard views. The skippers of the famed glass-bottom boats had to share their waterway with swimmers and those daring young people diving off a two-story platform. *Top, author's collection; bottom, Delee Perry collection.*

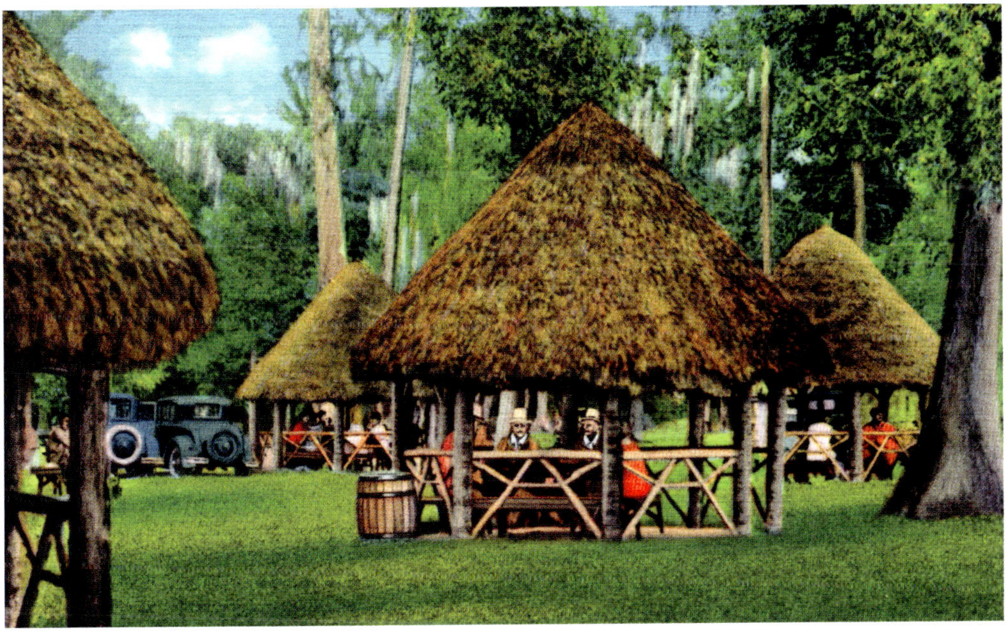

When not sloshing about in the water, tourists in the 1930s and '40s could enjoy a meal under these thatch-roofed picnic pavilions surrounded by moss-draped trees. *Author's collection.*

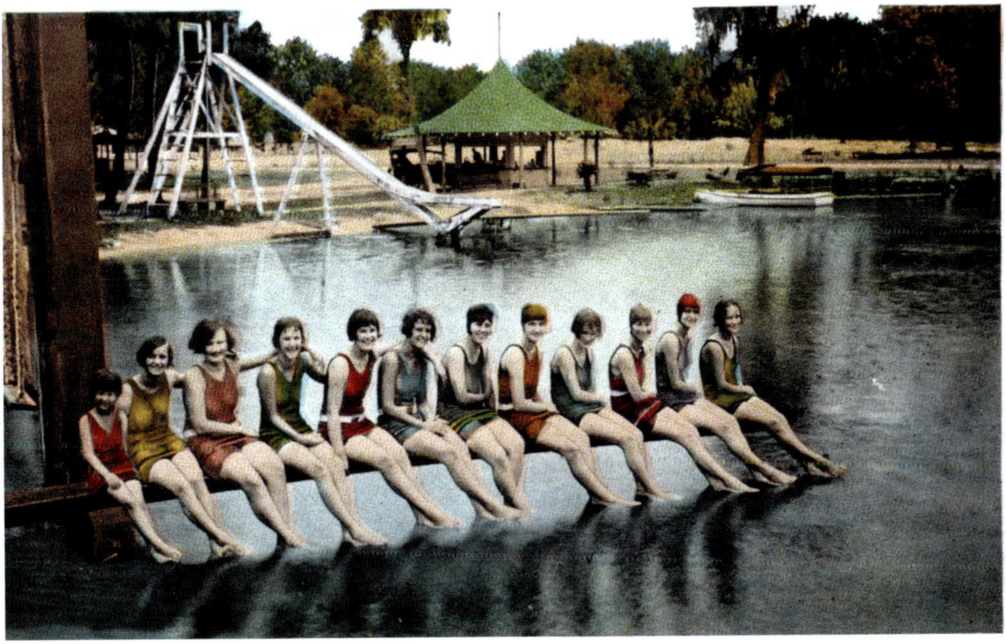

Of course, some folks in 1930, when this card was postmarked, might consider this much display of bare legs to rank high on the scandal meter...but Florida had long since discovered the best way to sell its myriad attractions, Silver Springs included. Notice the numerous pieces of playground equipment installed along the shores of the spring. *Delee Perry collection.*

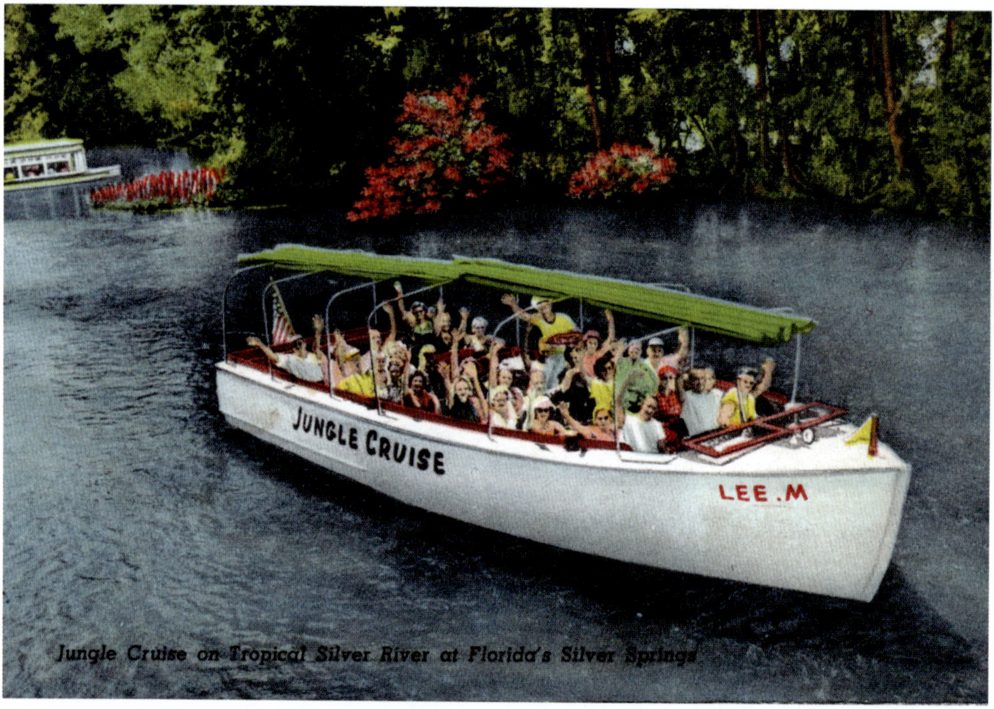
JUNGLE CRUISE
LEE. M
Jungle Cruise on Tropical Silver River at Florida's Silver Springs

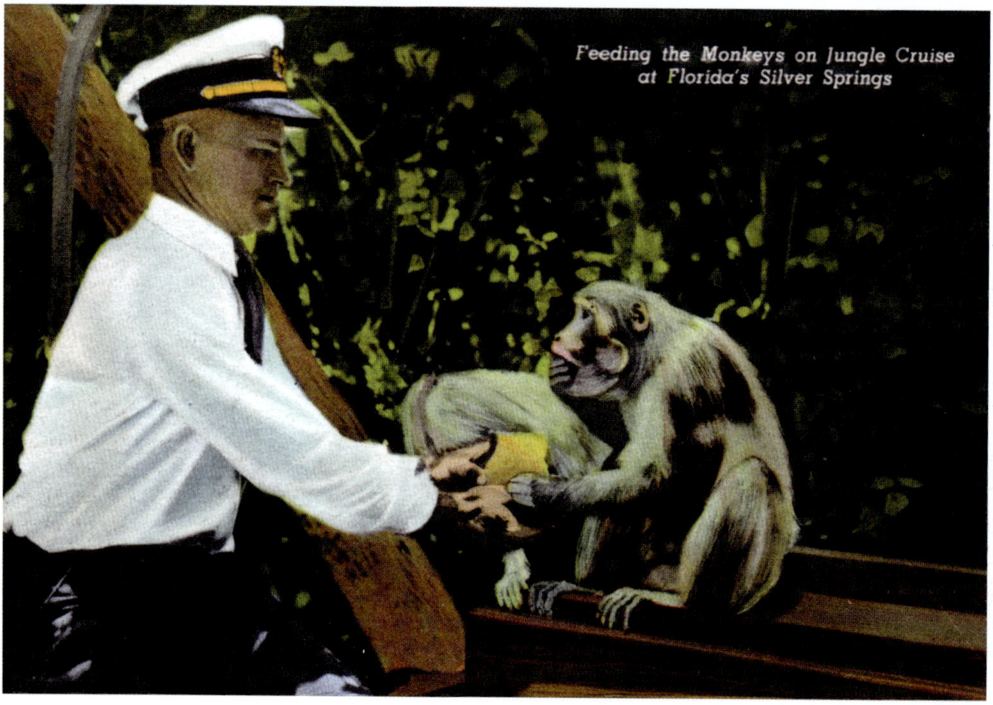
Feeding the Monkeys on Jungle Cruise
at Florida's Silver Springs

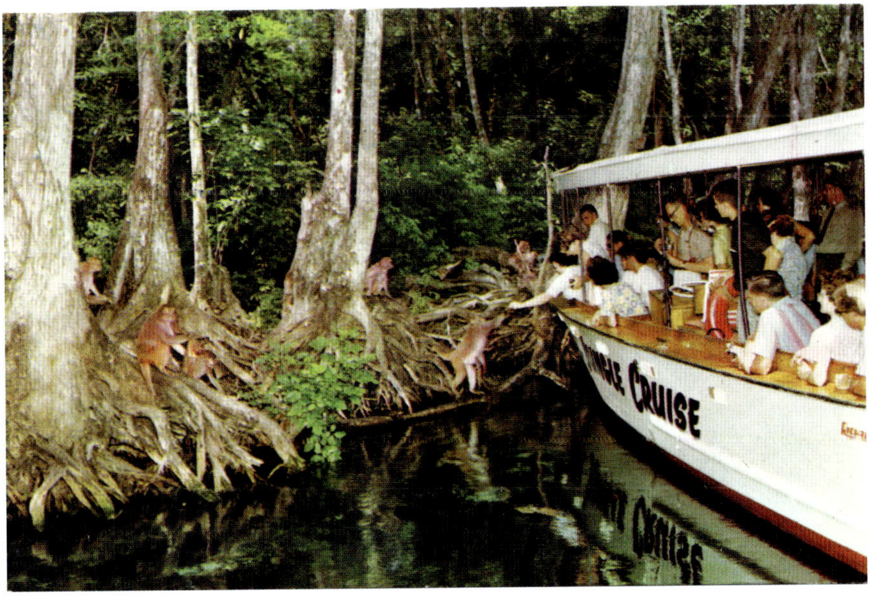

OPPOSITE, TOP: In the mid-1930s, an entrepreneur named Colonel Tooey—"Colonel" was actually his first name, not a title—started offering a "Jungle Cruise" that plied some of Silver Springs' backwaters, where the glass-bottom boats did not travel. Of course, Florida had plenty of jungle to go around, so there was room for all. *Author's collection.*

OPPOSITE, BOTTOM: To increase interest in his Jungle Cruise, Tooey imported rhesus monkeys and installed them on an island. They immediately escaped to shore, and their descendants still populate the jungle along the riverbank to this day, prompting warning signs to be posted throughout the park. *Author's collection.*

ABOVE: The Jungle Cruise became the longest-lived of all the ancillary attractions at Silver Springs. It operated all the way until the property became a Florida State Park in 2013. Vintage photos such as this one horrify today's park rangers, as human/monkey interaction is strictly forbidden—for the safety of both parties. *Author's collection.*

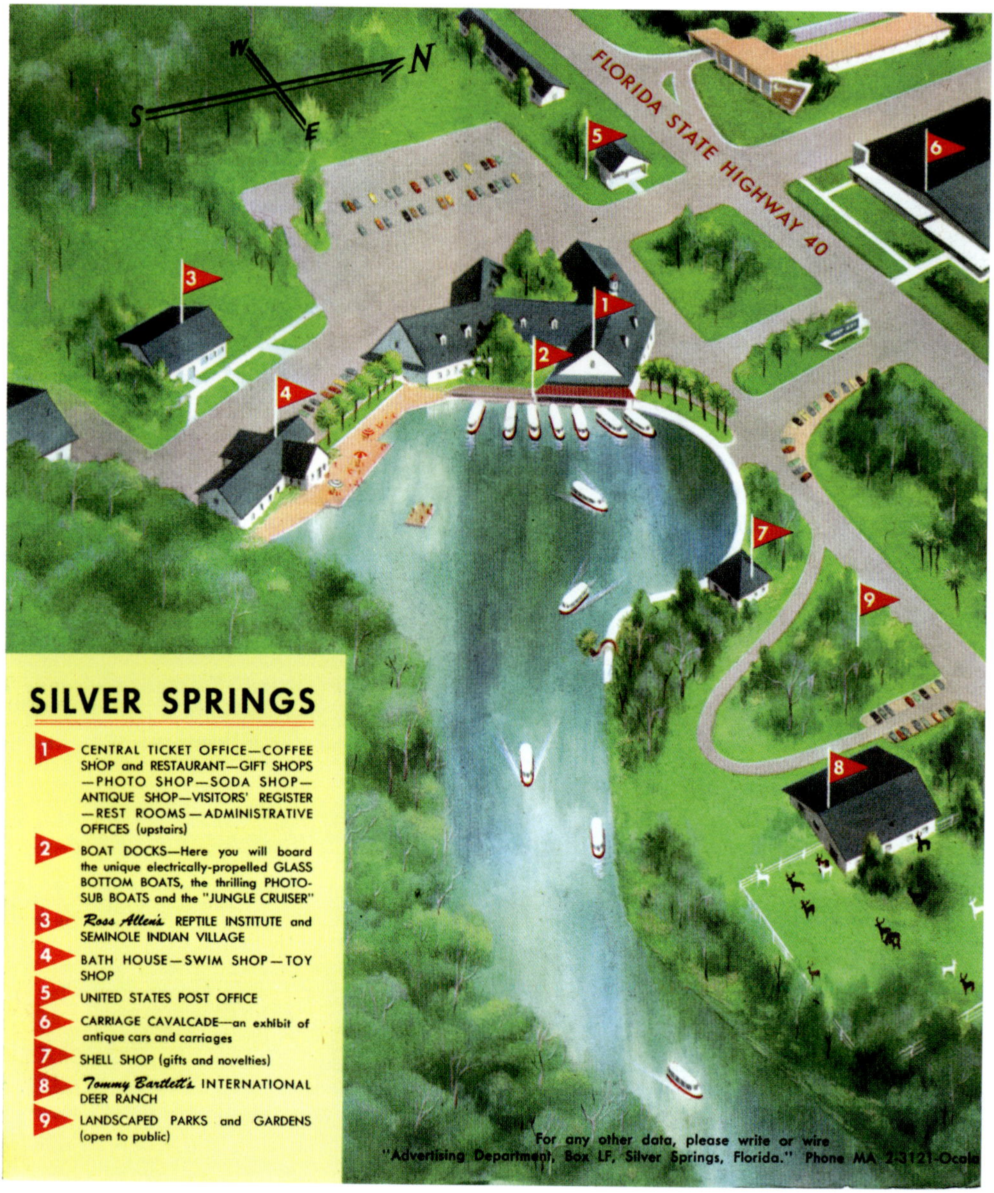

By the early 1950s, Silver Springs' Jungle Cruise had been joined by a number of other concessions, all of which will be explored in more depth in upcoming chapters. This park map from that period shows the relative locations of them all. *Author's collection.*

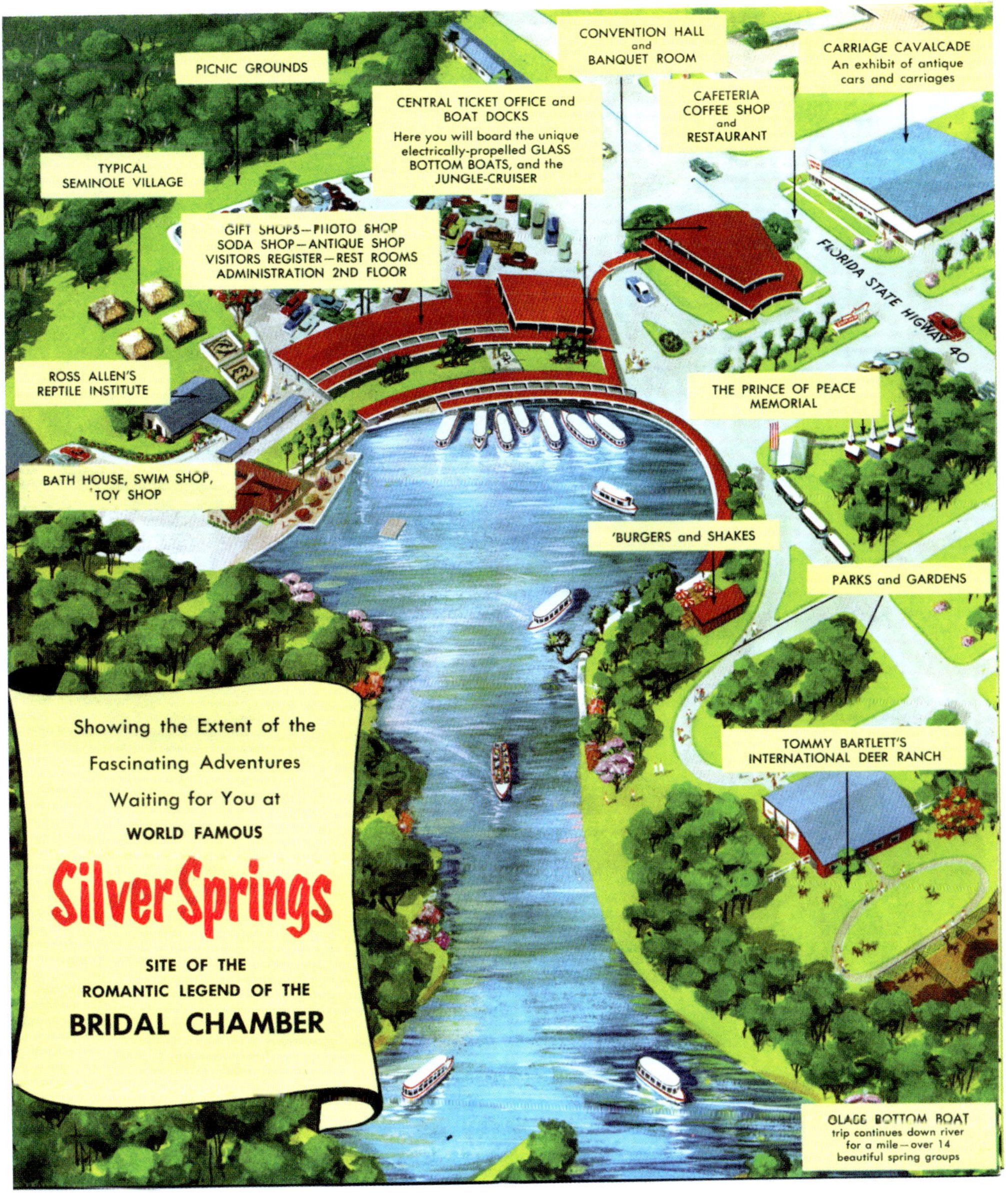

Here is an updated park map from just a few years after the previous one; as you can see, things had gotten a bit more crowded in the interim. The primary change had been due to a fire that consumed the original 1930s gift shops, restaurant and boat docks in 1955; hence, the new space age–style structures that replaced them. *Author's collection.*

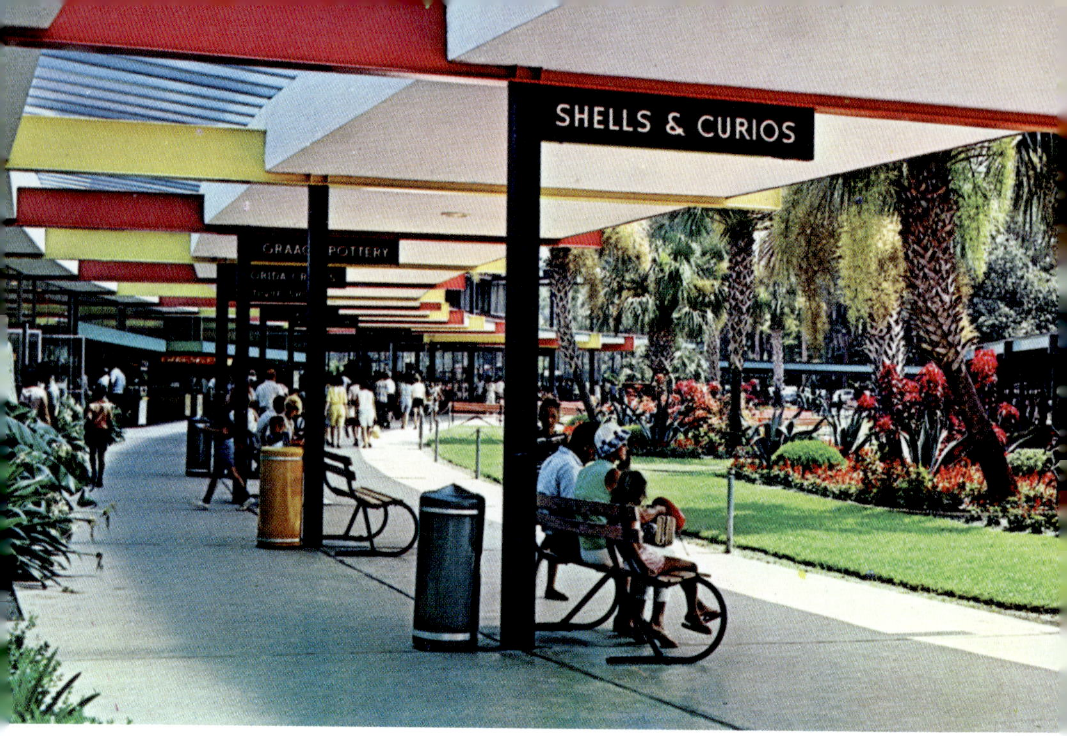

ABOVE: Here is the "promenade" as it was rebuilt after the 1955 fire. This view can still be enjoyed today, except that things are considerably less colorful, thanks to changing public tastes and the control of the Florida State Parks Department. *Author's collection.*

OPPOSITE, TOP: One "lost attraction" you will no longer find at Silver Springs is the traditional bumper sticker. At most major tourist attractions, it was customary to have a staff of workers place a bumper sticker on each car in the parking lot—no permission needed or granted. The blonde beauty doing the job here is Ginger Stanley, one of Silver Springs' major models of the era. *Ginger Stanley Hallowell collection.*

OPPOSITE, BOTTOM: Here is Ginger Stanley again, this time in glorious living color. Posters similar to this one were re-created as billboards throughout the South, but especially along Florida's many busy tourist highways. *Author's collection.*

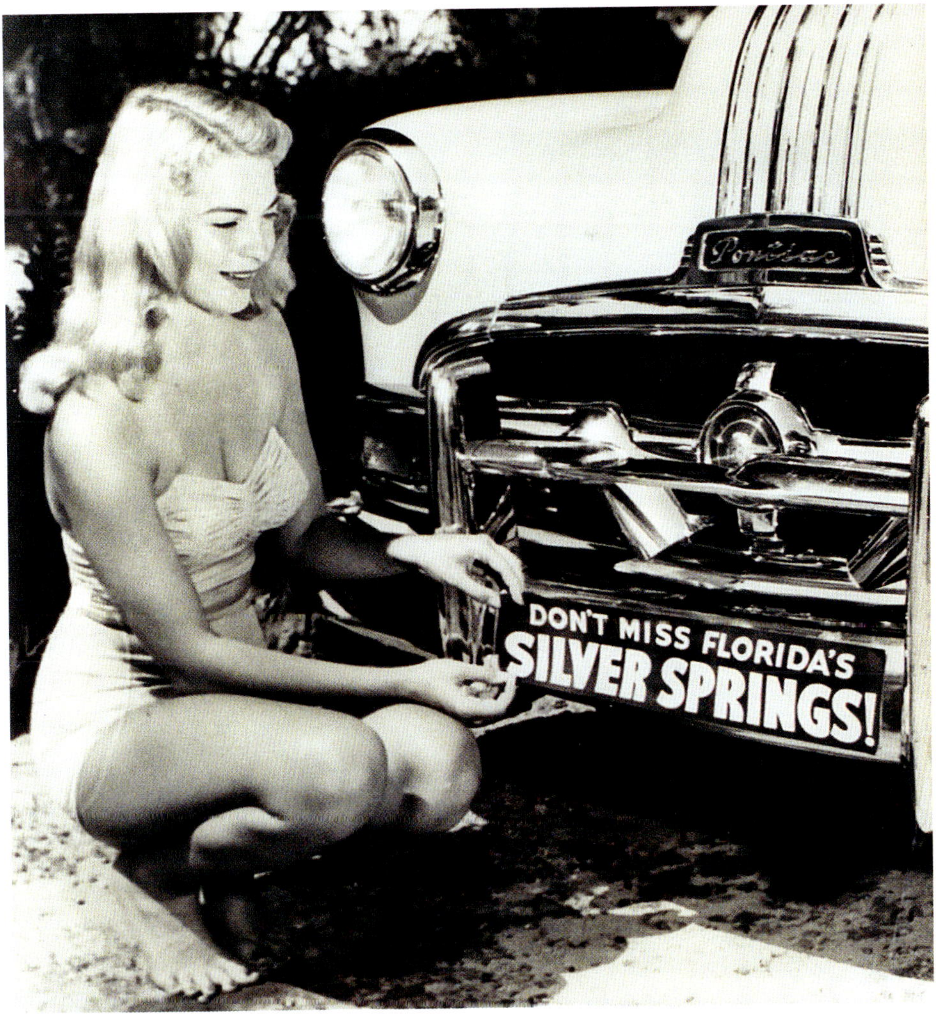
Pontiac
DON'T MISS FLORIDA'S
SILVER SPRINGS!

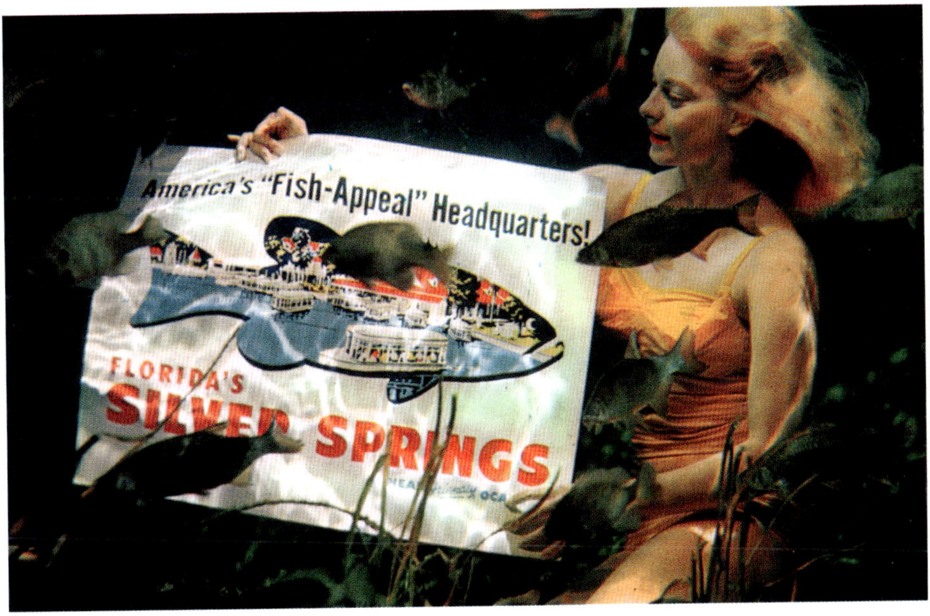
America's "Fish-Appeal" Headquarters!
FLORIDA'S

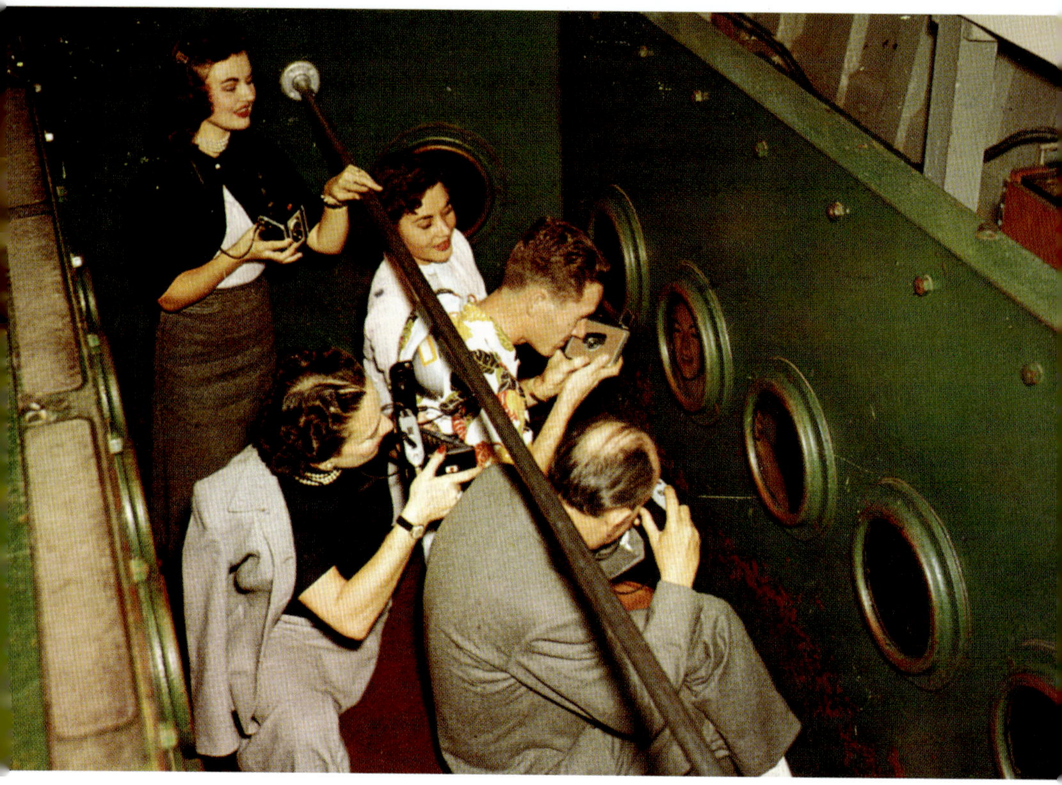

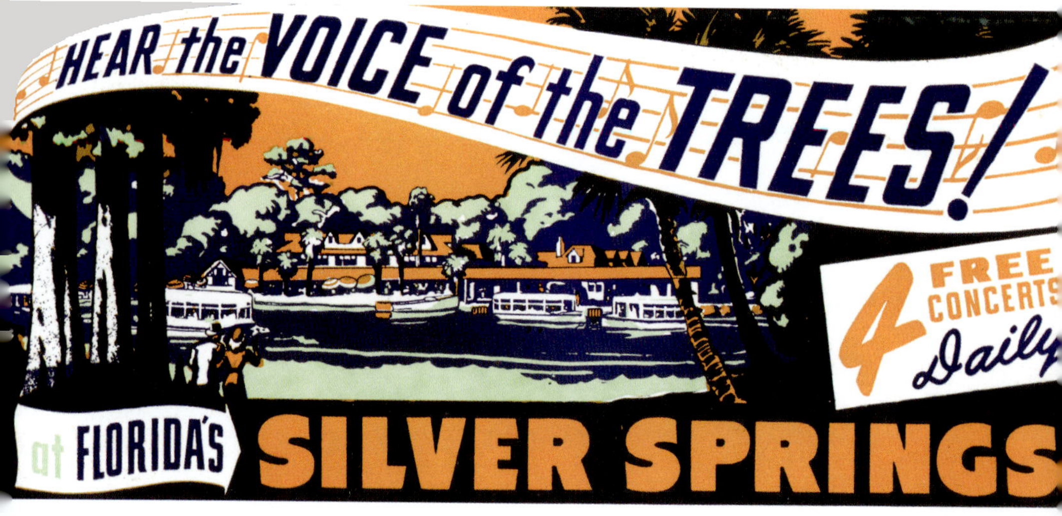
HEAR the VOICE of the TREES!
4 FREE CONCERTS Daily
at FLORIDA'S SILVER SPRINGS

OPPOSITE, TOP: An almost forgotten feature at Silver Springs was the "Photo-Sub," where tourists did not just look at the underwater world from a glass-bottom boat but were also actually submerged to view the sights through portholes. As we shall see several pages from now, this idea was actually lifted from another attraction that also later became a Florida State Park. *Delee Perry collection.*

OPPOSITE, BOTTOM: What in the name of the Wizard of Oz was the "Voice of the Trees," you ask? For a time in the 1950s, Silver Springs had hidden speakers among the branches, and chimes concerts would be given periodically throughout the day. *Author's collection.*

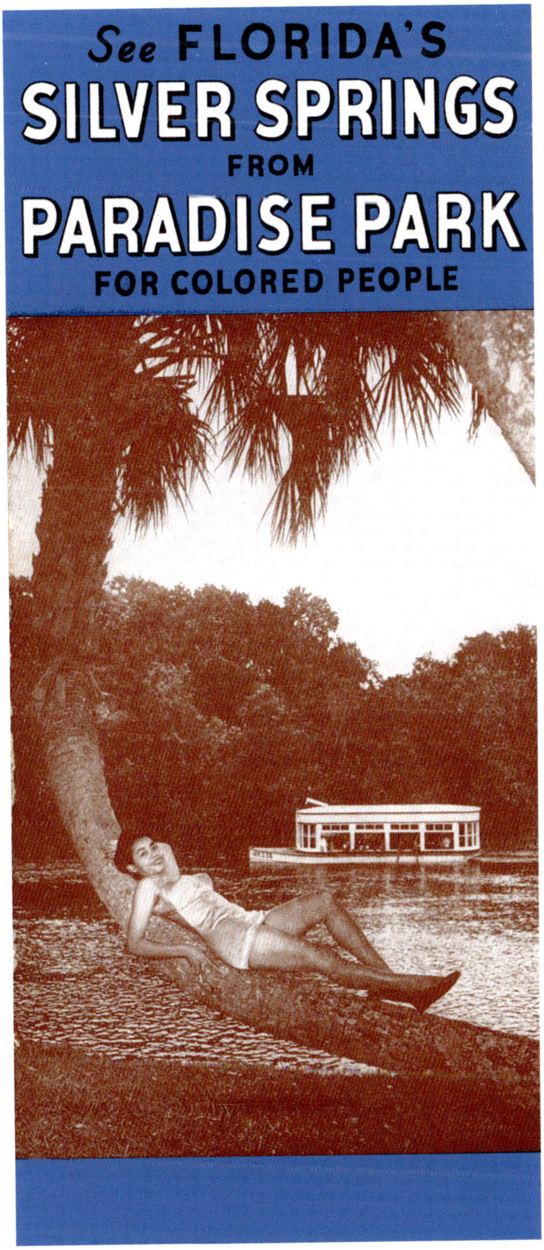

RIGHT: Some attractions are "lost" for good reason. Knowing the customs of the South at the time, it should not be surprising that those individuals who happened to not be white were prohibited from visiting Silver Springs proper. For them, the attraction's owners presented Paradise Park, which offered glass-bottom boat rides and several other attractions. Somewhat ironically, its thriving business was curtailed by the end of legalized segregation, and it closed in 1969. *Ken Breslauer collection.*

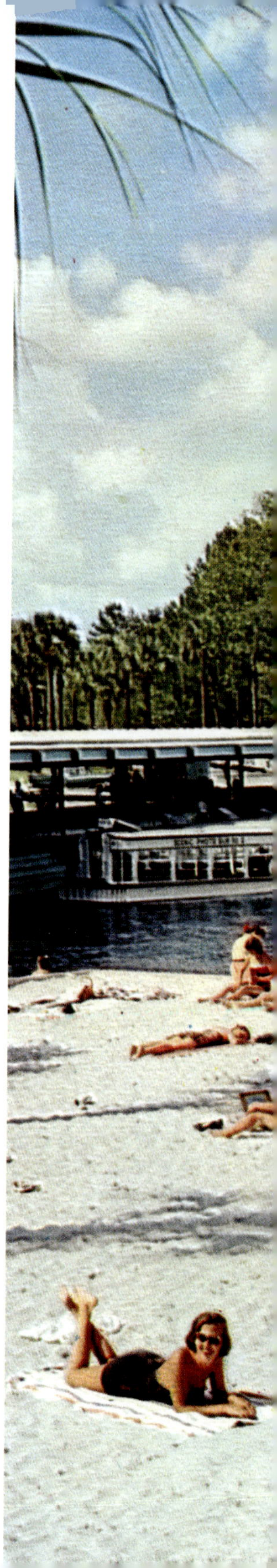

Naturally, many of the thousands of tourists who visited Florida annually were there to enjoy the white sand beaches. Since Silver Springs was in the center of the peninsula, an hour away from the nearest beach, the park did the next best thing and created a sandy white shoreline of its own. *Author's collection.*

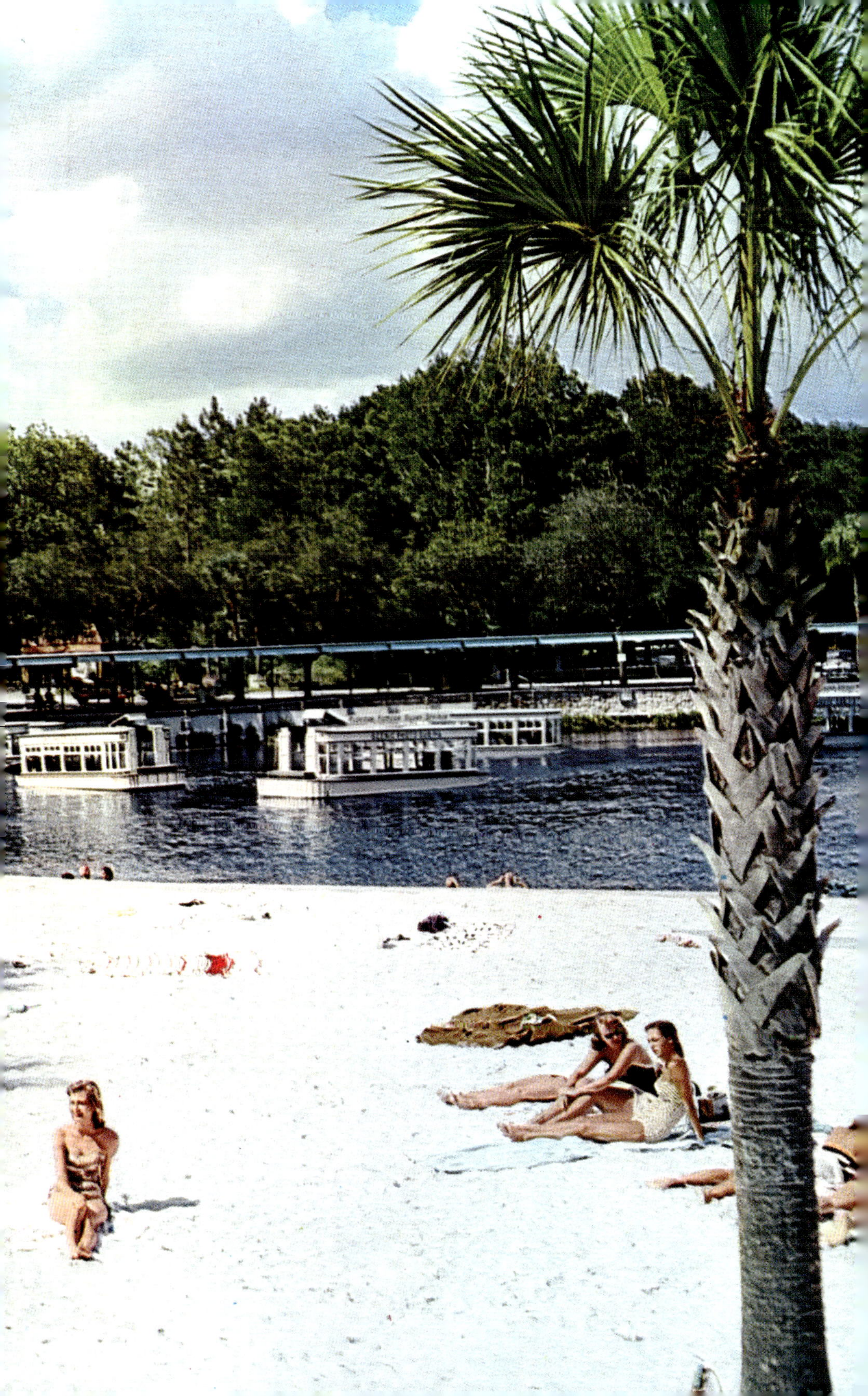

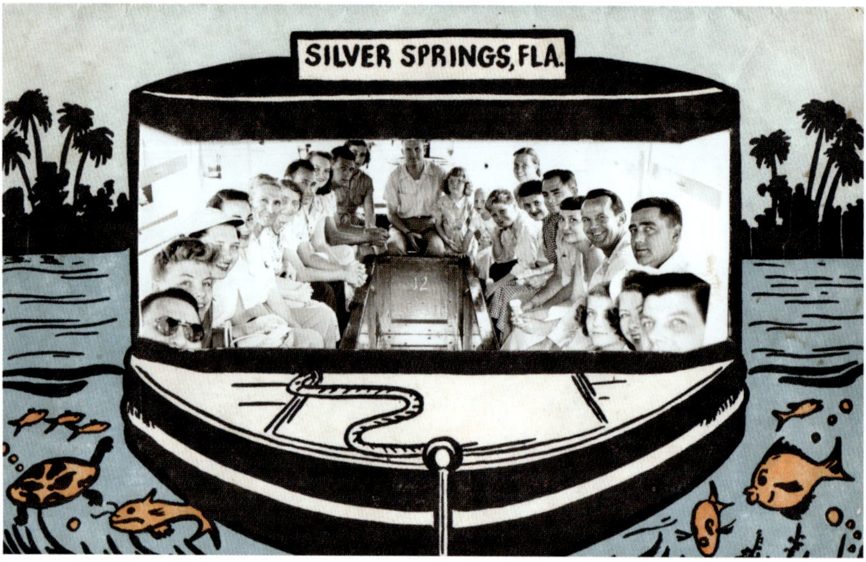

ABOVE: One tradition that faded away over time was the custom of having a group photo taken of each glass-bottom boatload of passengers. Once developed, the black-and-white photos could be purchased in a variety of colorful folders. The downside to this was that everyone ended up with photos in which they had no idea who 95 percent of the people were. *Author's collection.*

OPPOSITE, TOP: Underwater stunts were an everyday ritual for those who worked at Silver Springs. It was not unusual for a swimmer to suddenly appear in the porthole of the Photo-Sub or in the window of a glass-bottom boat, just to get a rise out of the tourists. *Author's collection.*

OPPOSITE, BOTTOM: Another facility for getting a good view of submarine life—whether human or piscatorial—was Silver Springs' "aquatarium," which allowed visitors to literally walk under water. As with some of the park's other attractions, this was a variation on an idea already being handled with great success at the Homosassa Springs park on the Gulf Coast side of Florida. *Author's collection.*

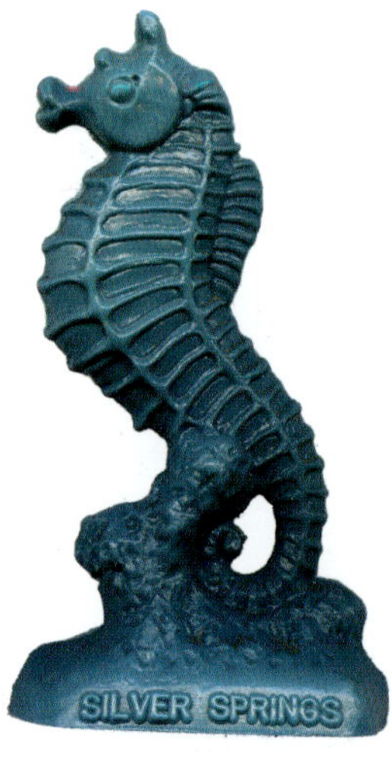

RIGHT: Does the name "Mold-a-Rama" mean anything to you? The company's coin-operated machines were staples of nearly every tourist attraction in the 1960s and can still be found occasionally today. With the deposit of the necessary funds, a mold would open, melted wax poured in and baked, and a hollow wax souvenir figure dropped out, all within the span of a few minutes. *Author's collection.*

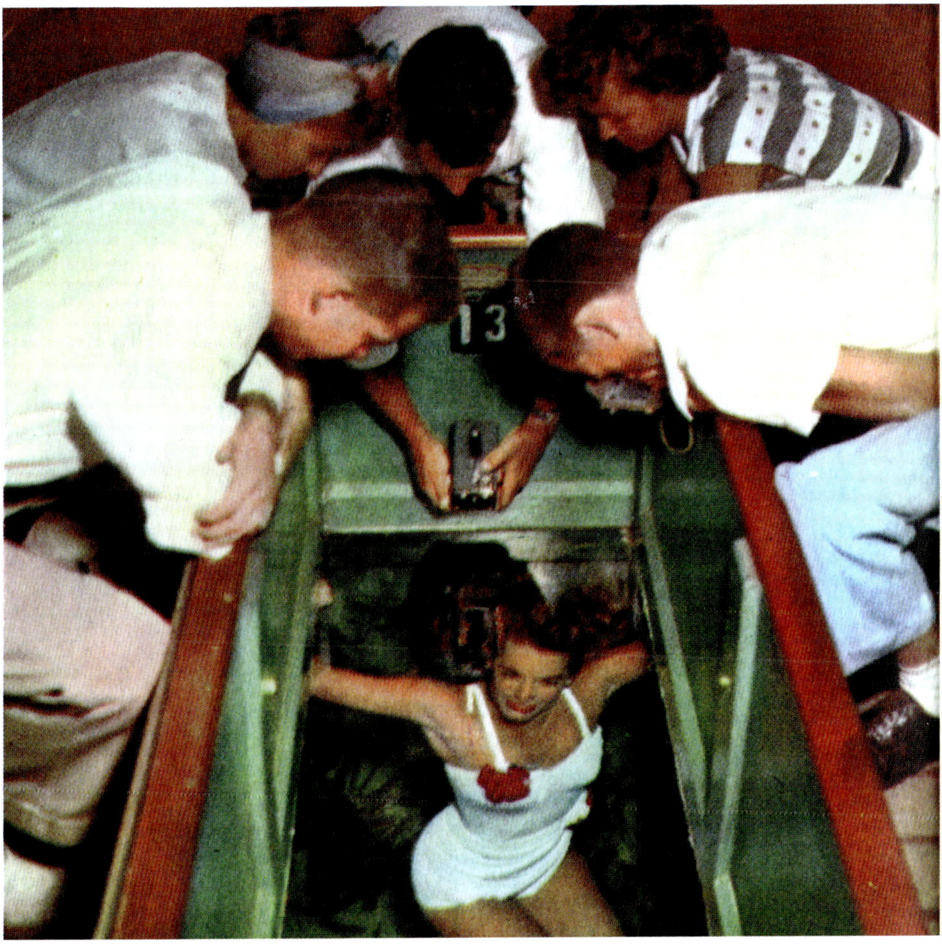

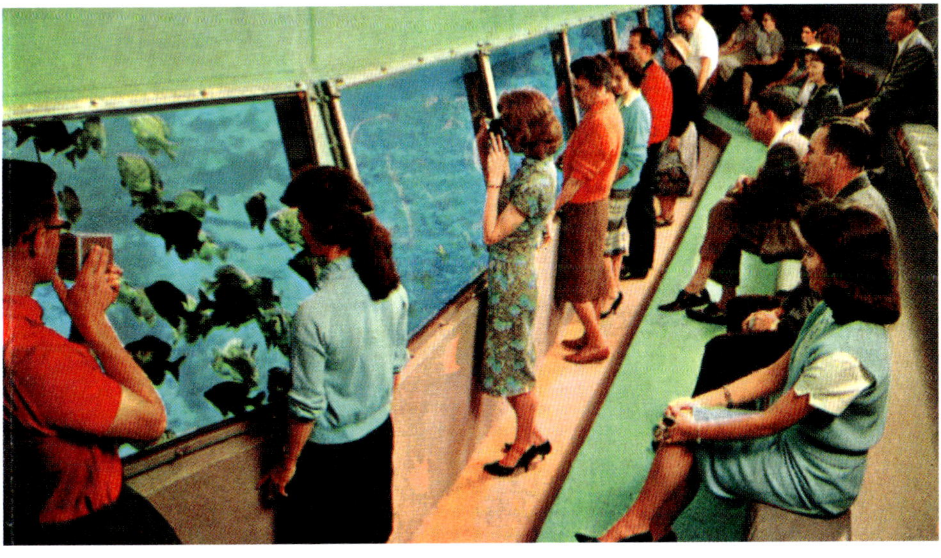

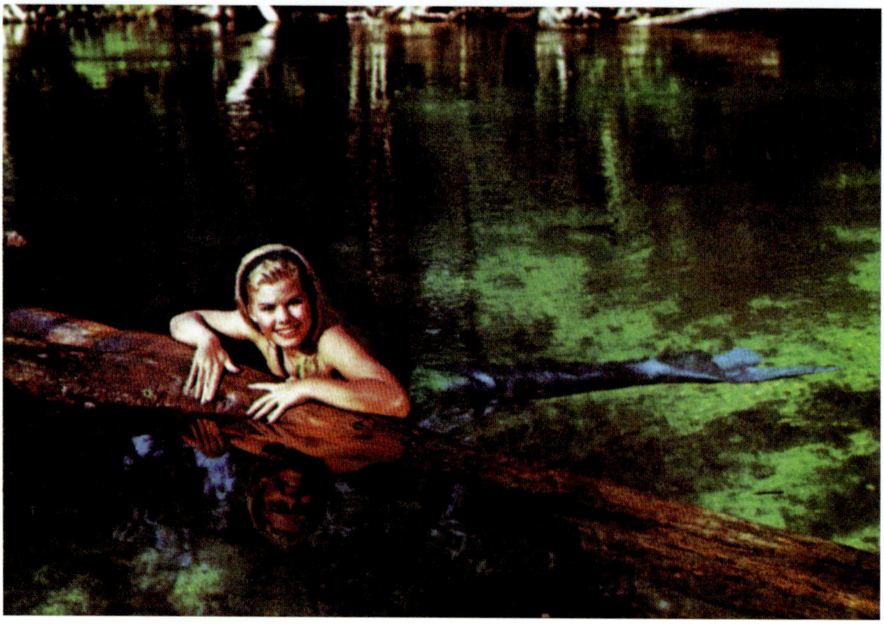

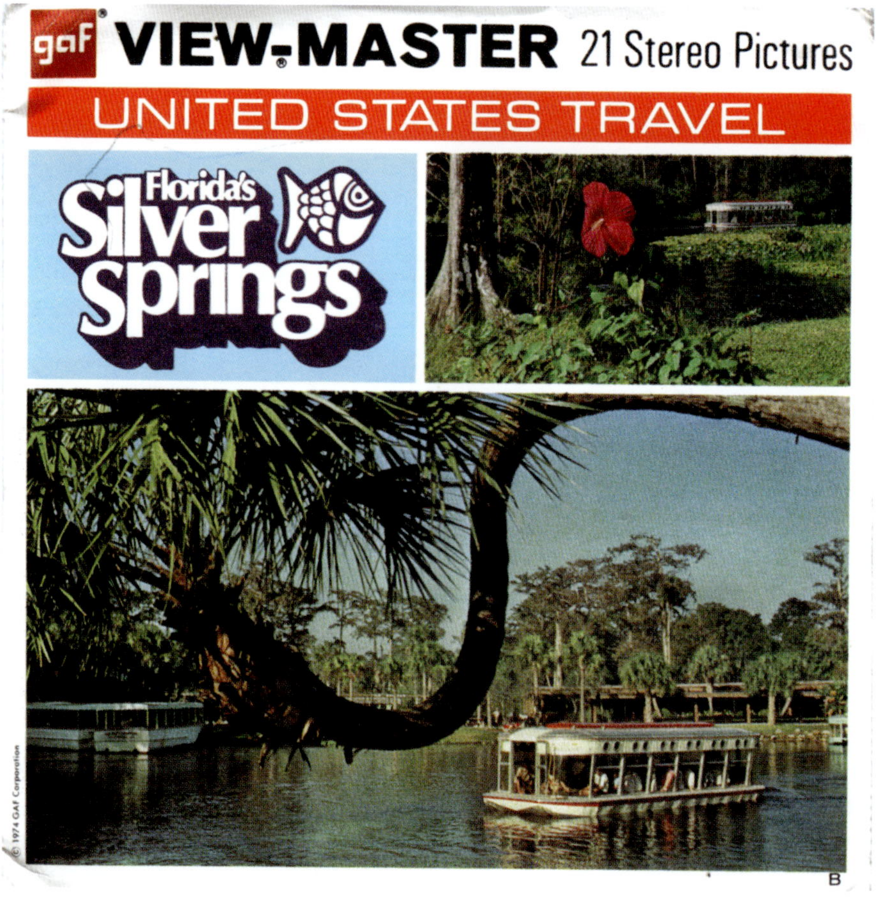
gaf
VIEW-MASTER 21 Stereo Pictures
UNITED STATES TRAVEL
Florida's Silver springs
© 1974 GAF Corporation
B

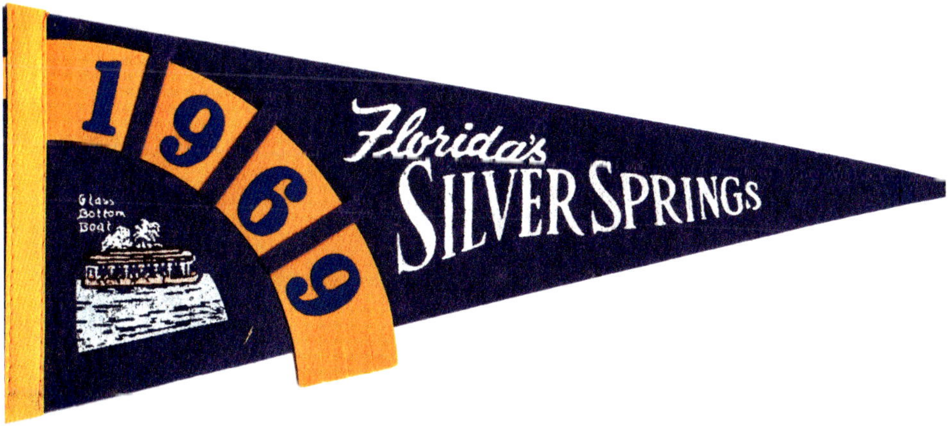

OPPOSITE, TOP: While many well-known movies and TV series were filmed at Silver Springs through the decades, there were also some that are forgotten today. One of those was *Mike and the Mermaid* (1964), which co-starred lovely Jerri Lynn Fraser as the second half of the title duo. *Author's collection.*

ABOVE: Felt pennants have long been a fixture of any attraction's souvenir shop. As you can see, there was a period when Silver Springs' pennants were customized annually to commemorate the year of that visit. *Author's collection.*

OPPOSITE, BOTTOM: Another ubiquitous souvenir was the packet of three View-Master reels. The goggle-eyed fish seen as part of the Silver Springs logo on this 1970s example was featured on numerous pieces of merchandise during this era. *Author's collection.*

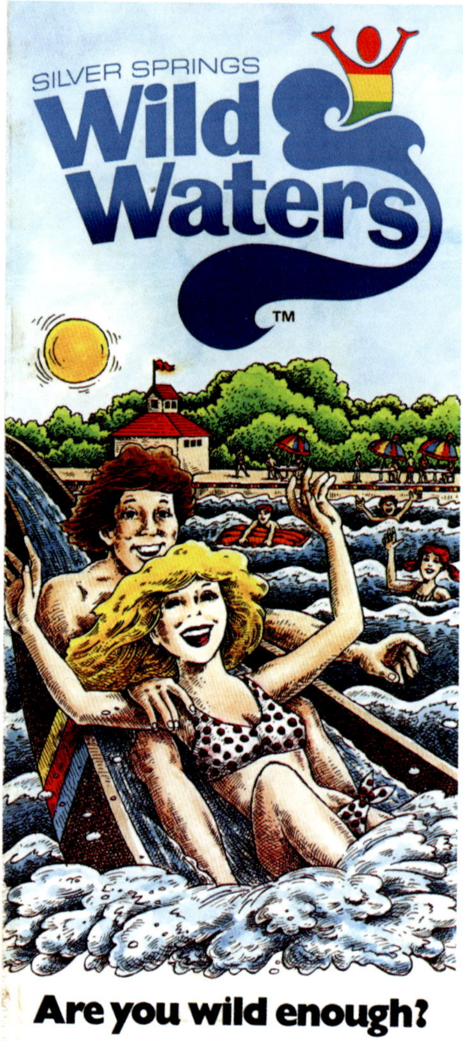

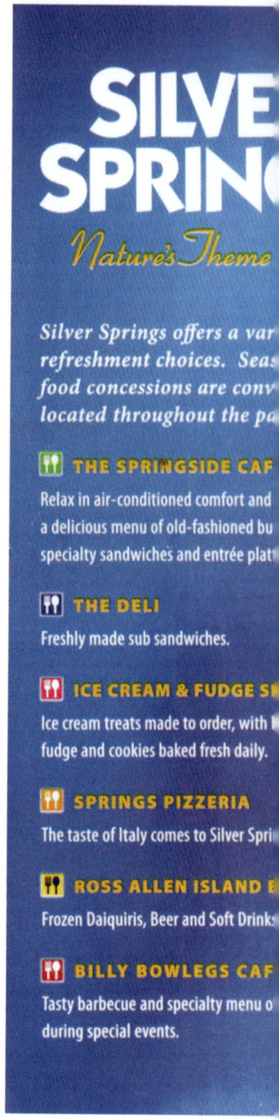

ABOVE: There was a nationwide craze for water parks in the late 1970s, and Silver Springs' answer was Wild Waters, a splashy second park located on the other side of the parking lot from the original attraction. Opened in 1978, it produced glass-bottom boatloads of soaking youngsters for nearly forty years. *Author's collection.*

OPPOSITE, TOP: Comparing this park map from 2006 with the 1950s examples shown earlier truly indicates how desperately Silver Springs was trying to compete with central Florida's multimillion-dollar theme park industry—and that does not even include the Wild Waters section. When Silver Springs became a Florida State Park in 2013, one of the first orders of business was to remove any of the remaining artificial attractions that had been grafted onto the property. *Author's collection.*

OPPOSITE, BOTTOM: Since a water park hardly fit the "naturetainment" theme of a state park, Wild Waters was closed after the 2016 season and scheduled for demolition. It would join its earlier brethren, such as the Deer Ranch and the Reptile Institute, as a lost attraction on Silver Springs' property. *Author's collection.*

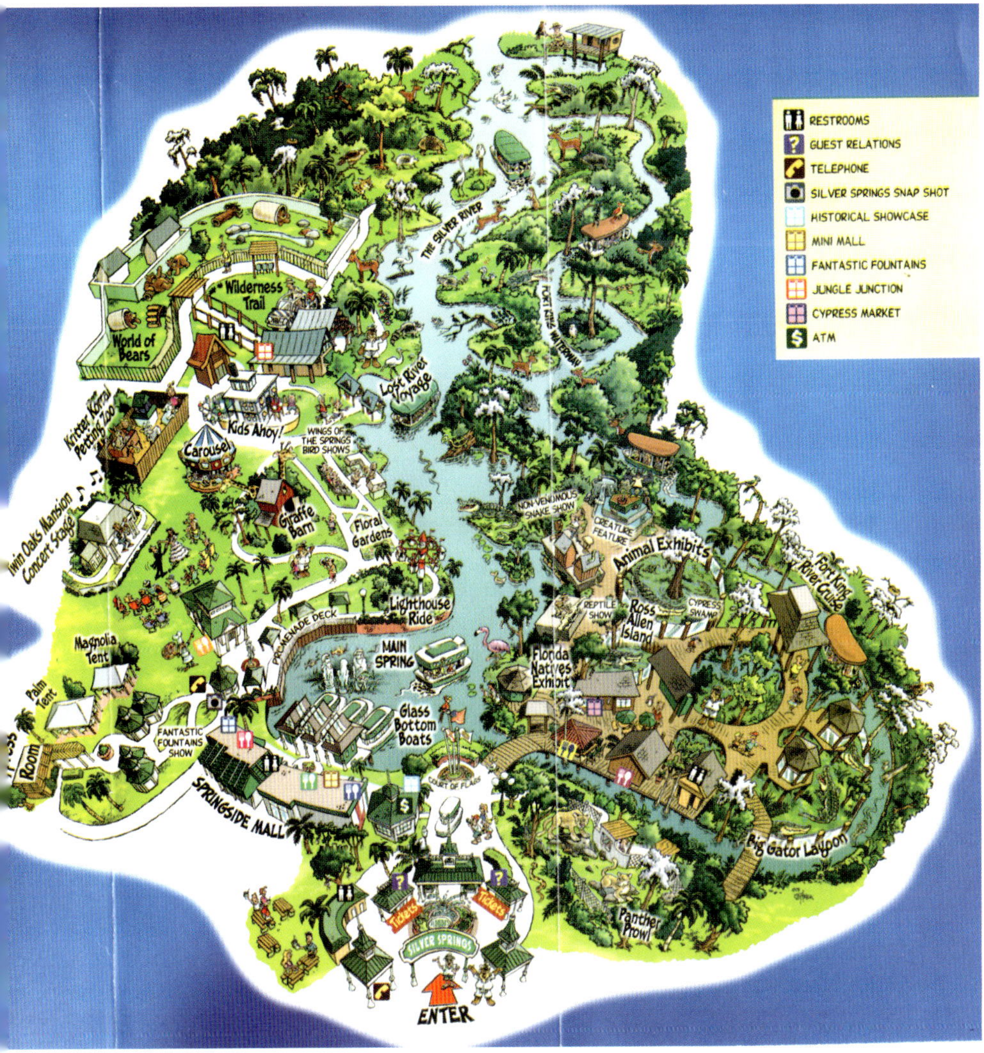

RESTROOMS
GUEST RELATIONS
TELEPHONE
SILVER SPRINGS SNAP SHOT
HISTORICAL SHOWCASE
MINI MALL
FANTASTIC FOUNTAINS
JUNGLE JUNCTION
CYPRESS MARKET
ATM
World of Bears
Wilderness Trail
The Silver River
Fort King Waterway
Lost River Voyage
Kids Ahoy!
Kritter Korral Petting Zoo
Carousel
Wings of the Springs Bird Shows
Concert Stage
Giraffe Barn
Floral Gardens
Non-Venomous Snake Show
Creature Feature
Animal Exhibits
Fort King River Cruise
Lighthouse Ride
Promenade Deck
Main Spring
Reptile Show
Ross Allen Island
Cypress Swamp
Florida Natives Exhibit
Magnolia Tent
Palm Tent
Room
Fantastic Fountains Show
Glass Bottom Boats
Court of Flags
Springside Mall
Big Gator Lagoon
Panther Prowl
Tickets
Tickets
Silver Springs
ENTER

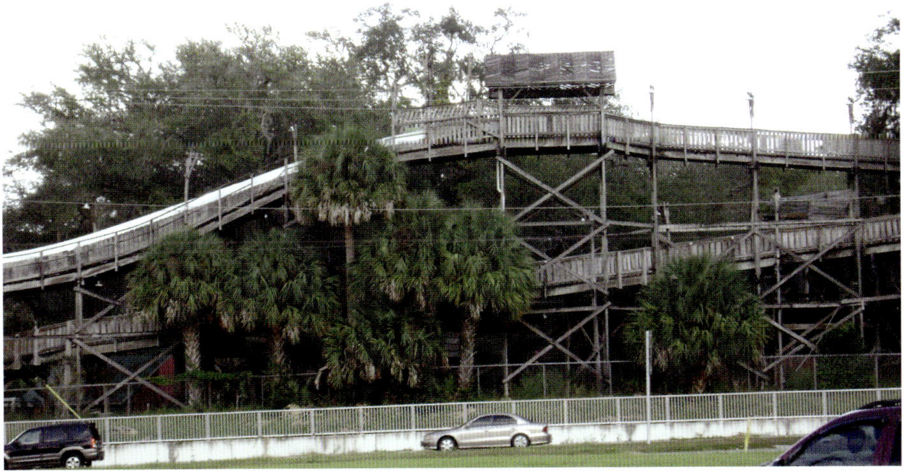

CHAPTER TWO

Ross Allen's Reptile Institute

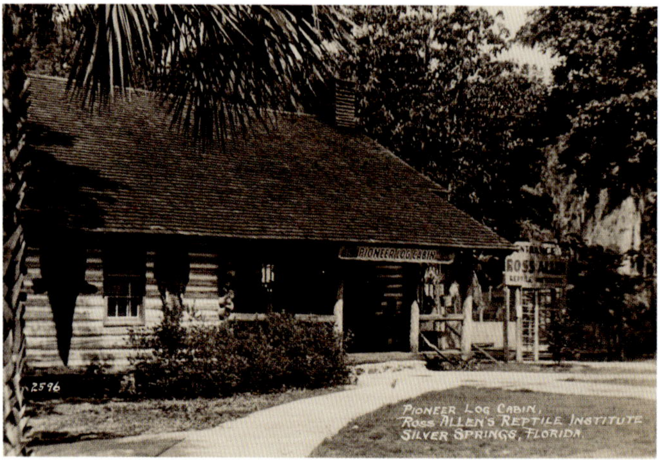

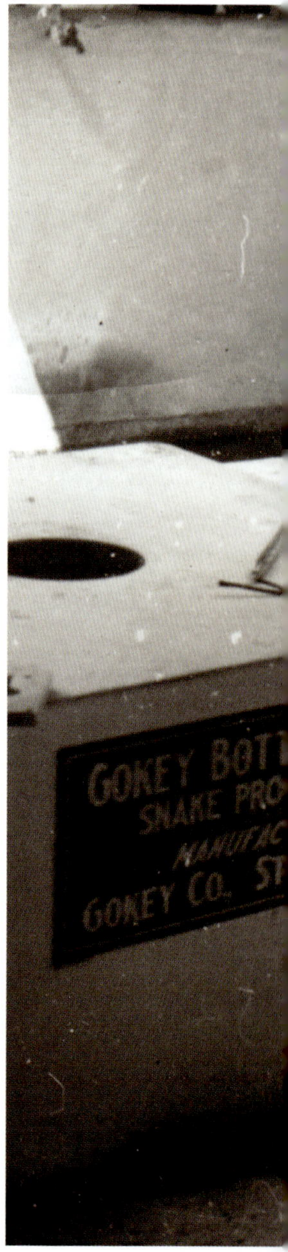

ABOVE: The Silver Springs property gained its first ancillary attraction in 1930, when herpetologist Ross Allen established his Reptile Institute on the west side of the main spring. By the middle of the decade, Allen had constructed this log cabin to serve as the entrance to his domain. *Delee Perry collection.*

OPPOSITE: It did not take long for Ross Allen's Reptile Institute to become nationally famous. Once, famed cartoonist and collector of curiosities Robert Ripley was asked what had been the most frightening experience of his career. Believe it or not, he replied, "Being in Ross Allen's snake pit when all the lights went out." *Delee Perry collection.*

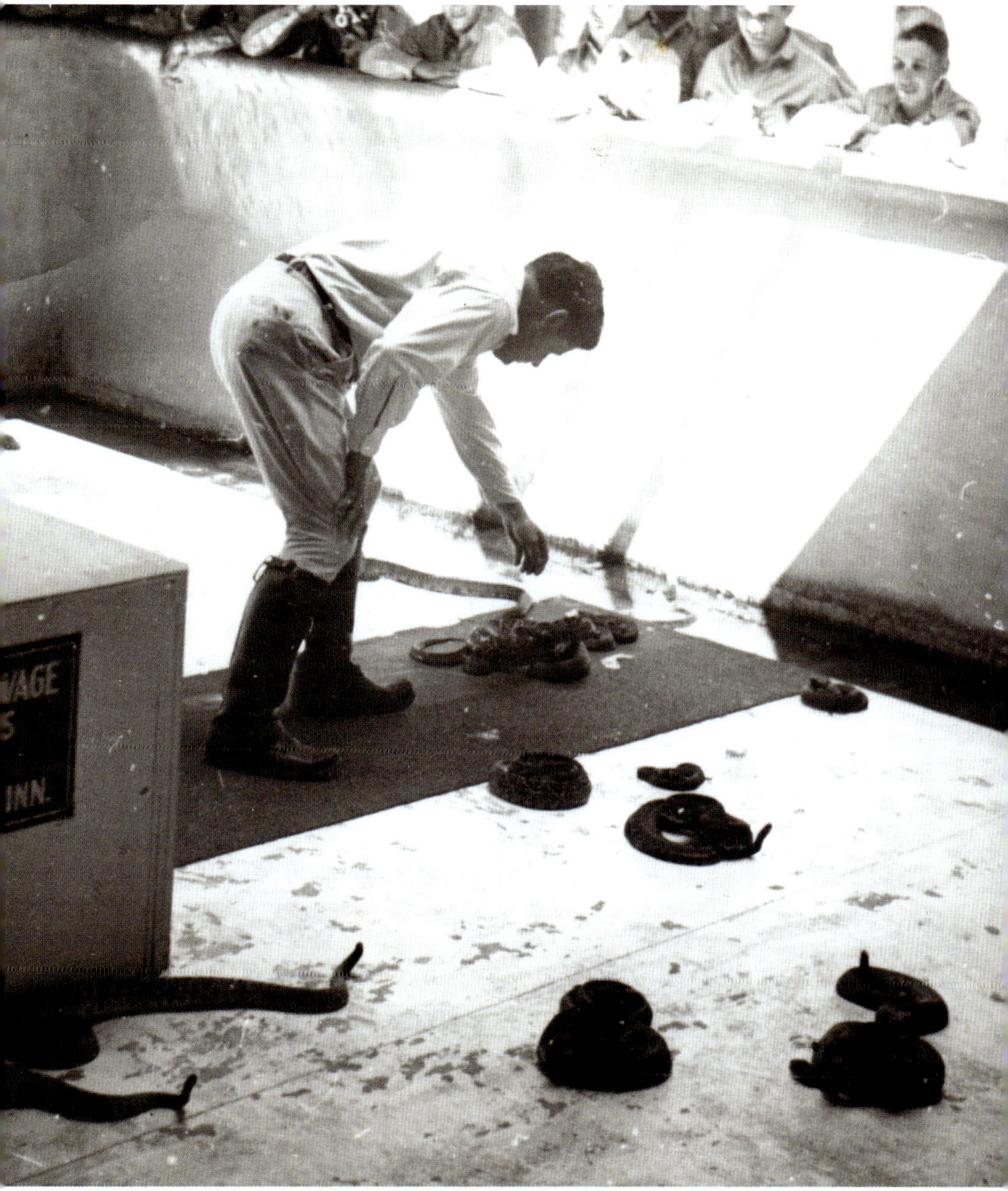

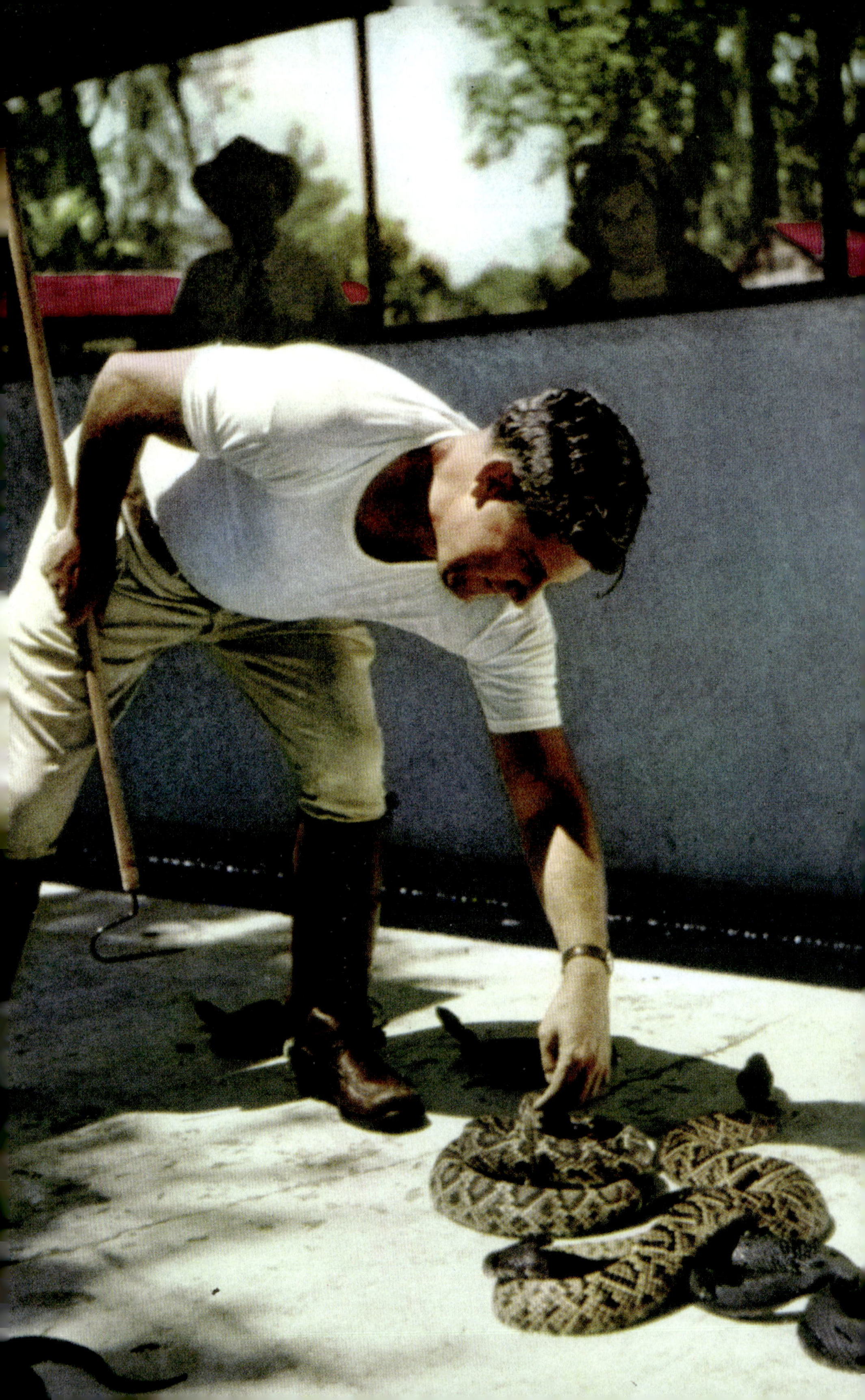

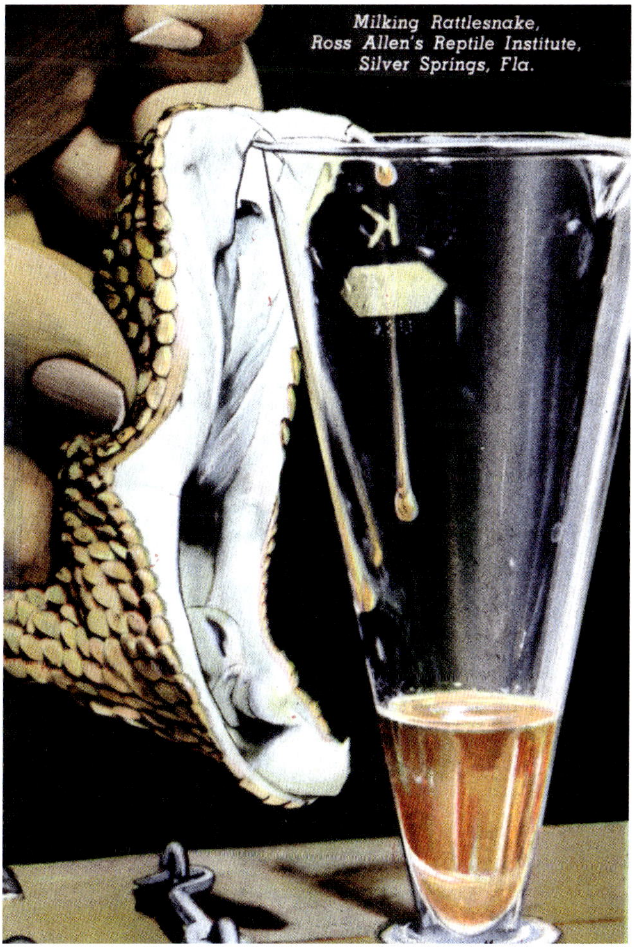

OPPOSITE: Ross Allen and his rattlesnakes were certainly not the normal sort of attraction for vacationing families. There were reptile farms and snake pits at many different roadside businesses, but none with the sheer scope and number of specimens of his springside exhibit. *Author's collection.*

ABOVE: More than just for show, Ross Allen's regularly scheduled demonstrations of "milking" rattlesnake venom had a very necessary and practical side. The extracted poison was used to create various types of lifesaving antidotes for those who were unfortunate enough to encounter the reptiles somewhere other than at a tourist attraction. *Author's collection.*

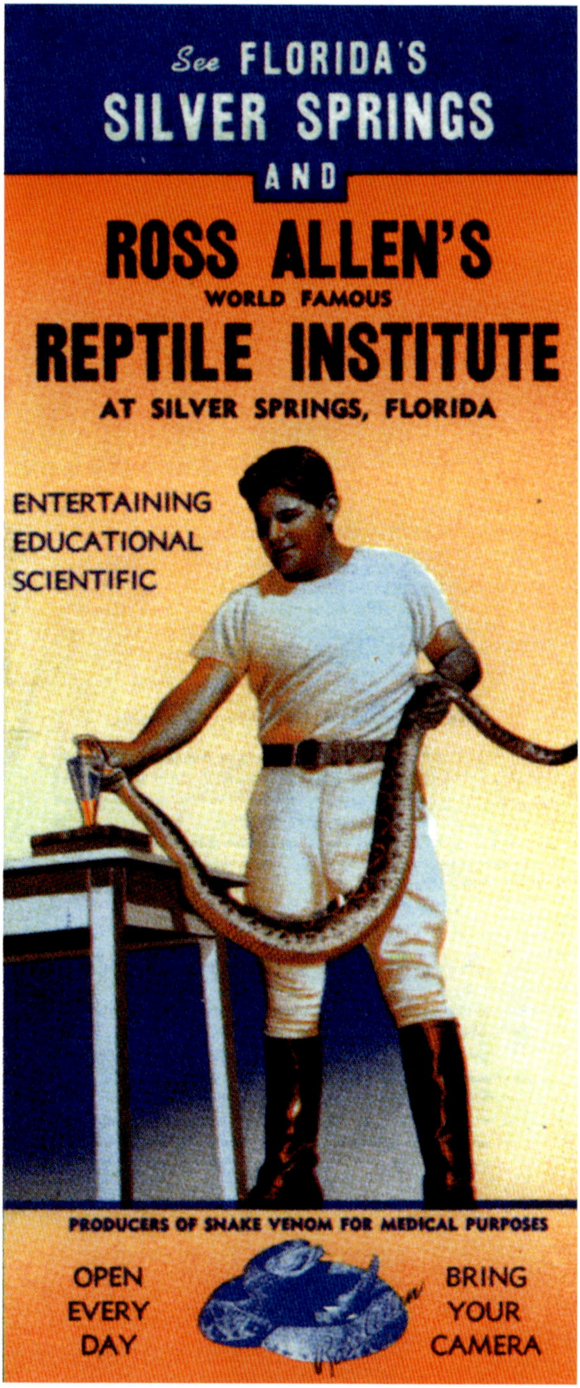

RIGHT: As this 1930s brochure indicated, the Reptile Institute could soon be justified in calling itself "World Famous." Apparently there were enough tourists who were not creeped out by creepy crawlers to maintain its success for decades. *Author's collection.*

OPPOSITE, TOP: Eventually, the Reptile Institute began to add various features unrelated to rattlesnakes and their ilk. One resident that could be dangerous but cuddly at the same time was Tom, a Florida panther. Ross Allen seemingly had a way with practically any living creature, whether it had four feet, two feet or no feet. *Delee Perry collection.*

OPPOSITE, BOTTOM: Among the Reptile Institute residents that fell into the feathered friends category were the exotic parrots and macaws that quite willingly posed for photos with tourists of all types—and stripes, judging by the lady in the white shorts. *Delee Perry collection.*

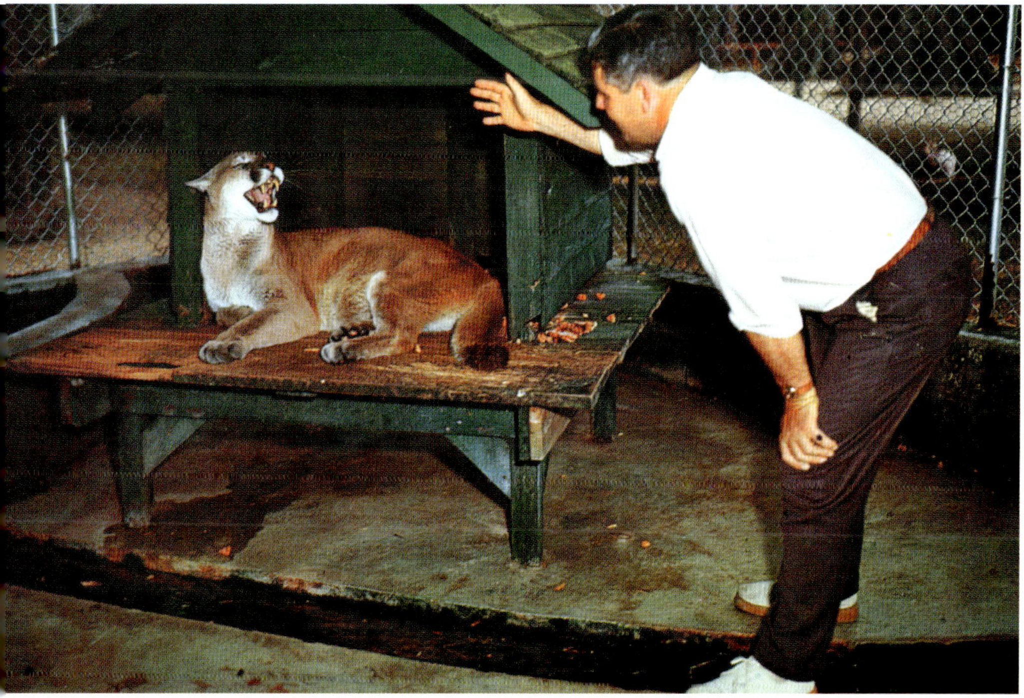

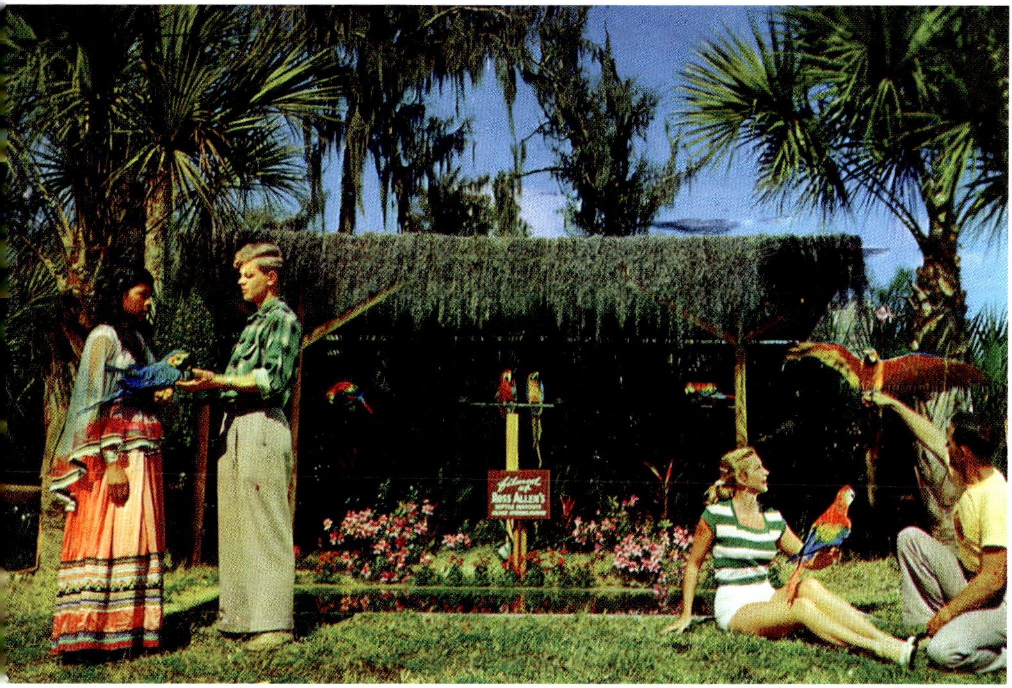
ROSS ALLEN'S

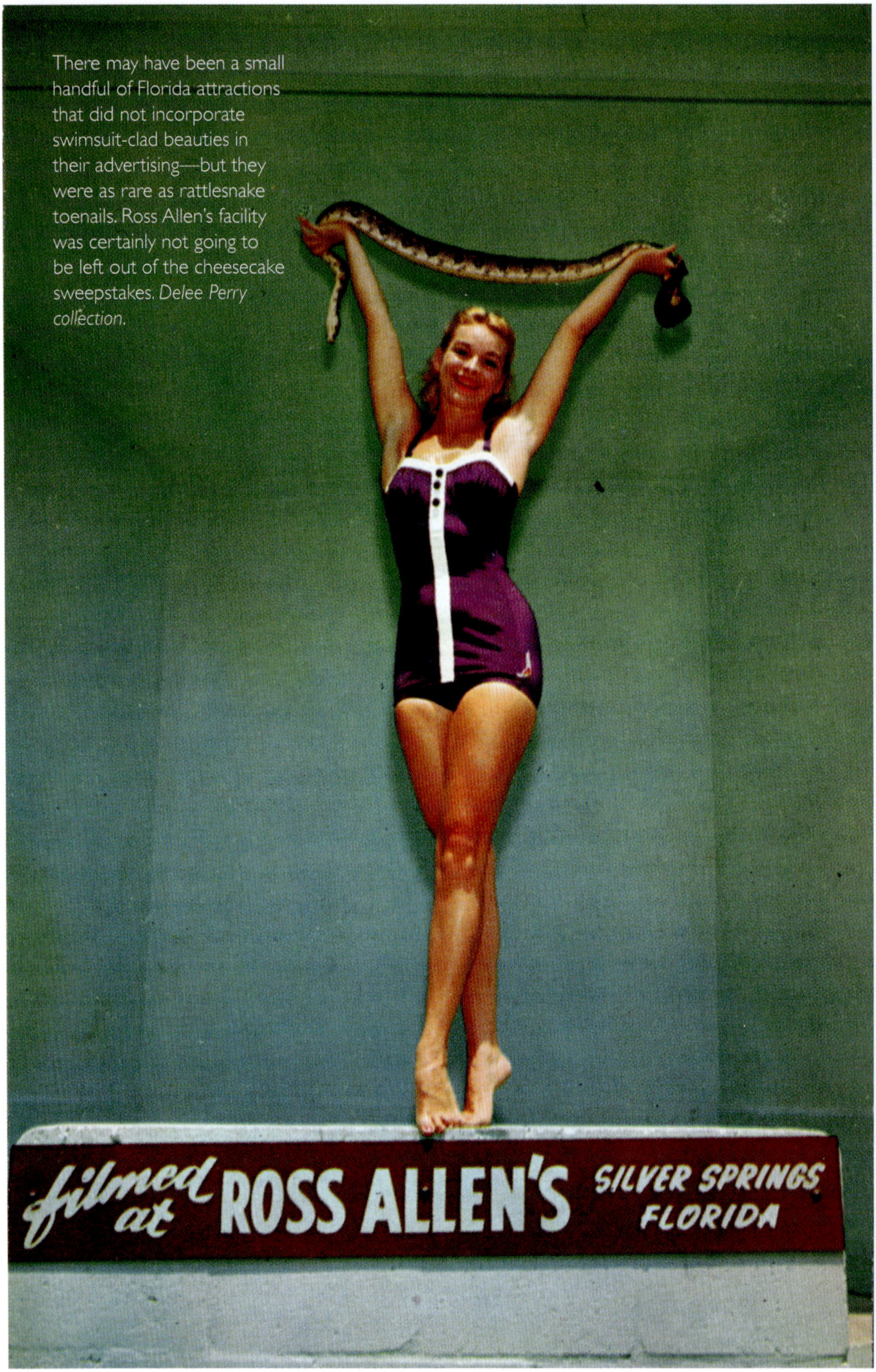

There may have been a small handful of Florida attractions that did not incorporate swimsuit-clad beauties in their advertising—but they were as rare as rattlesnake toenails. Ross Allen's facility was certainly not going to be left out of the cheesecake sweepstakes. *Delee Perry collection.*

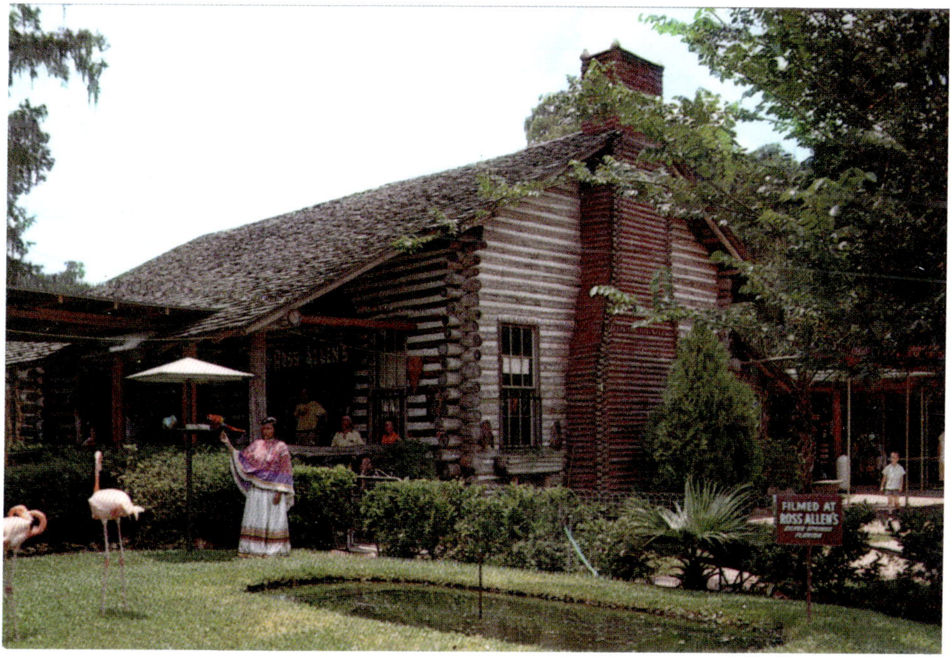

The 1935 log cabin that was the Reptile Institute entrance was still serving as the gift shop thirty years later. This postcard was one of a very few non-black-and-white views of the site, although it must be admitted that the pink flamingos helped add a splash of color to the otherwise drab tone of the building. *Author's collection.*

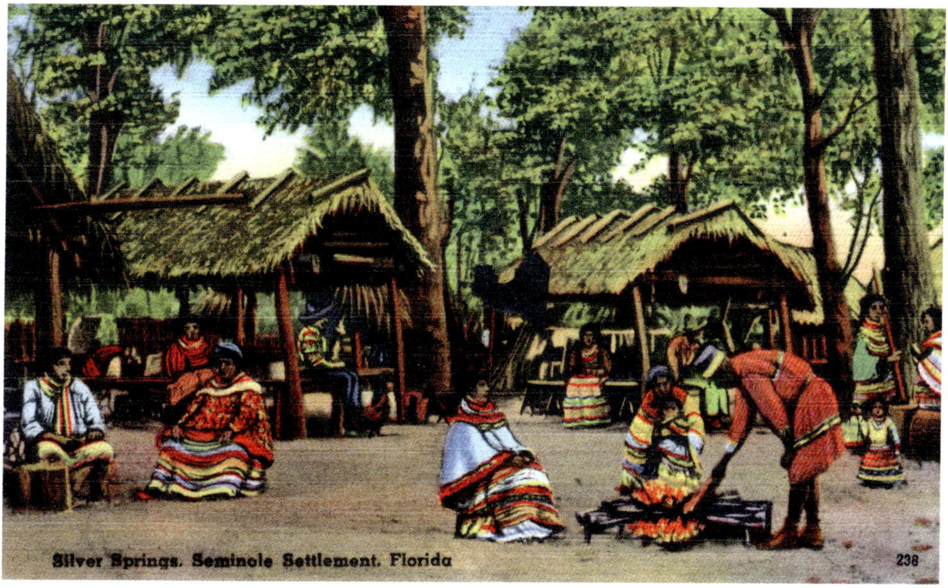

A decidedly non-reptilian feature of the Reptile Institute was the "genuine" Seminole Village. A number of similar attractions could be found in southern Florida and the environs of the Everglades, but the one at Silver Springs was unique for its part of the state. *Delee Perry collection.*

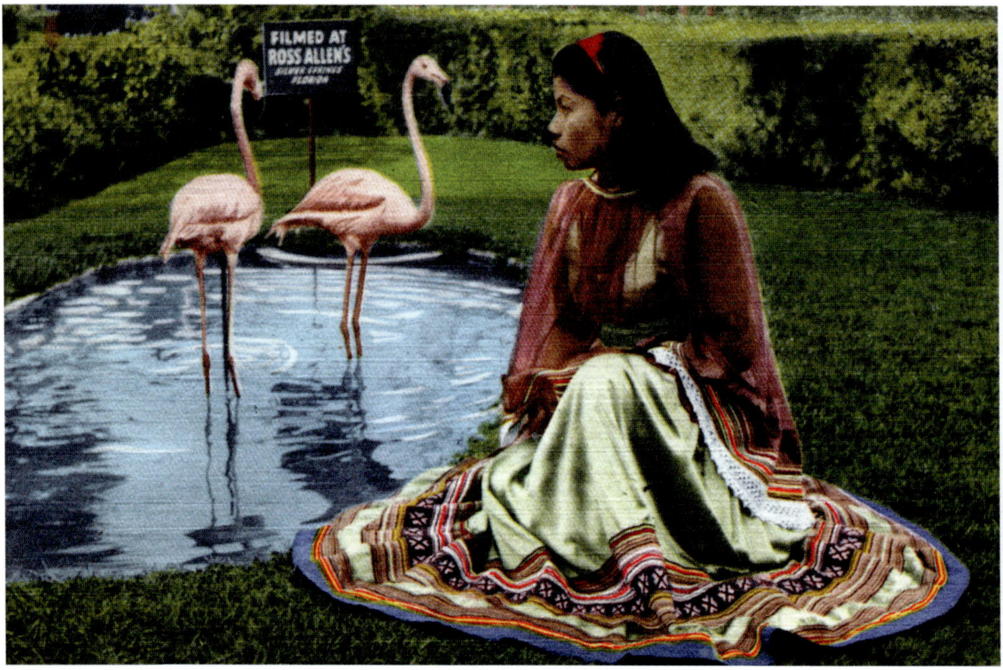

ABOVE: Admittedly, the idea of putting human beings on display seems more than a bit outdated today. However, it is important to remember that the Seminoles who populated Ross Allen's village were, in reality, employees, doing their jobs, just as the boat captains and gift-shop workers engaged in their duties elsewhere in the park. *Delee Perry collection.*

OPPOSITE: Although the goal of the Seminole Village was to make it appear that the inhabitants lived in it and perpetuated the traditions of their ancestors, the truth was that the parts seen by the public were the "stage," to put it in theatrical terms. Behind barriers were the true living spaces, providing privacy from any unwanted prying eyes. *Author's collection.*

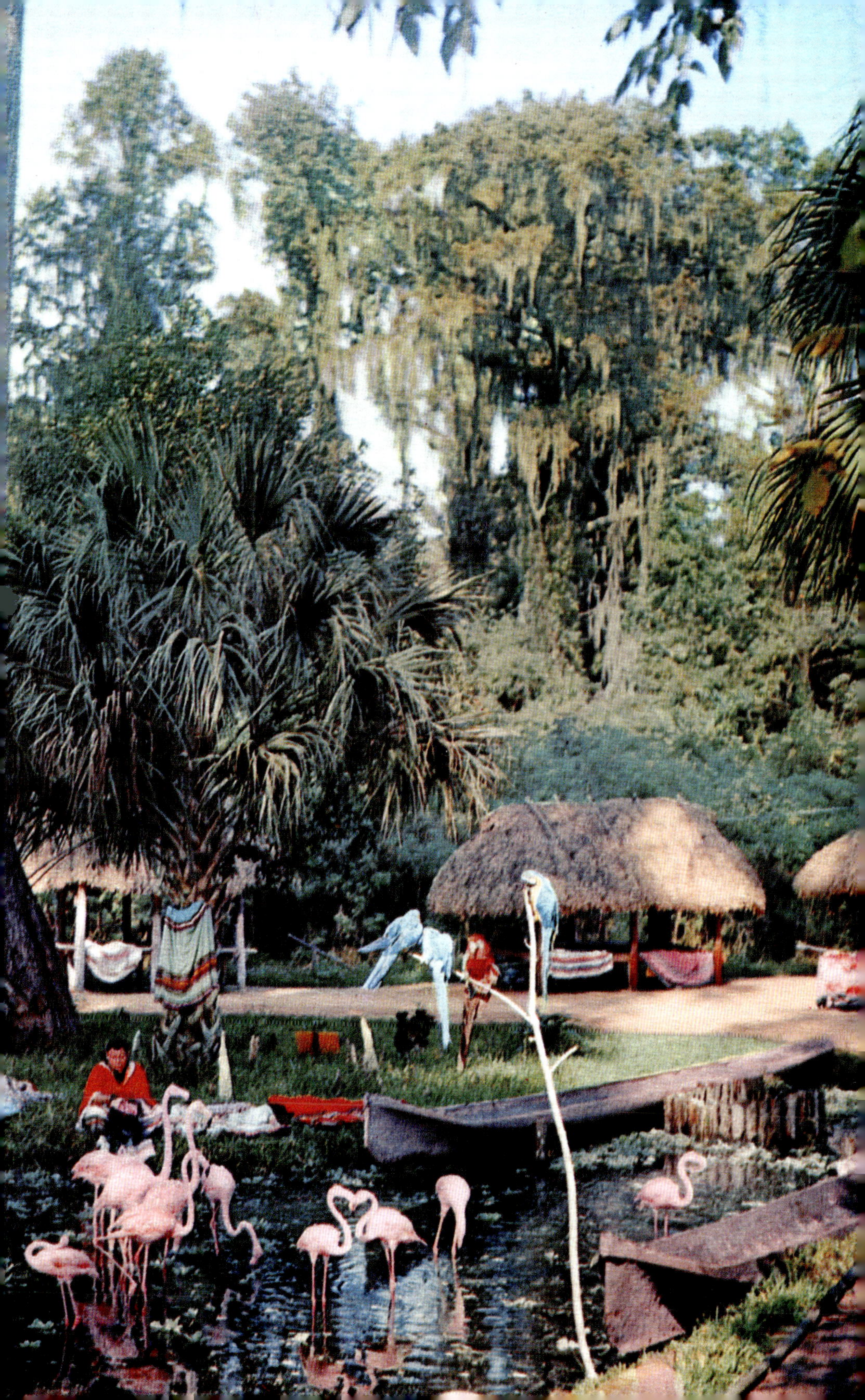

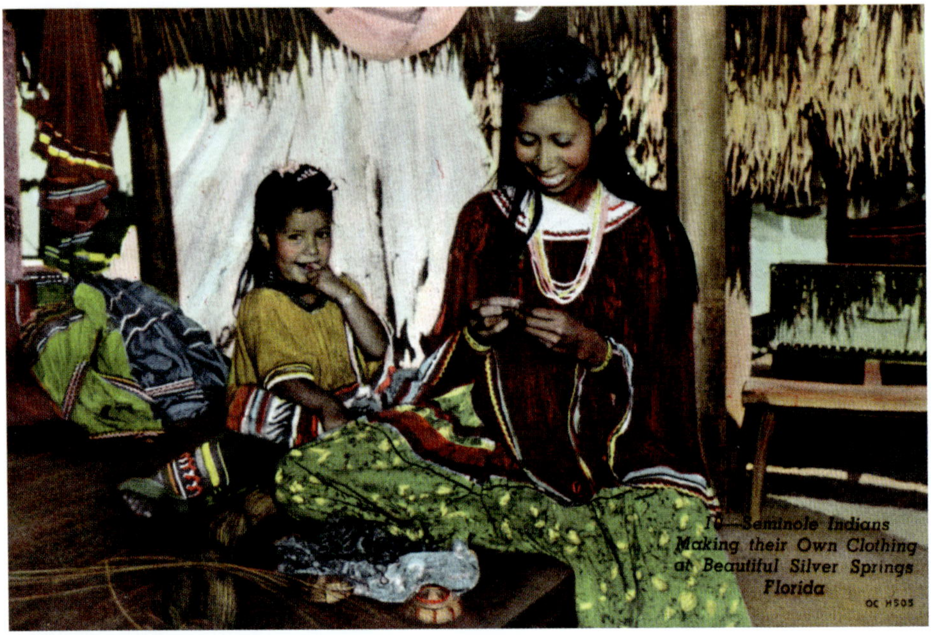

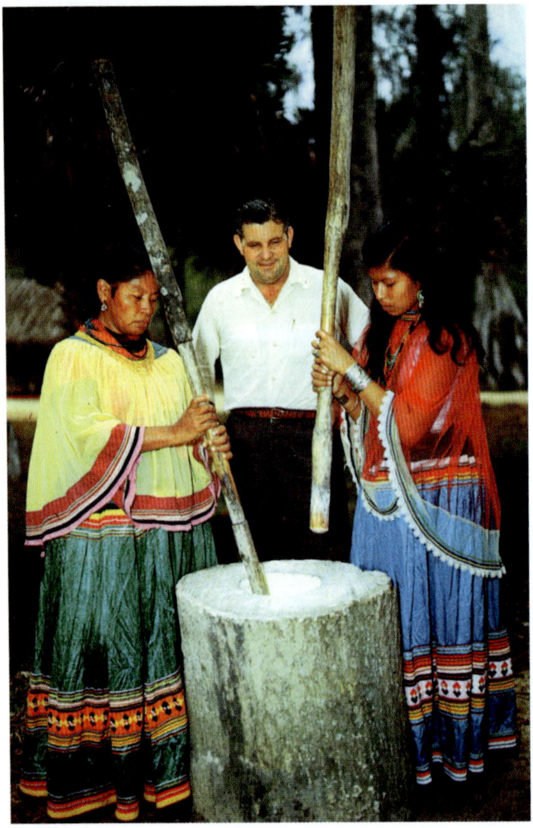

There were a great many similarities between Ross Allen's Seminole Village and the cultural exhibitions that went on in Cherokee, North Carolina. In both, the residents made their living by demonstrating the methods their forefathers had developed, from creating their own fabulously colored clothing to showing how their food was prepared. At least the Seminoles had one advantage, in that their culture was more or less accurately represented, whereas in Cherokee, the Native Americans elected to take on the appearances of Plains Indians—the image the public expected after years of exposure to Western movies and TV shows. *Delee Perry collection.*

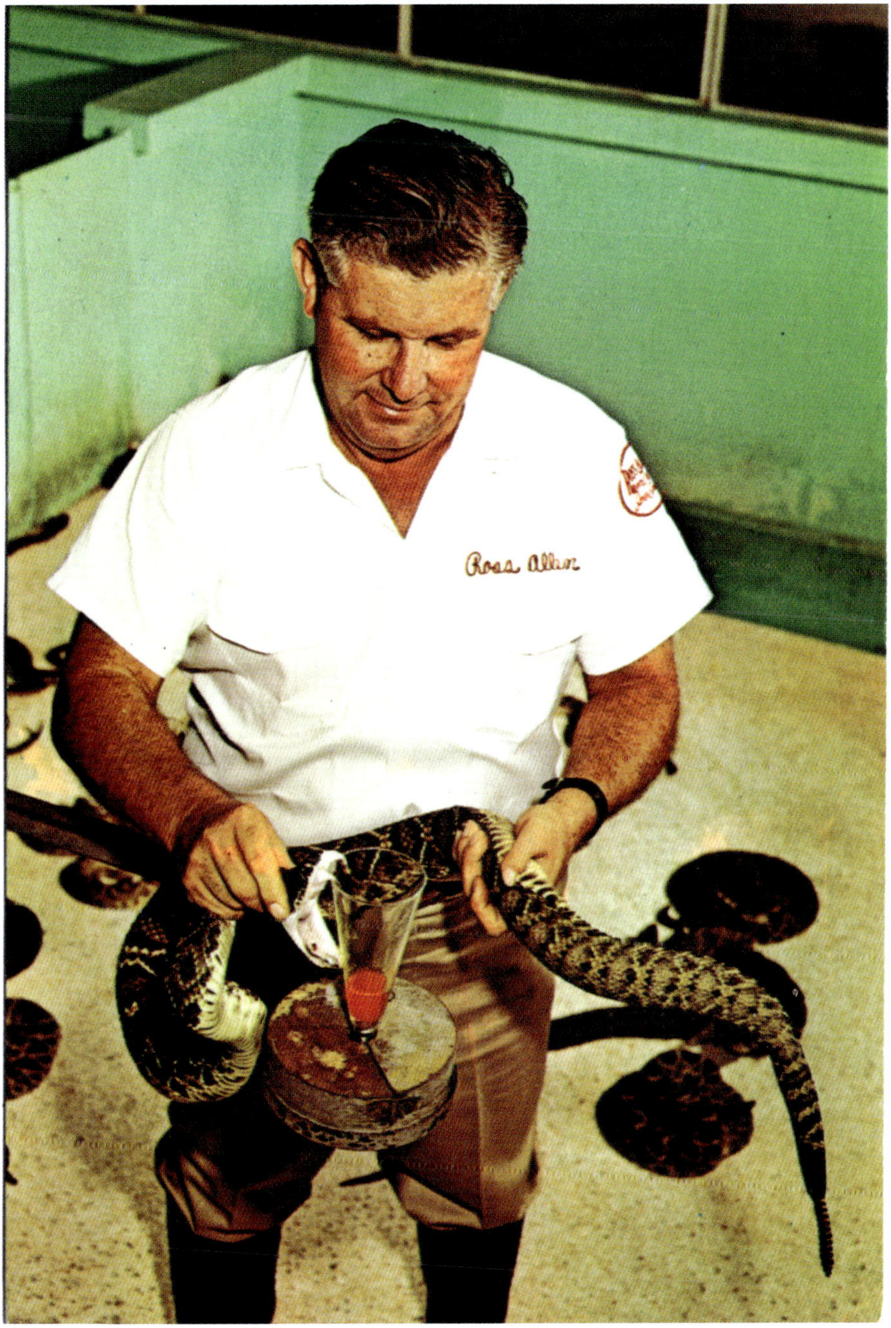

Like most of the other add-on attractions surrounding Silver Springs, the Reptile Institute was closed in the mid-1970s. Ross Allen went on to develop another proposed attraction, known as Alligator Town U.S.A., alongside I-75 at Lake City. But the world-famous herpetologist passed away in May 1981, before his replacement park could open. *Delee Perry collection.*

CHAPTER THREE

Tommy Bartlett's Deer Ranch

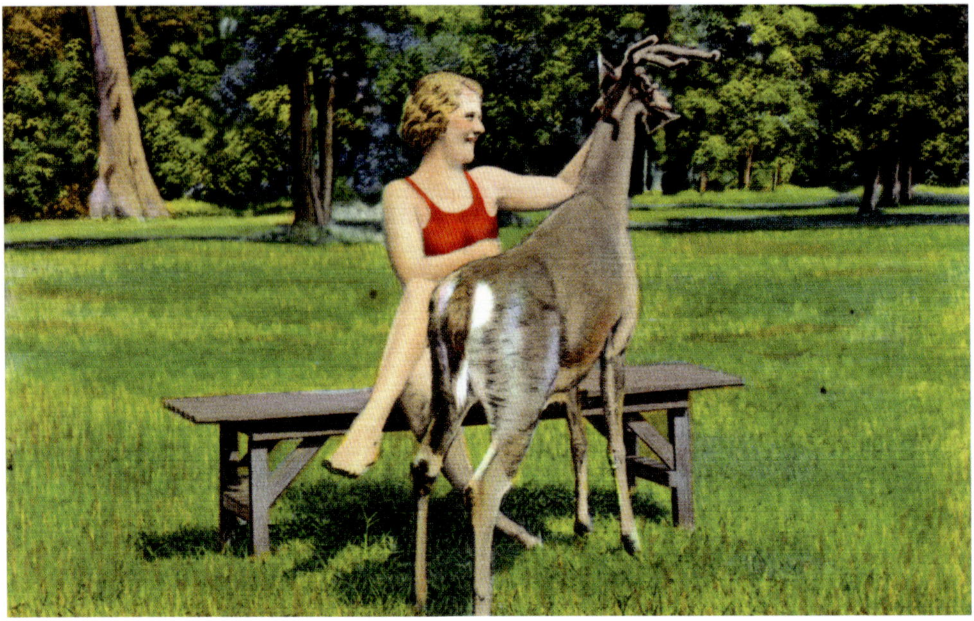

As far back as this 1935 postcard, Silver Springs had a few tame deer—this one was "Bill"—on-site to interact with visitors (and, almost as often, with models). It would be almost twenty years before the concept developed into anything more permanent. *Author's collection.*

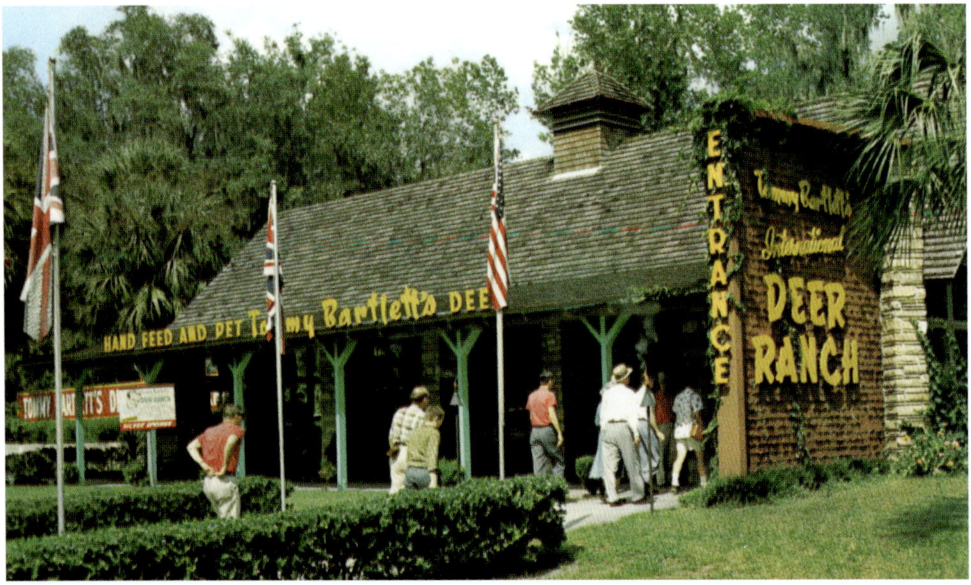

Tommy Bartlett was a popular CBS-TV and radio personality and had made a second career out of the attractions he owned in the tourism-happy world of the Wisconsin Dells. Eyeing the lucrative Florida market, in 1954, he established his Deer Ranch on the side of Silver Springs opposite the Reptile Institute. *Author's collection.*

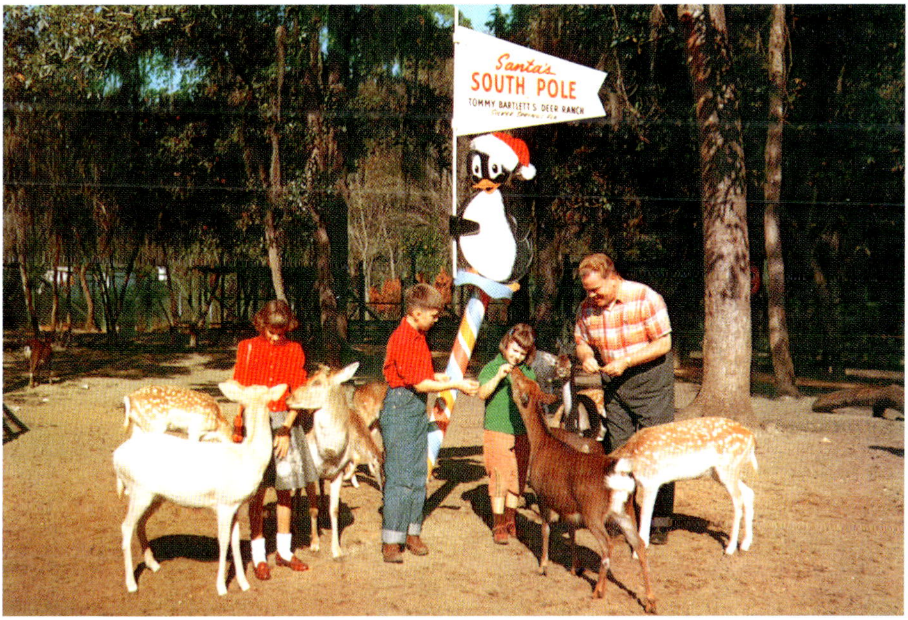

With little but the tame deer to furnish a connection, the Tommy Bartlett Deer Ranch (that is Bartlett in the checkered shirt) employed an incongruous Christmas theme. Its Santa's South Pole display was a popular spot for photos, both professional and tourist-made. *Author's collection.*

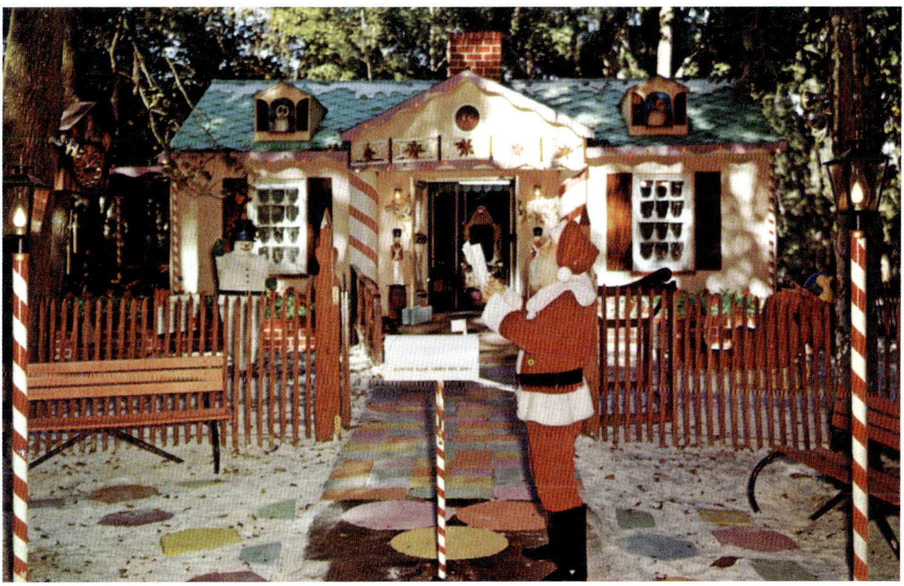

Jolly old St. Nick had his own residence at the Deer Ranch, where the beloved gift-bringer must have felt right at home surrounded by the cousins of Dancer, Prancer and Rudolph. *Author's collection.*

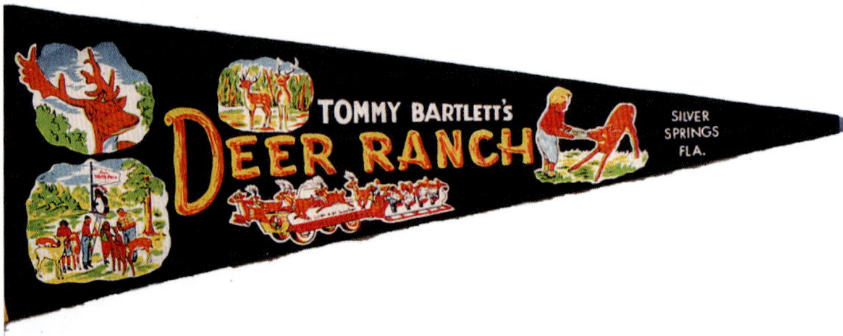

TOP: Earlier we saw an example of Silver Springs' souvenir felt pennants; now here is one that was sold at the Deer Ranch. It is printed in loud, fluorescent colors, which make it look even more amazing under black light than in normal illumination. *Author's collection.*

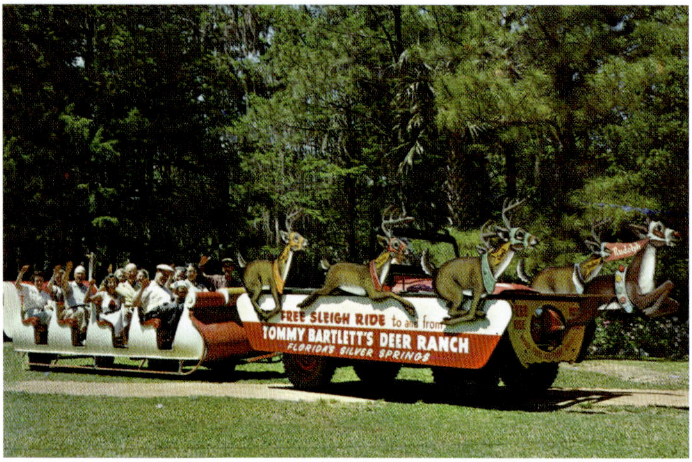

MIDDLE: Many of the displays at the Deer Ranch, including Santa's South Pole and this simulated sleigh ride, were the work of artist Vincent "Val" Valentine. He arrived in Silver Springs around 1955 and immediately set about creating pieces for most of the area attractions. *Author's collection.*

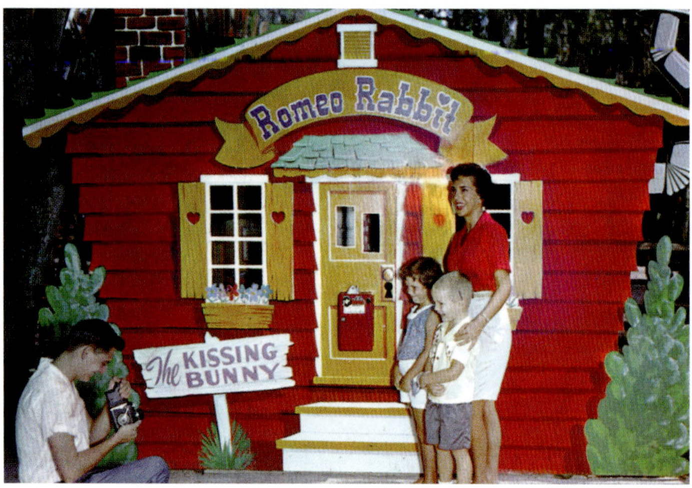

BOTTOM: Val Valentine created imaginative settings for the Deer Ranch's collection of trained animals. The critters received their education from animal behaviorist Keller Breland, who simultaneously operated a Hot Springs, Arkansas attraction known as the I.Q. Zoo. *Author's collection.*

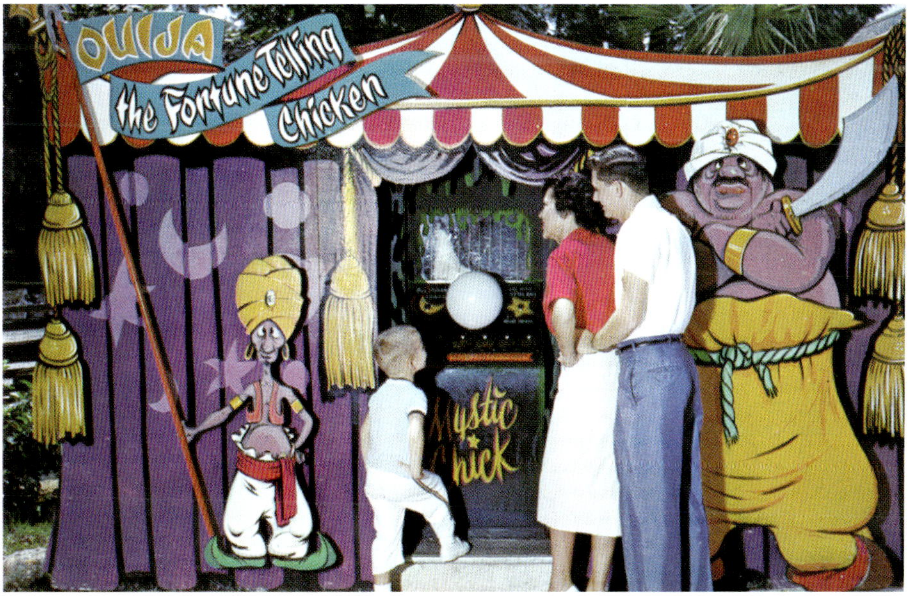

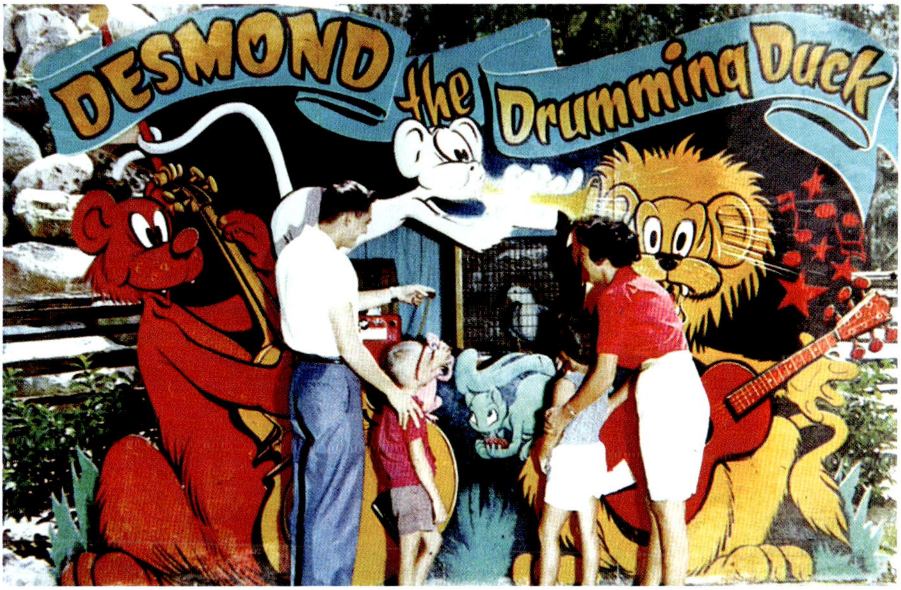

In the late 1930s and early 1940s, Val Valentine had served as an artist at the Max Fleischer animation studio in Miami, working on the *Popeye* and *Betty Boop* cartoons. Many of his designs for the Tommy Bartlett Deer Ranch clearly show his background in the animated cartoon industry, some even resembling specific characters from the films. *Author's collection.*

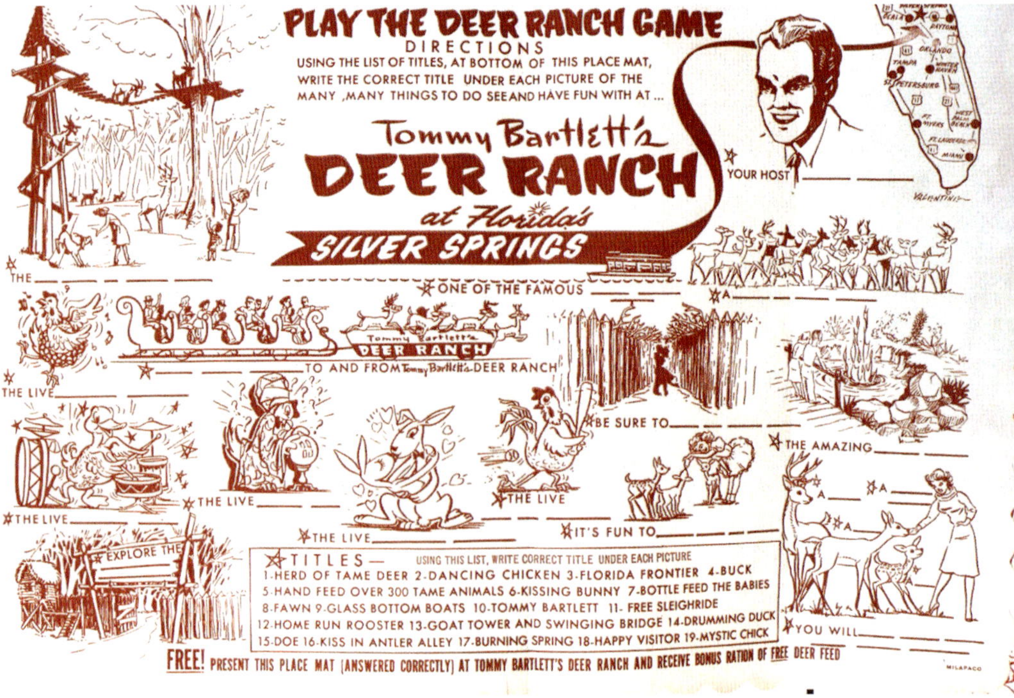

A popular form of advertising various Florida attractions was the use of paper placemats in hundreds of restaurants (in the days before fast food and chains were the most common places to chow down). Val Valentine drew this one for the Deer Ranch. Provided that you answered the trivia questions correctly, it could be presented at the gate for an extra supply of deer feed. *Author's collection.*

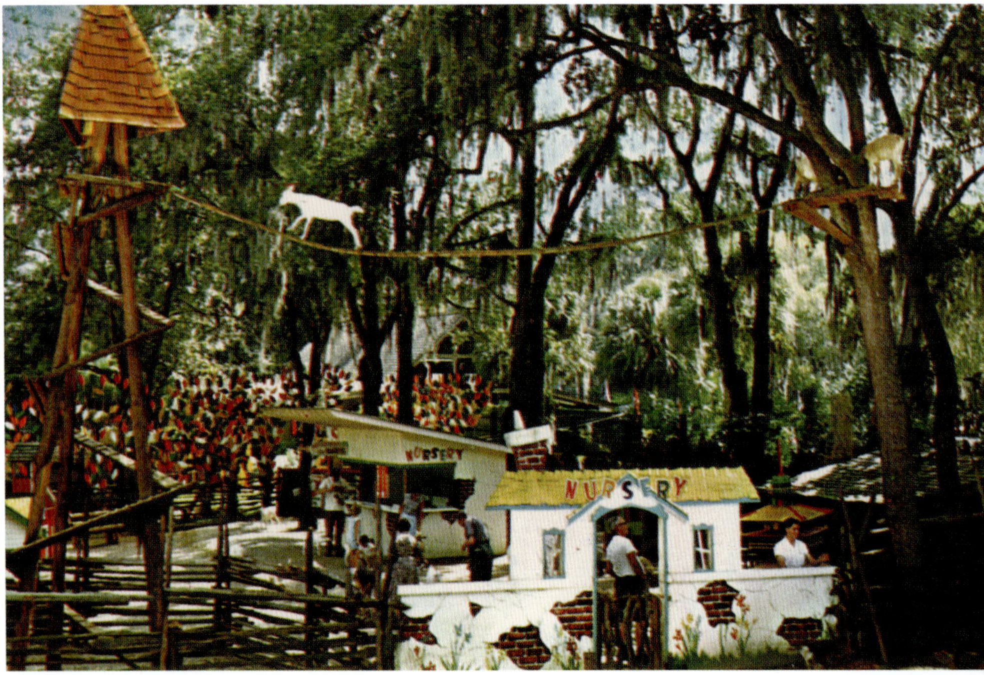

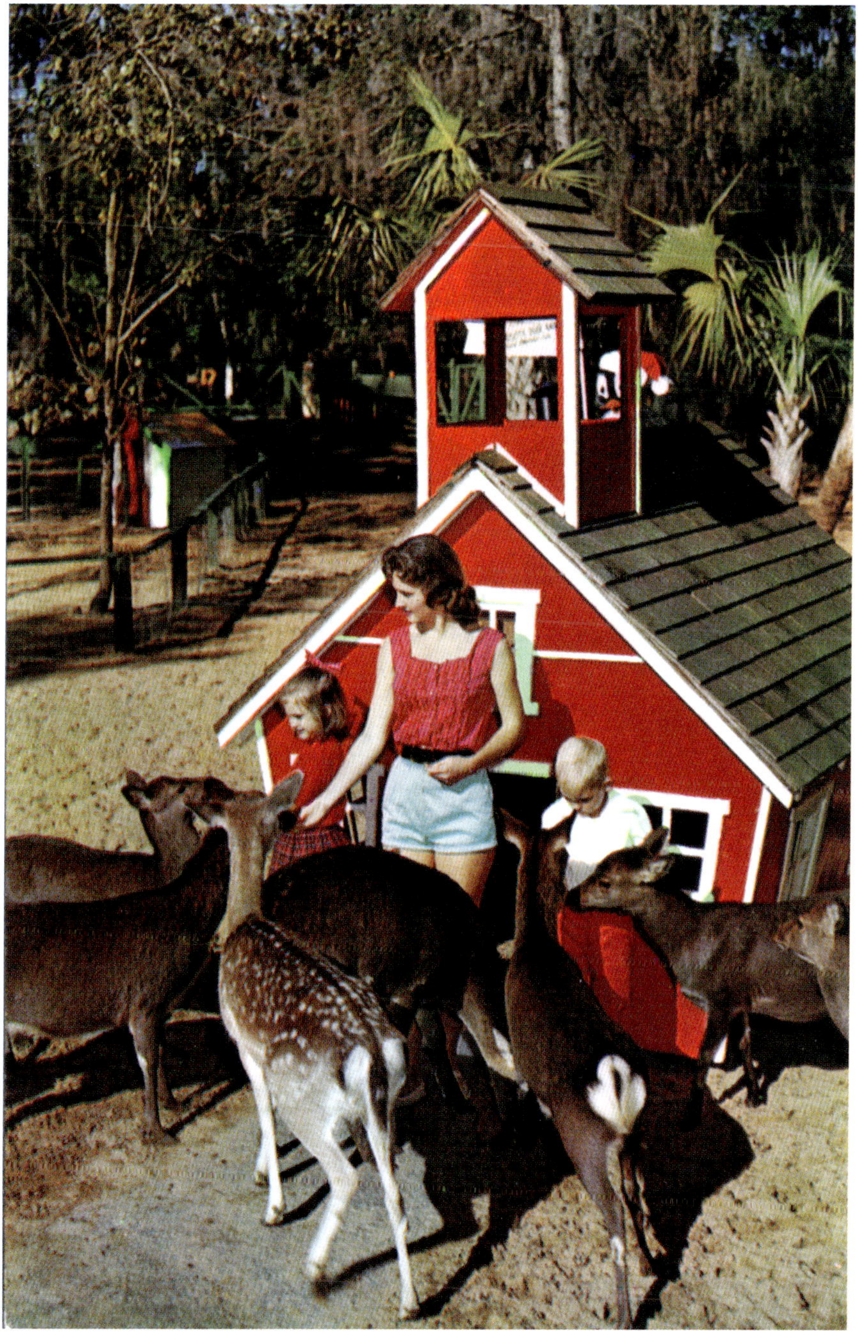

That bonus deer feed could come in handy once one glimpsed the sheer number of furry, four-footed friends that made the Deer Ranch their home. Besides the starring deer, there were baby goats and other farm animals just waiting for the endless parade of human beings whose sole purpose for existence—as far as they were concerned—was to feed them. *Opposite, bottom: Delee Perry collection; above: author's collection.*

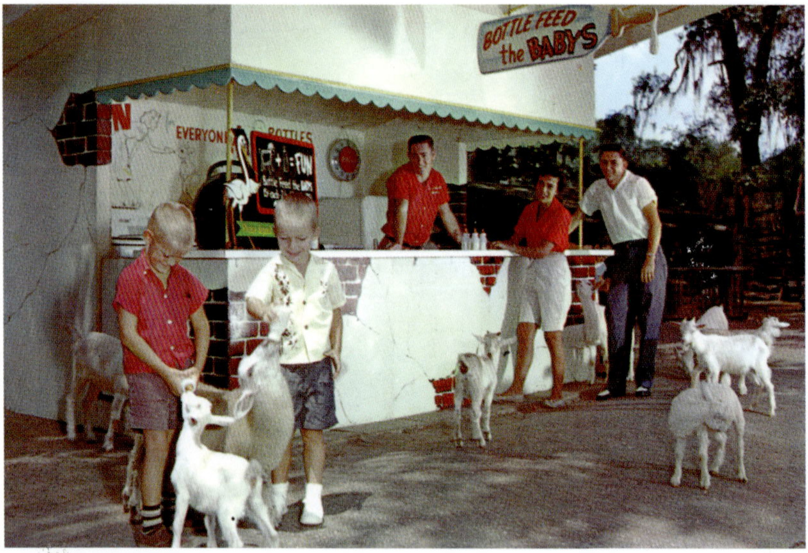
BOTTLE FEED
the BABY'S
BOTTLES

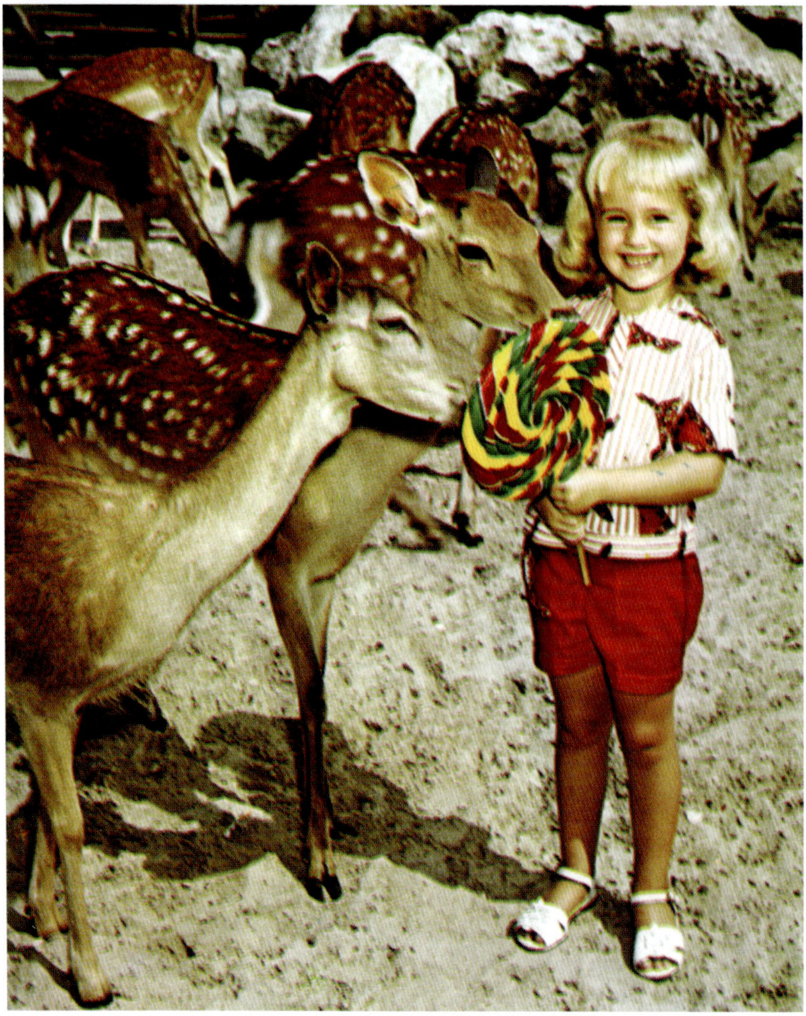

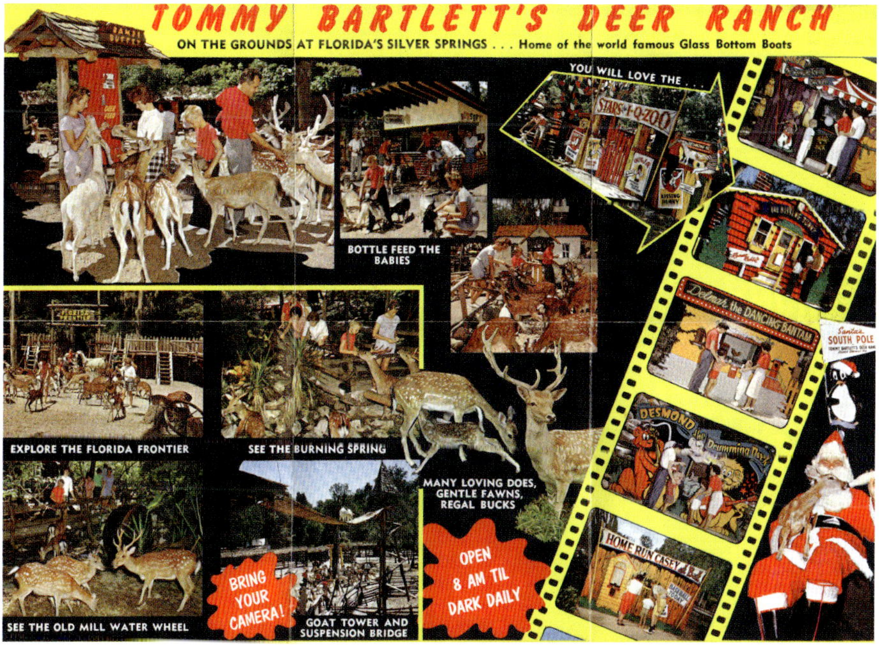

OPPOSITE, TOP: Yes, folks could interact with the denizens of Tommy Bartlett's Deer Ranch in a way that few would desire to try across the way at Ross Allen's Reptile Institute. Naturally, being hand-fed all day was a good way to produce some spoiled animals that rivaled their visitors. *Delee Perry collection.*

OPPOSITE, BOTTOM: This classic Deer Ranch postcard contains so much cuteness that it's hard to swallow it all in one dose. Even though rainbow-striped lollipops were not normally on the deer's recommended diet list, this photo makes it appear that, once they have finished it off, they might start eating their smiling blonde visitor next. *Author's collection.*

ABOVE: After ABC assumed control of Silver Springs in 1962, one of its first actions was to remove the Tommy Bartlett name, since he was an established personality for rival network CBS. It was then known simply as the International Deer Ranch until it closed, along with most of the other ancillary attractions, around 1975. Into the 1980s and '90s, some of the enclosures were still being used for Silver Springs' continuing animal population, but all traces have now been sent back to the North Pole with Santa and his helpers. *Author's collection.*

CHAPTER FOUR

The Prince of Peace Memorial

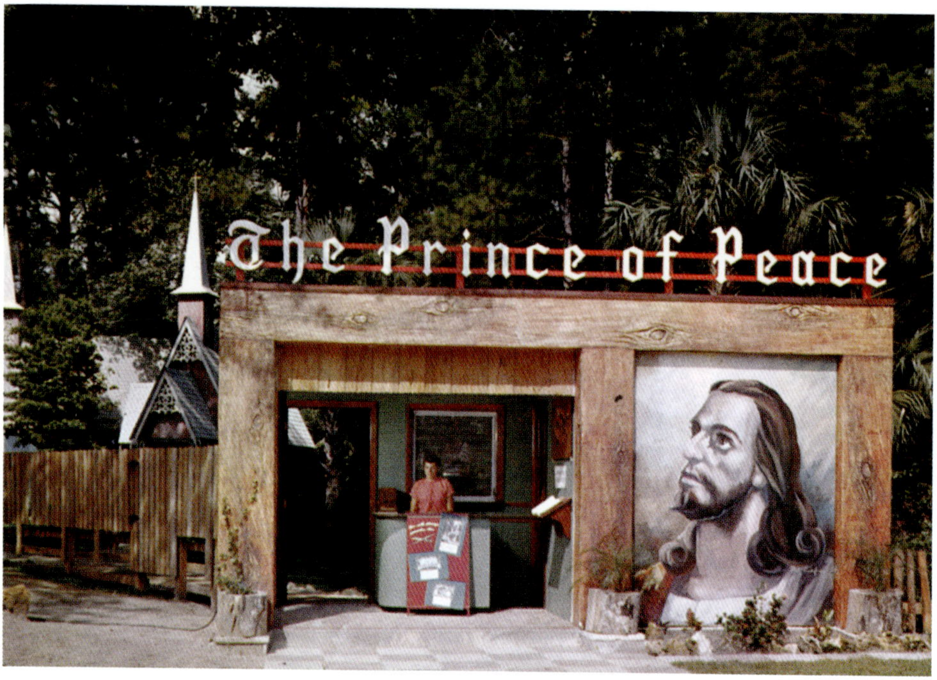

ABOVE: At the same time that the Deer Ranch hoofed its way into the neighborhood, another, even more unusual attraction was added to Silver Springs' roster—the Prince of Peace Memorial. With an entrance like this, even tourists named Thomas could have no doubts about its theme. *Author's collection.*

OPPOSITE: Contrary to what one might have expected, rather than being housed in a single building, the Prince of Peace Memorial was spread among a series of small chapels. In its peaceful setting, each chapel added another chapter and verse to the story of the life of Christ. *Delee Perry collection.*

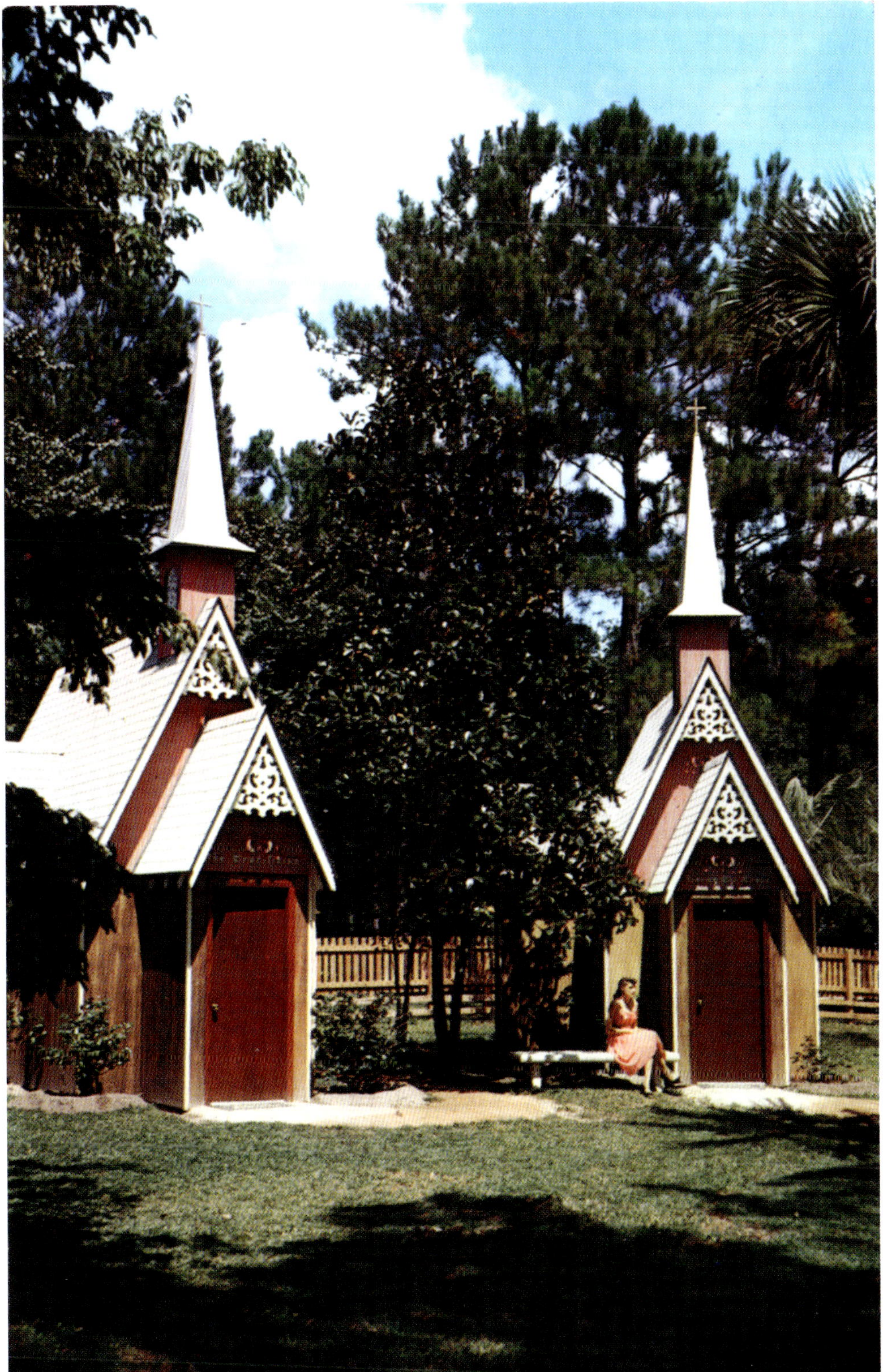

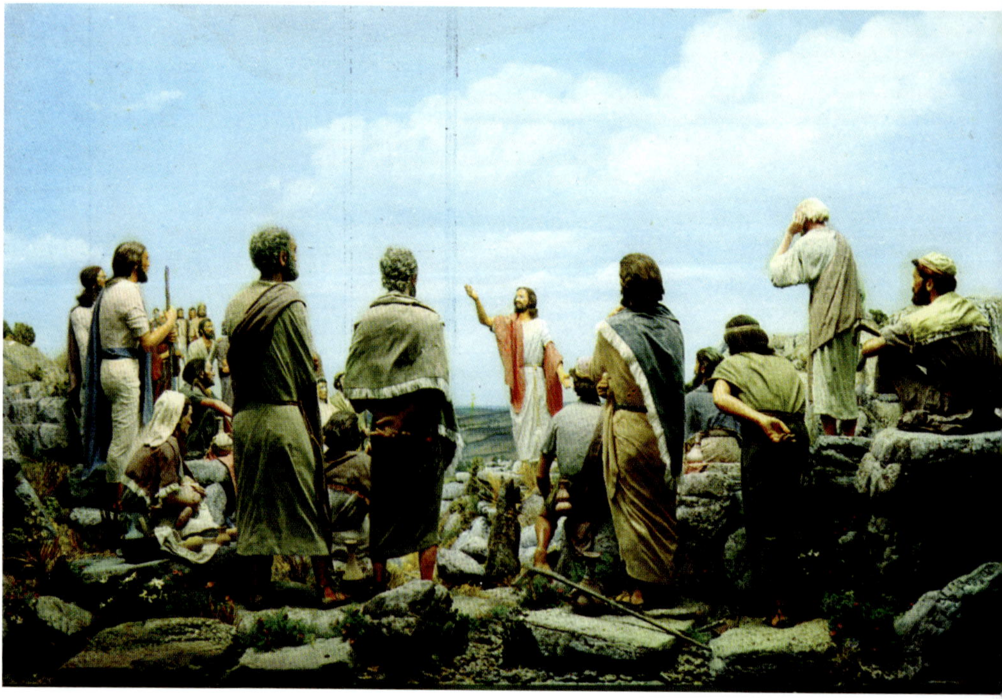

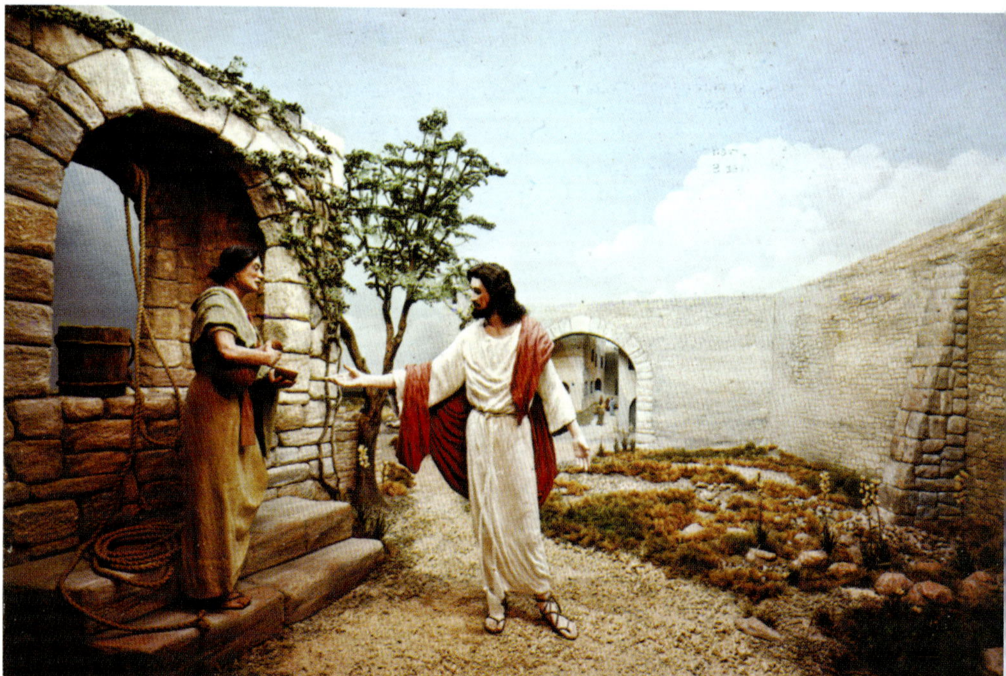

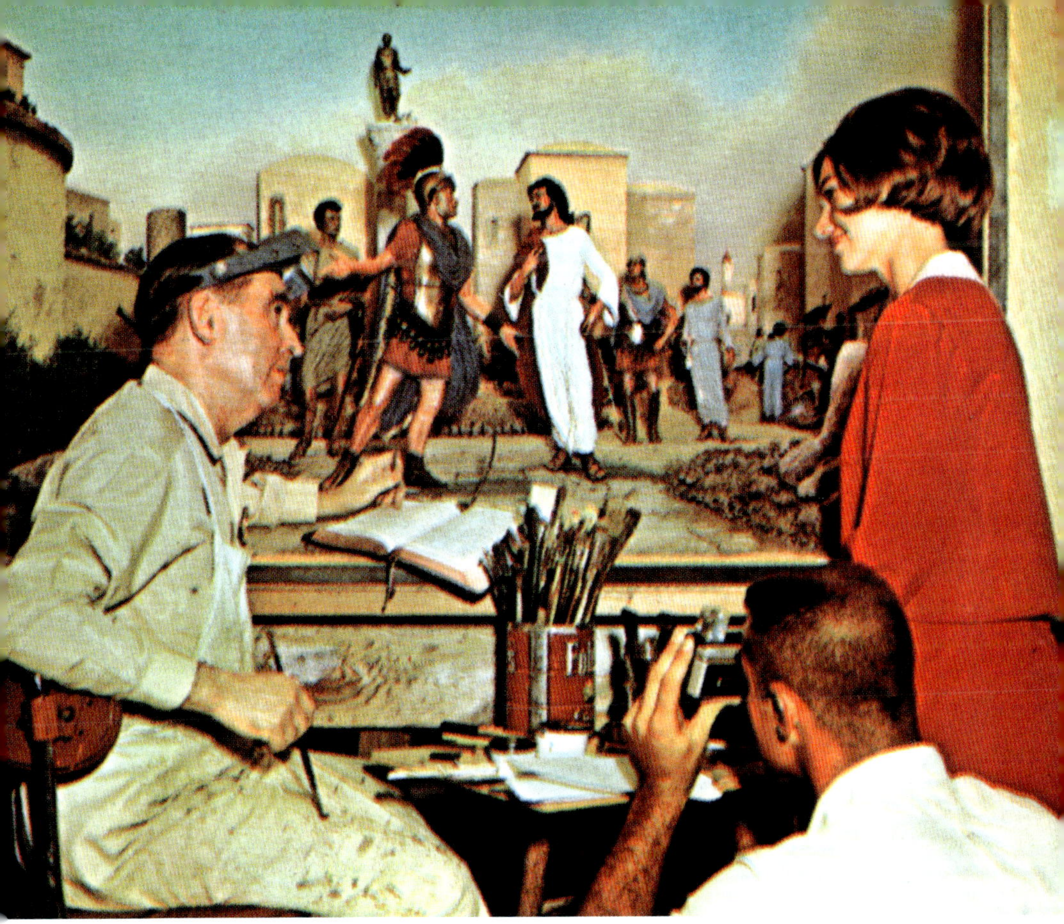

OPPOSITE: From looking at photos of the Prince of Peace dioramas, it would be easy to mistake them for scenes from a wax museum. Actually, each figure was hand-carved from wood, and the scenes were not much larger than a tabletop. *Both, Delee Perry collection.*

ABOVE: This posed publicity photo of the woodcarver, Paul Cunningham, is really the only way to get an idea of the true size of his delicate creations. *Author's collection.*

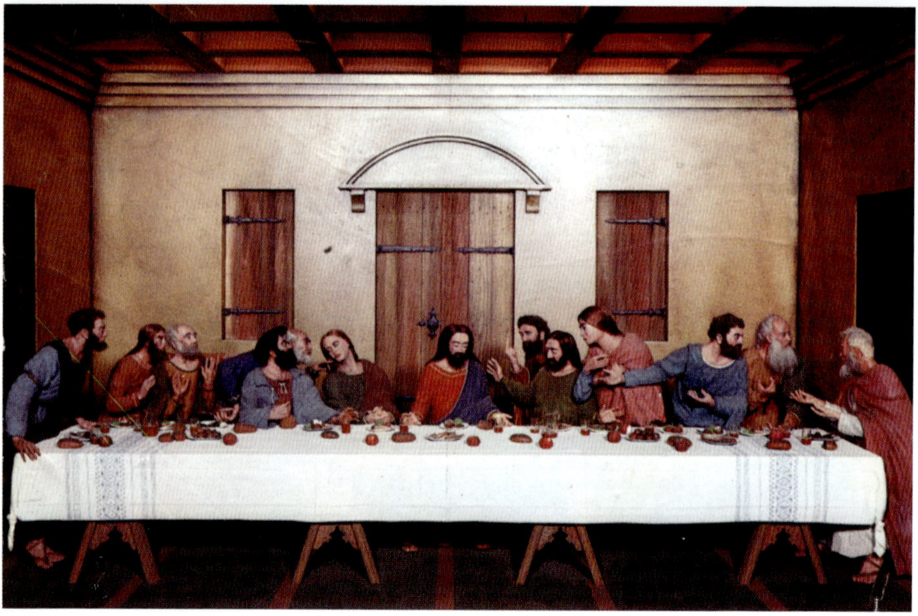

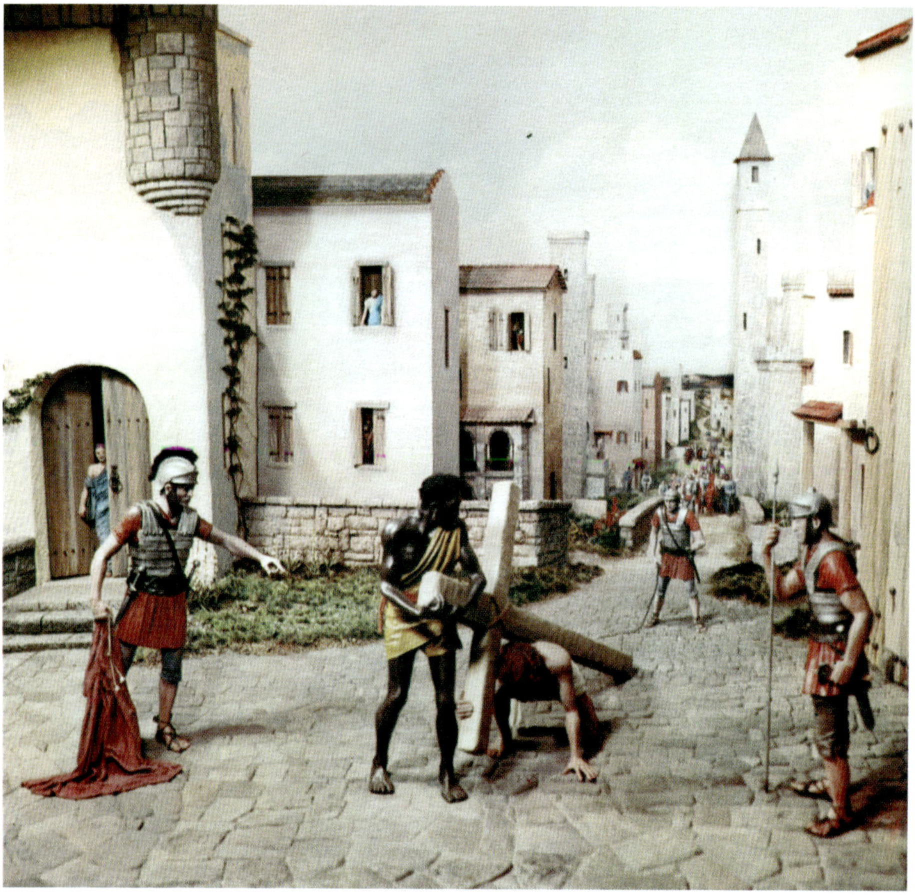

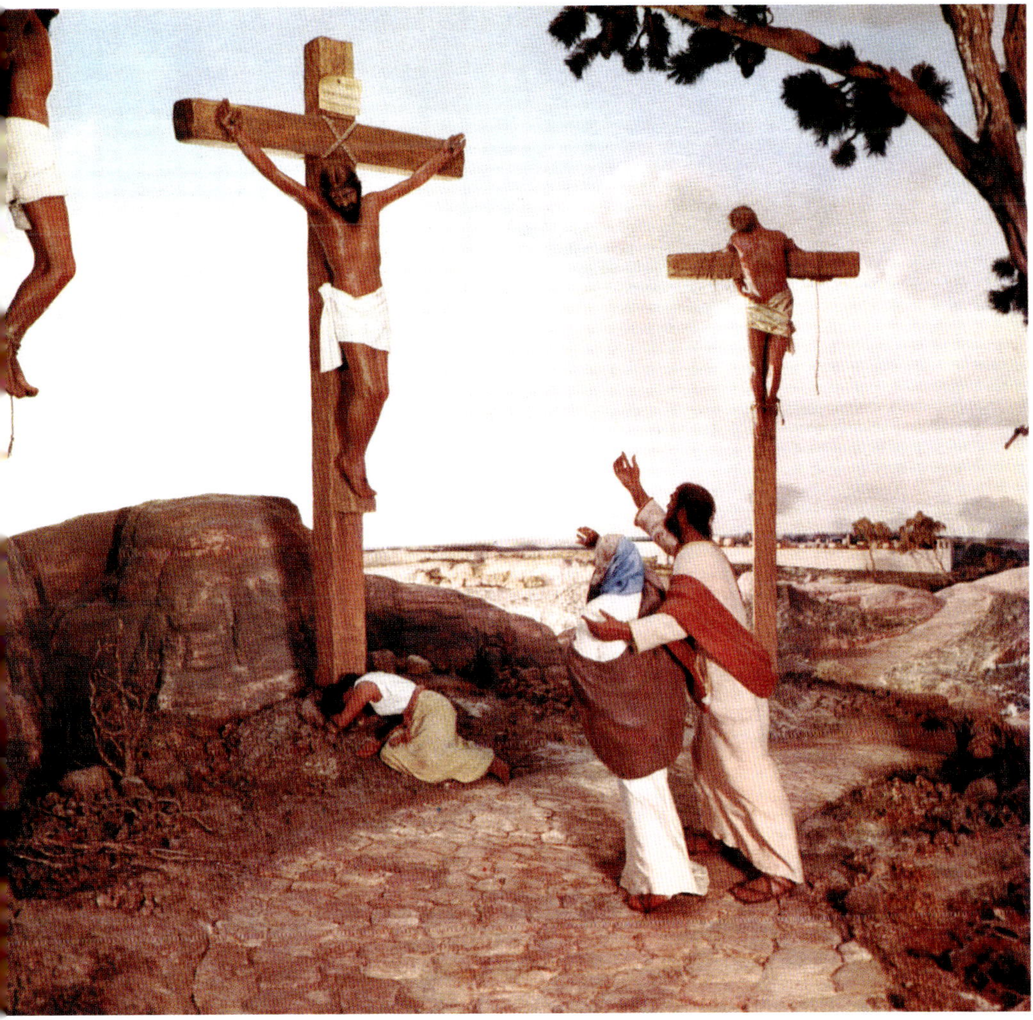

OPPOSITE: The amount of detail in each of the Prince of Peace dioramas was incredible—and probably easier to absorb through these photos than it would have been when moving through the various chapels. Whereas most of the scenes were Cunningham's own visualizations of the biblical accounts, he obviously could not resist the temptation to re-create da Vinci's *Last Supper*—probably one of the most-imitated works of art in history. *Author's collection.*

ABOVE: While we all know how the Bible ends the life of Christ, things are not so certain when it comes to the fate of the Prince of Peace carvings. When ABC-TV divested Silver Springs of its concessionaires in the 1970s, Paul Cunningham took his dioramas on the road in a series of traveling trailers. They were last reported as residing at a religious retreat somewhere in the Carolinas; hopefully, they are still in storage somewhere, awaiting their own possible resurrection. *Delee Perry collection.*

CHAPTER FIVE

The Early American Museum

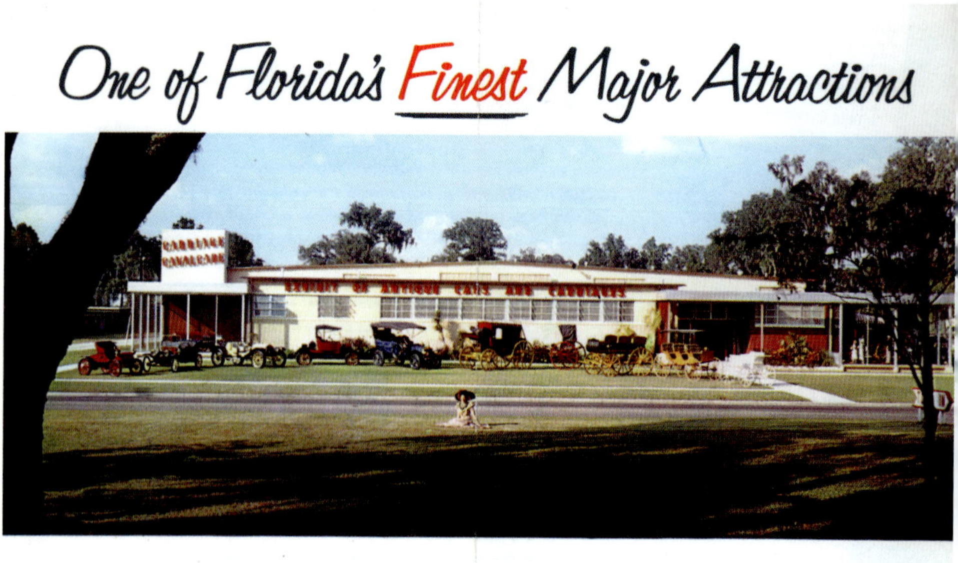

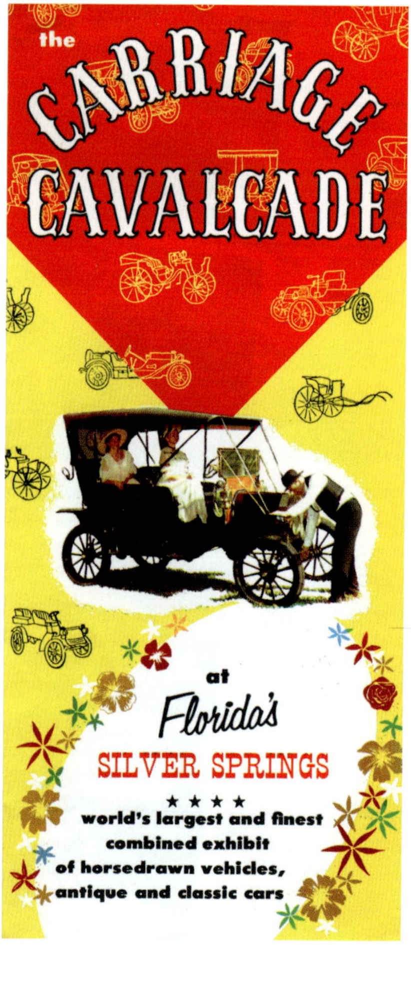

ABOVE: One ancillary Silver Springs attraction was not located on the property surrounding the springs, but instead across Highway 40, facing Silver Springs' main entrance. When it opened in 1953, it was known as the Carriage Cavalcade—but that was far from the only name it would carry in its history. *Author's collection.*

LEFT: Originally, the Carriage Cavalcade was intended as a showcase for the antique car collection of oil tycoons Sam and Vernon Jarvis. As this 1950s brochure touted, the display consisted of vehicles of all types, from horse-drawn carriages to Model Ts and beyond. *Author's collection.*

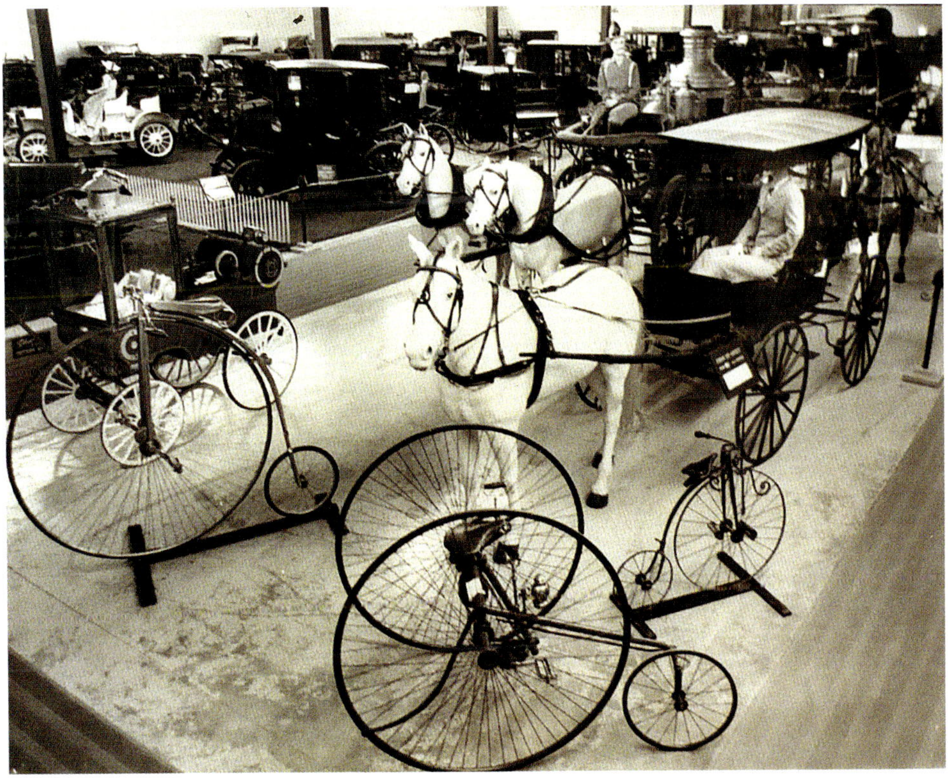

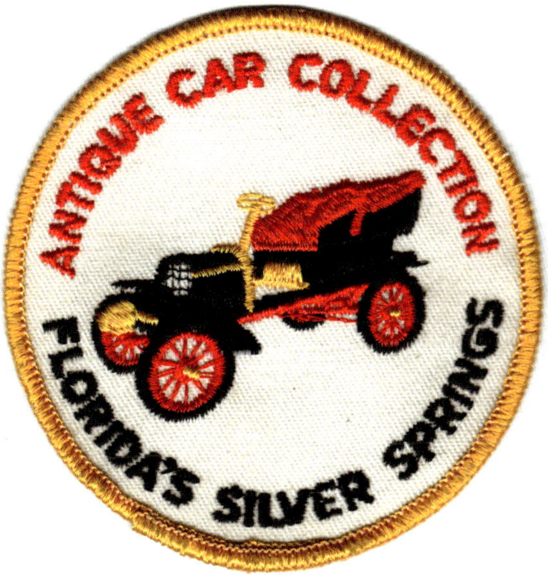

ABOVE: The wide-open floor space and aisles of the Carriage Cavalcade provided plenty of room for the displayed vehicles to spread out. Even artificial horses had to be incorporated, since it would have looked rather silly for a buggy to be sitting with nothing in its traces. *Author's collection.*

LEFT: As the 1950s blended into the 1960s, the Carriage Cavalcade began to similarly morph into new themes and even new names. For a while, it carried the enigmatic and almost unpronounceable moniker "Cavalcadia," which would have done little to persuade tourists to visit. At the time this embroidered patch was being sold as a souvenir, the maker had gone with the more generic "Antique Car Collection" without trying to be catchy about it. *Author's collection.*

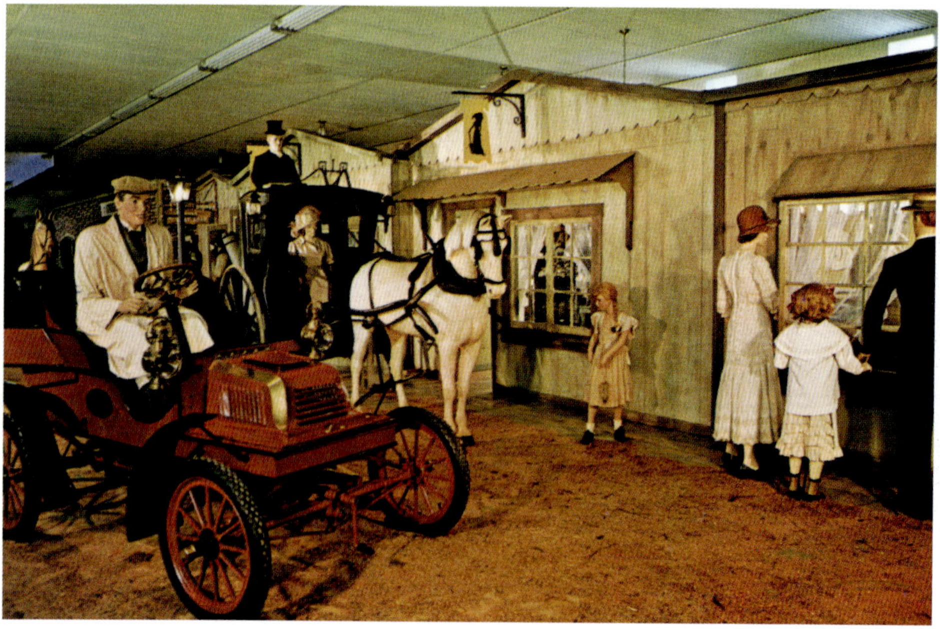

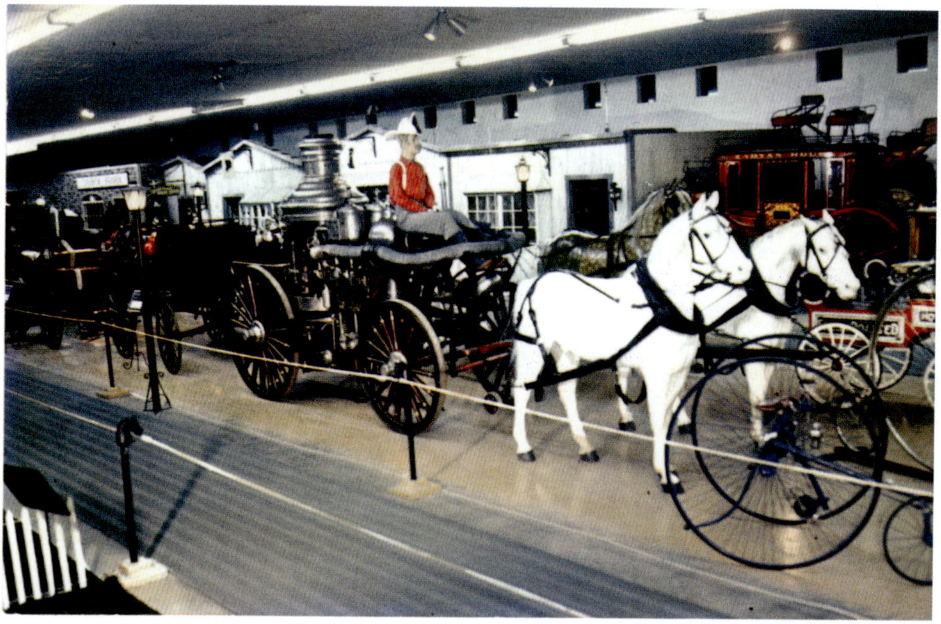

Other changes taking place in the 1960s involved building more and more scenic displays to give the historic vehicles some context. A row of shopfronts with simulated muddy streets was a terrific way to illustrate the days when motor vehicles were beginning to compete with horses for dominance of the nation's fledgling highways. *Author's collection.*

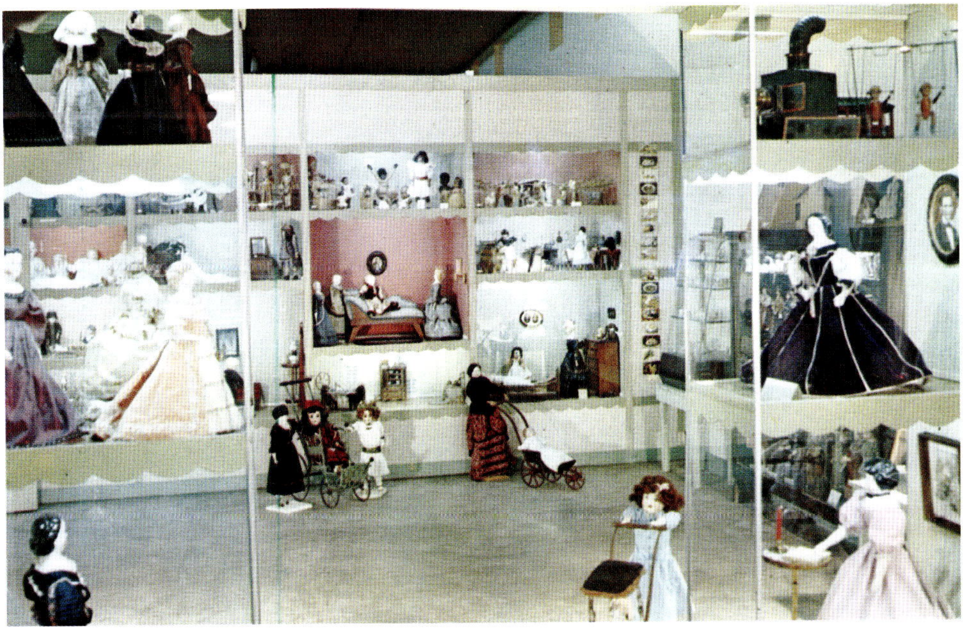

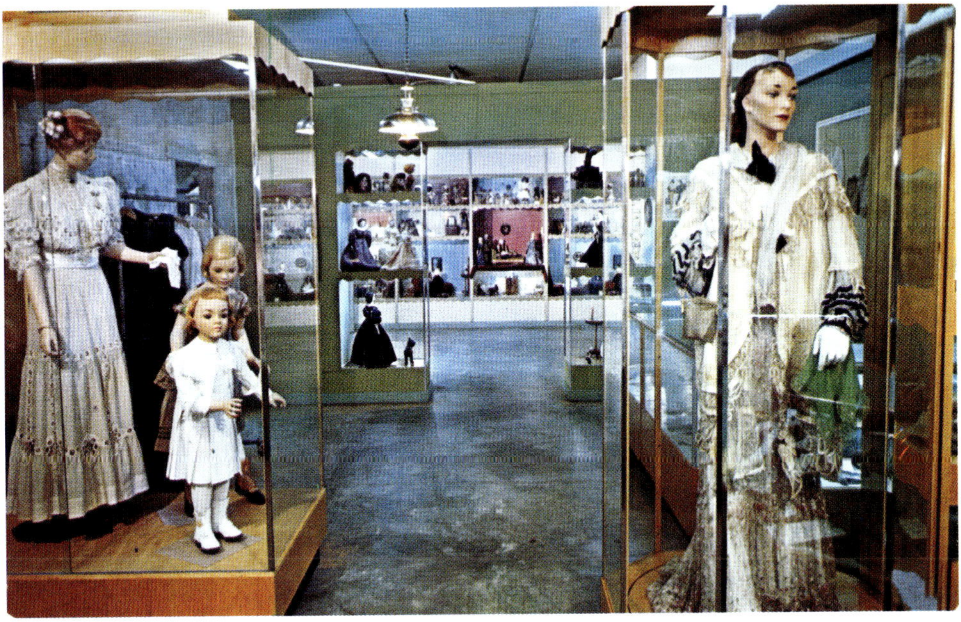

Besides improving the display space, the new museum also branched into other areas of history. Much publicity was given to its collections of antique toys and clothing ("from Grandma's day," according to the ads). What is ironic is that the cars, toys and clothing of the 1950s and '60s, when the museum operated, are now museum pieces and historic artifacts themselves. Time marches on. *Author's collection.*

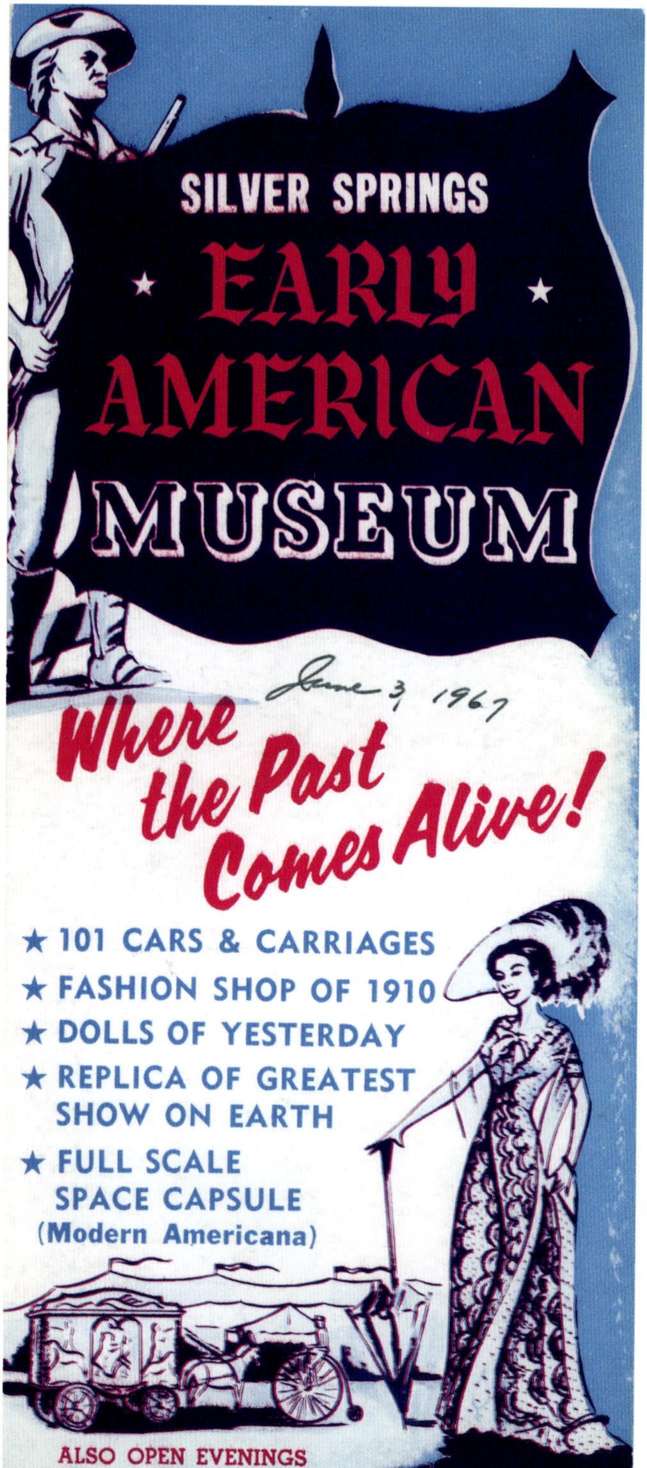

Finally, the former Carriage Cavalcade (aka Cavalcadia) had broadened its focus so widely that it had to adopt a new name: the Silver Springs Early American Museum, with seemingly something to offer every member of the family. *Author's collection.*

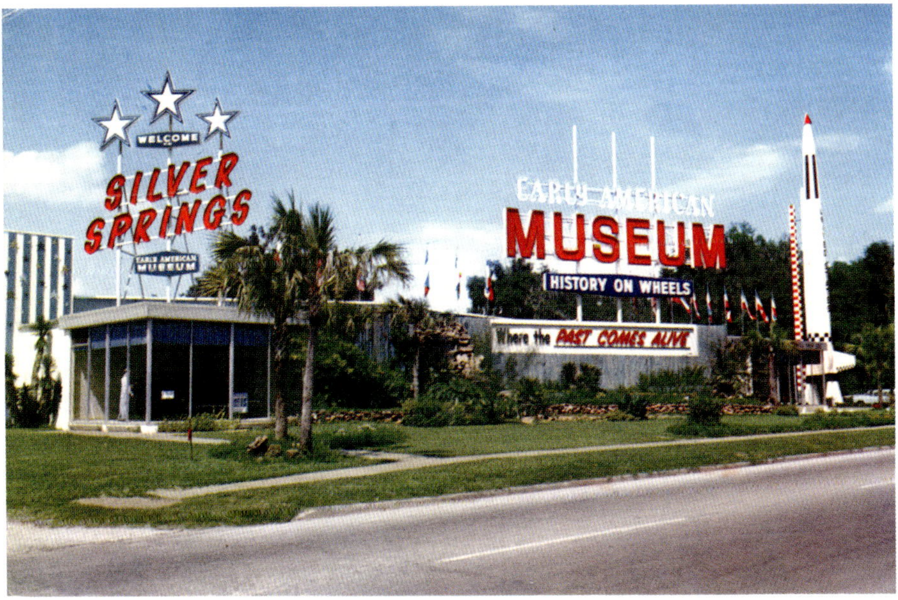

Along with its new name, the Early American Museum got what might have been the flashiest neon signage to be found anywhere along Highway 40 leading to Silver Springs. Pay special attention to that replica rocket in the parking lot; you will be seeing it again very shortly. *Author's collection.*

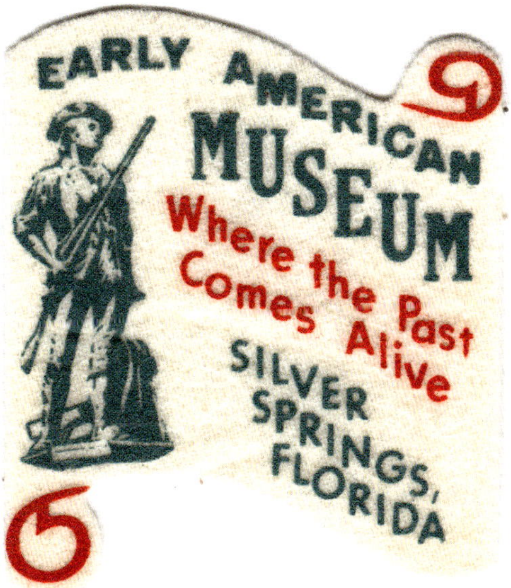

In retrospect, it is somewhat amusing to note that as a logo, the Early American Museum seemed to take its own name literally and incorporated the familiar image of the Revolutionary War minuteman. In reality, the museum's cars, toys and clothing dated from the late 1800s and early 1900s, long after the minutemen had hung up their muskets. *Author's collection.*

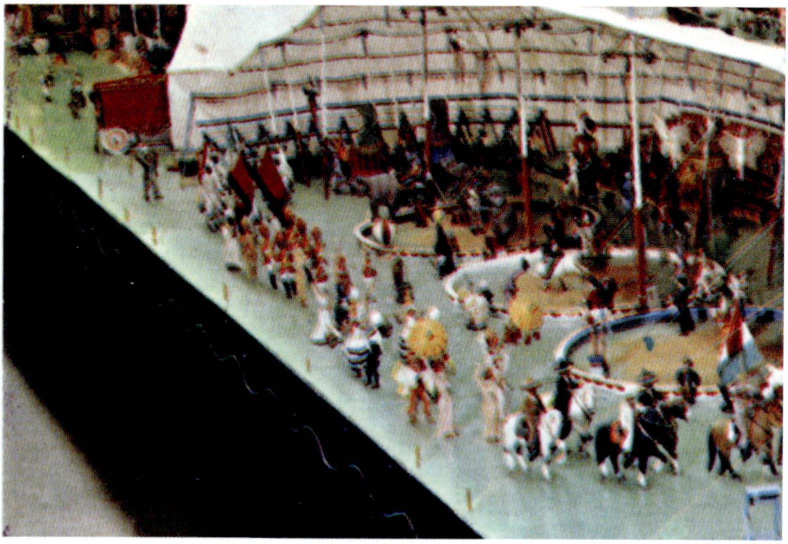

Kids who were dragged into the Early American Museum by their parents might well have been bored by all the moldy history. For them, there was an incredible hand-carved circus occupying a room of its own. A series of buttons along the handrails could be used to make the different parts of the circus come to life in crude animation. *Author's collection.*

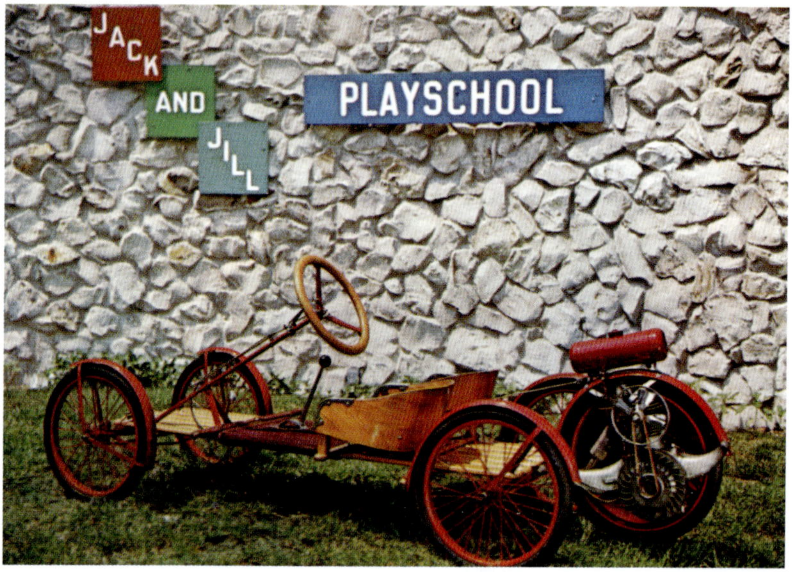

Speaking of youngsters, for this postcard, the Early American Museum took one of its display pieces, a vintage kiddie car, and positioned it with another "lost attraction" of the Ocala area, the Jack and Jill Playschool. Remember that public school kindergarten was still relatively rare at the time, making private preschool facilities a profitable enterprise. *Author's collection.*

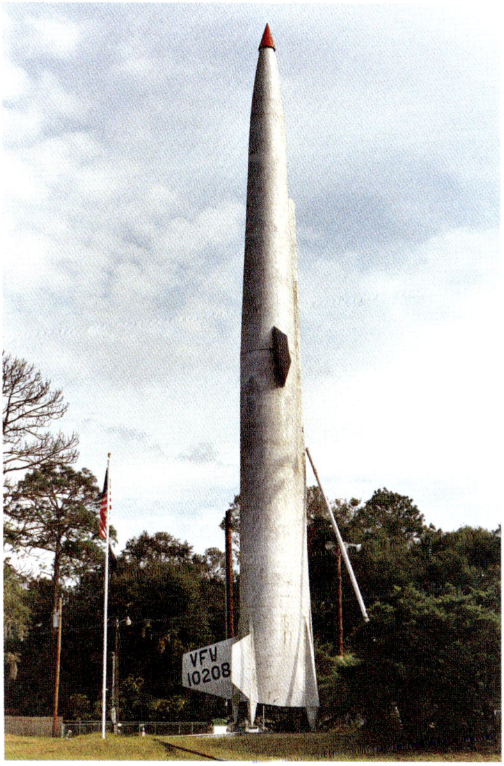

The Early American Museum stuck around a bit longer than some of the other Silver Springs border attractions, finally auctioning off its displays in 1983. Remember the rocket? Today, it sits outside a VFW lodge in Salt Springs, while its concrete supports and the tall pole that held it upright can still be seen in the weedy, overgrown former museum parking lot. *Author's collection.*

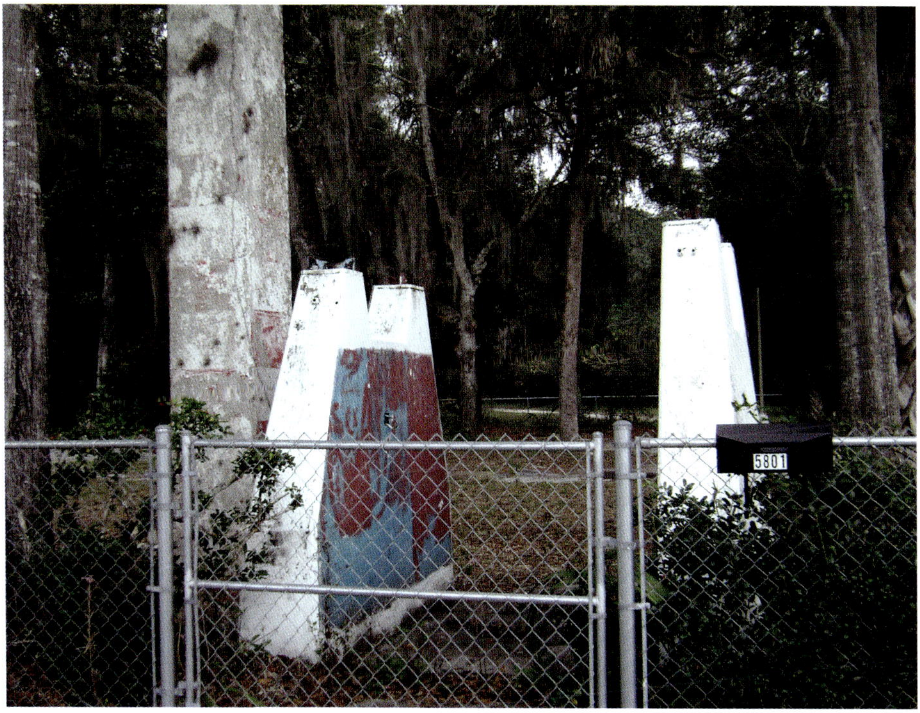

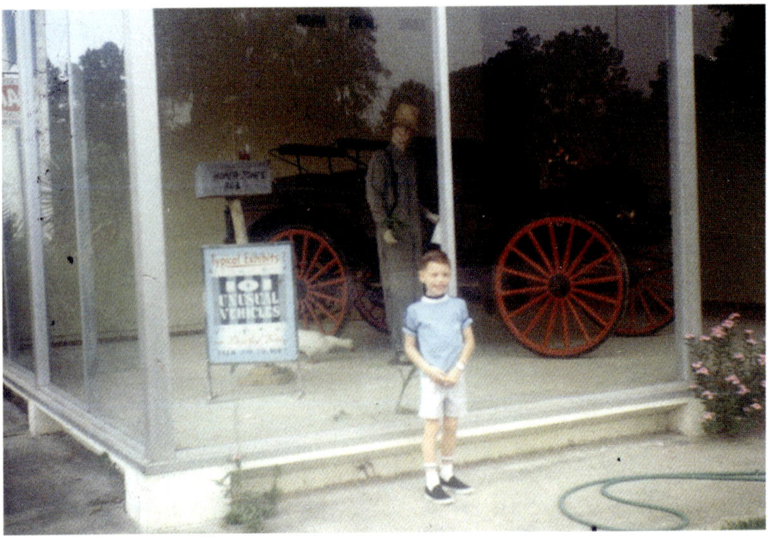

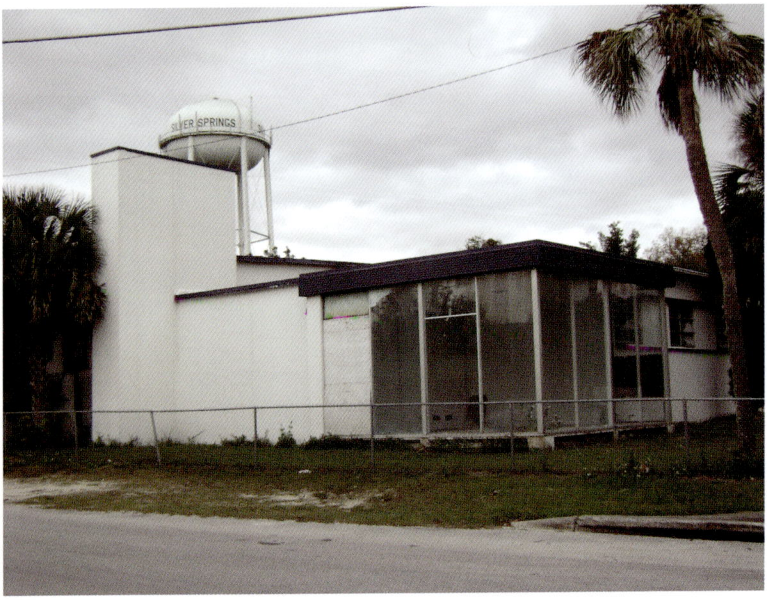

The former Early American Museum building has housed a number of other, non-tourism-related businesses since 1983, but it currently sits mostly empty. There is your author in 1970, posing with one of the museum's display windows. In the other photo, you see that same window today—looking rather melancholy without the classic cars and vintage clothes. *Author's collection.*

CHAPTER SIX

Six Gun Territory

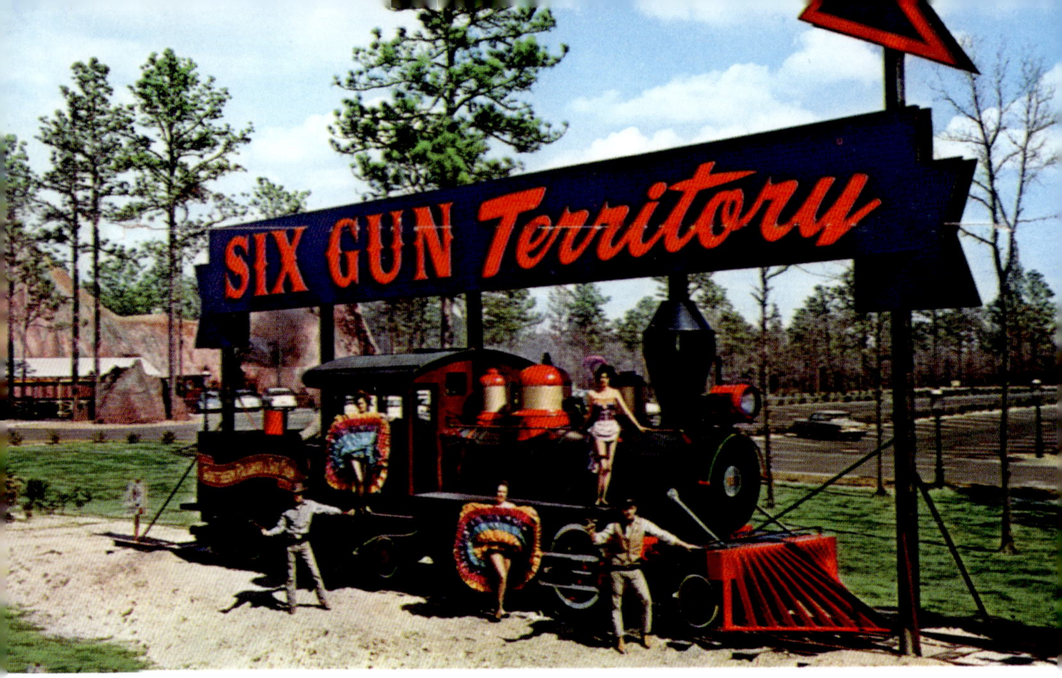

In 1963, the cowboys, Indians, outlaws and saloon girls of the mythical Old West came a-ropin' and a-ridin' into the Silver Springs neighborhood with the opening of Six Gun Territory. The sprawling theme park homesteaded an enormous piece of property alongside State Highway 40 a couple of miles west of the Silver Springs entrance gate. *Author's collection.*

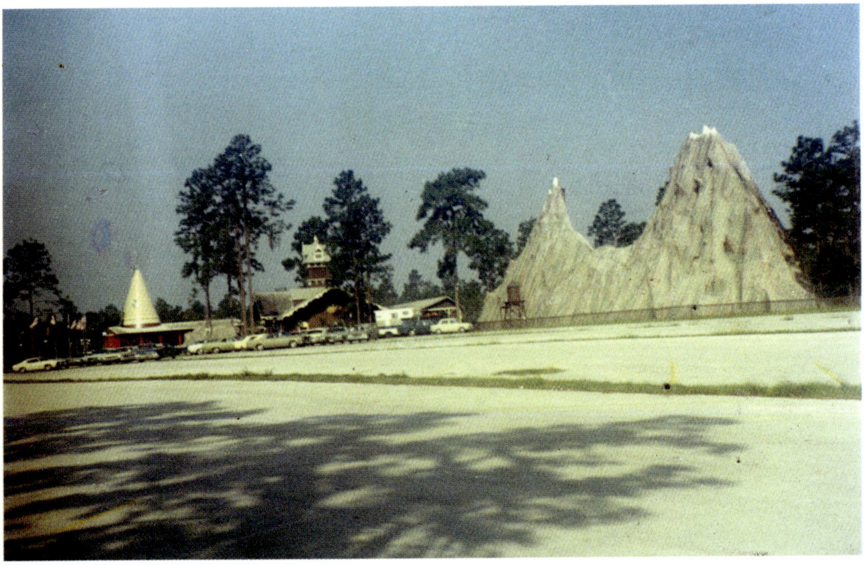

Six Gun Territory was a project of R.B. Coburn, who had already produced one hit attraction with his Ghost Town in the Sky at Maggie Valley, North Carolina. The size of that park was necessarily limited by its mountaintop locale, but Coburn had all the room he could possibly need with Six Gun, spreading it out over some two hundred vast acres. *Author's collection.*

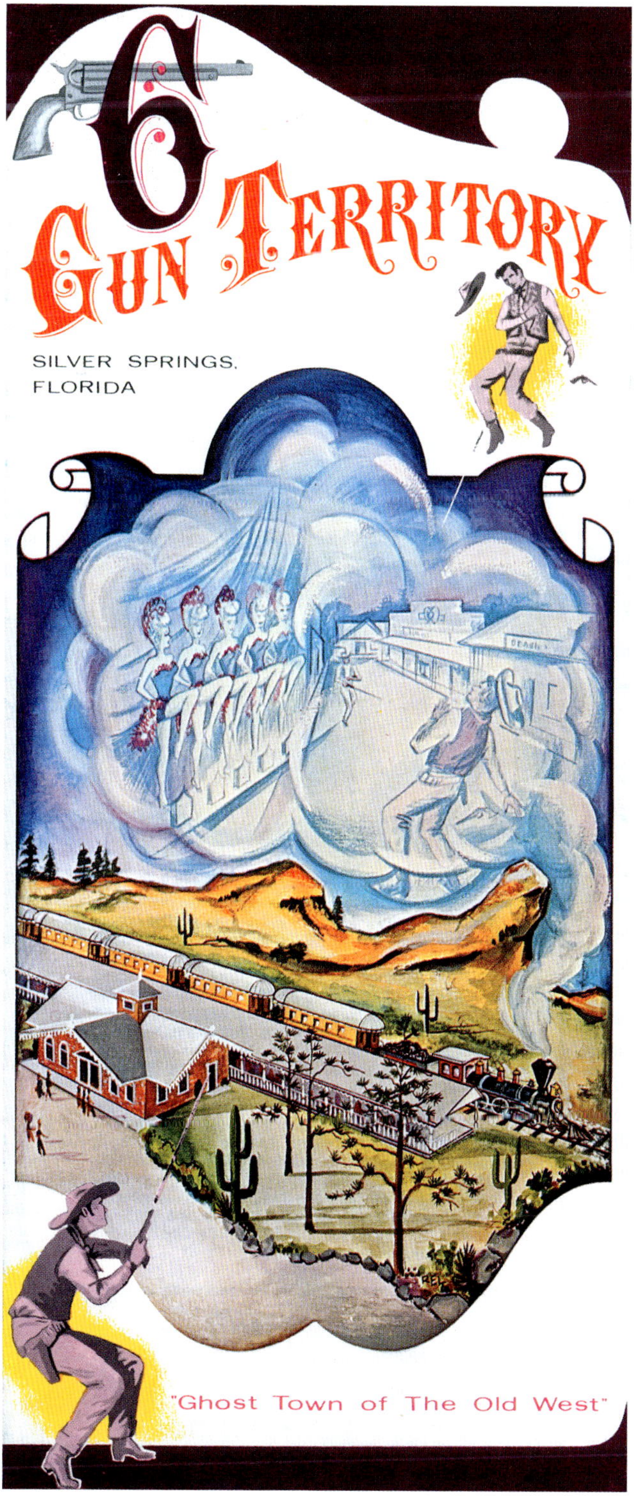

This was the earliest brochure for the new Six Gun Territory, when taking the train was the only choice for traveling from the parking area back into the past—and back into the property as well, where the simulated Western town sat. *Author's collection.*

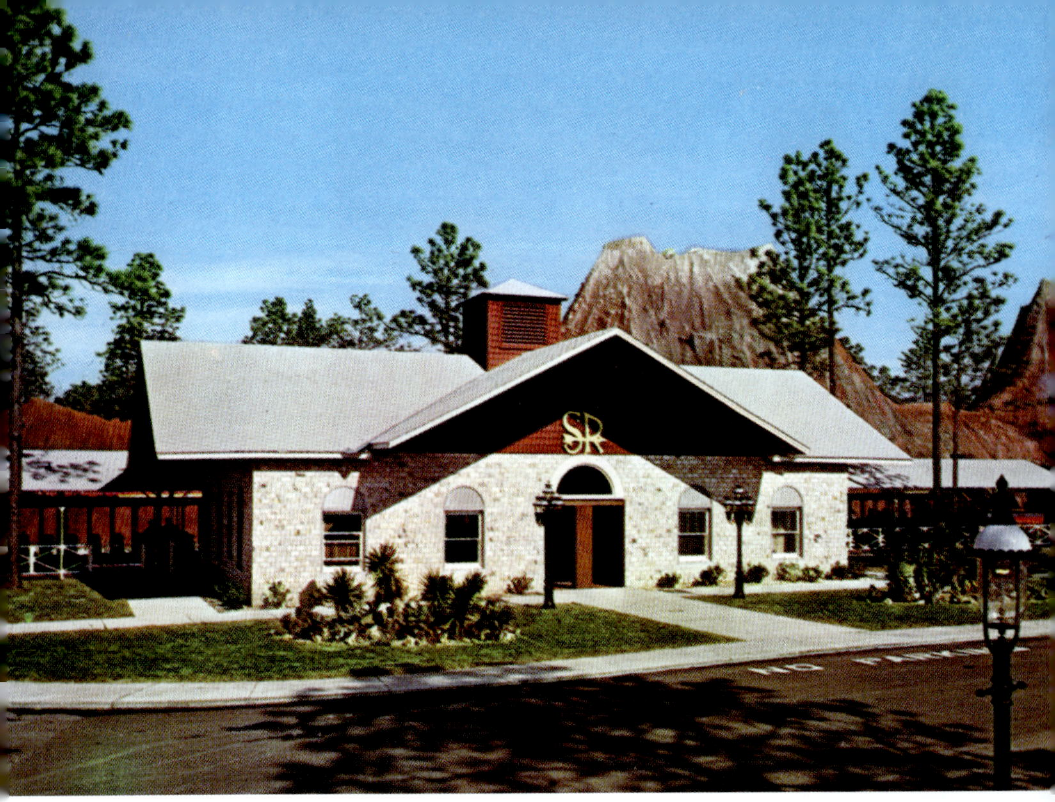

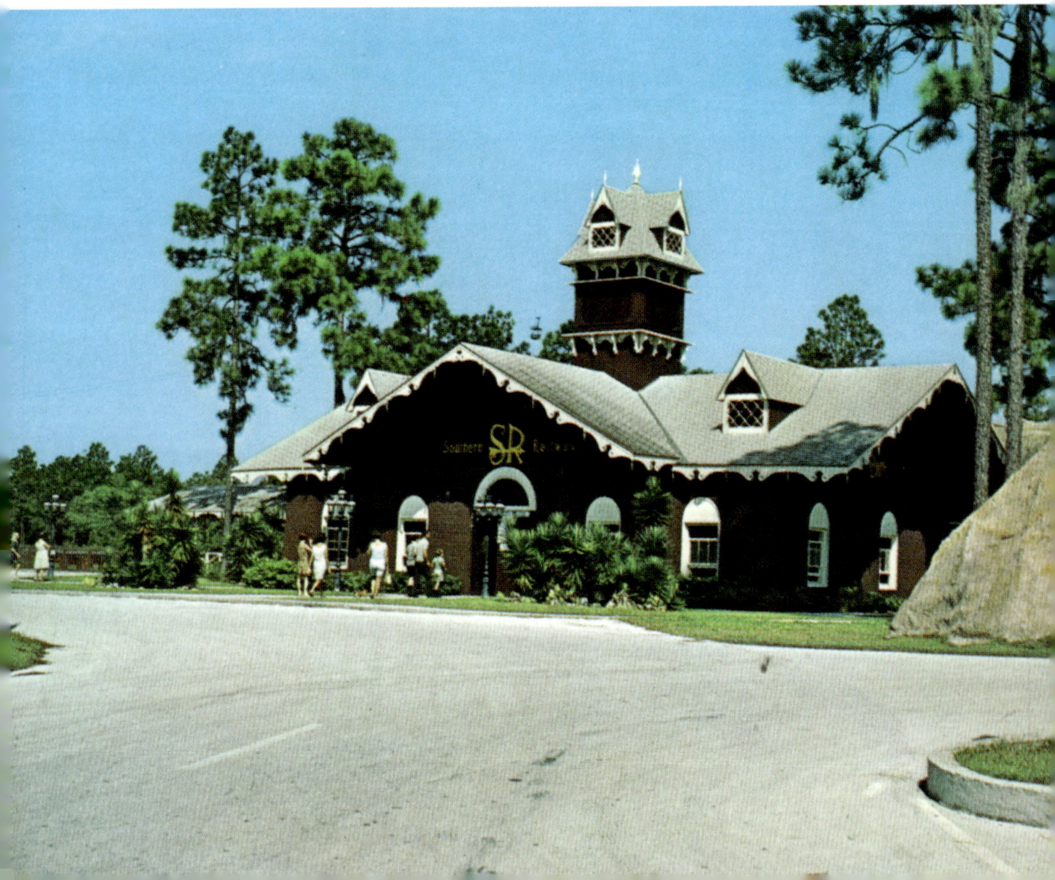

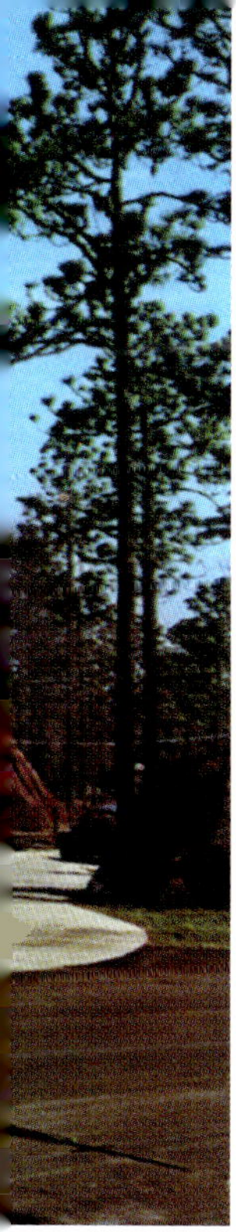

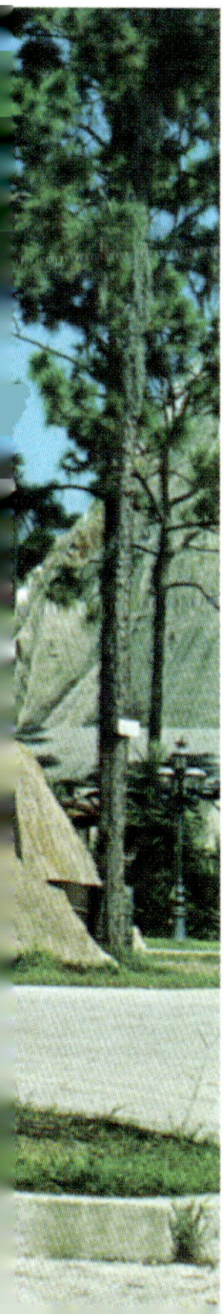

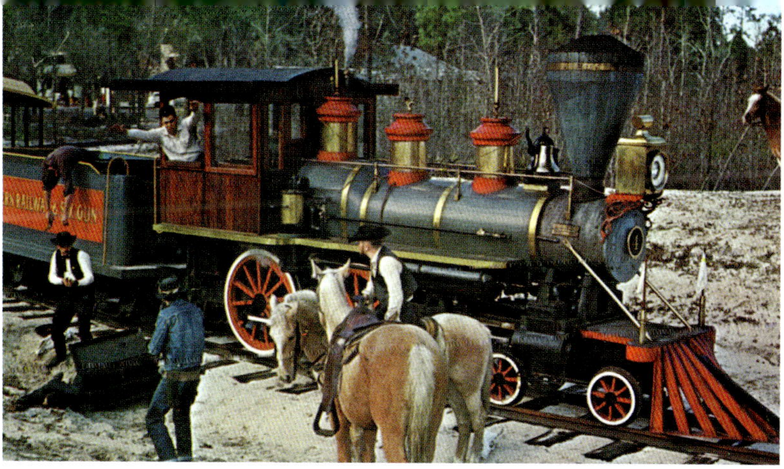

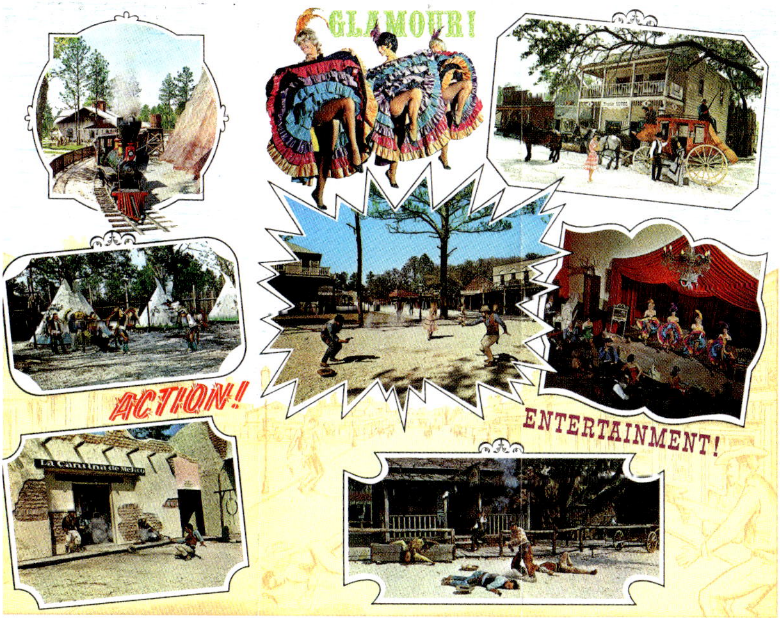

OPPOSITE: The journey into the past quite naturally began at the railroad depot. Yes, both photos are of the same building. When the park opened in 1963, the depot looked something like a branch bank, but by the end of the decade, it had been retrofitted with architectural details to give it a more nostalgic patina. *Top, Delee Perry collection; bottom, author's collection.*

ABOVE, TOP: As with any typical Western park, the trip from State Highway 40 to the territorial lands was fraught with peril. Along with static dioramas of frontier scenes, the train was consistently held up by ornery owlhoots or renegade Native Americans. Somehow, the passengers survived every time. *Author's collection.*

ABOVE, BOTTOM: Not everyone in the neighborhood was thrilled with the opening of a theme park costing nearly $2 million to build—especially when it was not on Silver Springs' property or even within sight of the entrance gate. Some of the existing attractions, the Deer Ranch in particular, fought to have Six Gun's construction permits denied, but the promise of new tourist revenue won out. *Author's collection.*

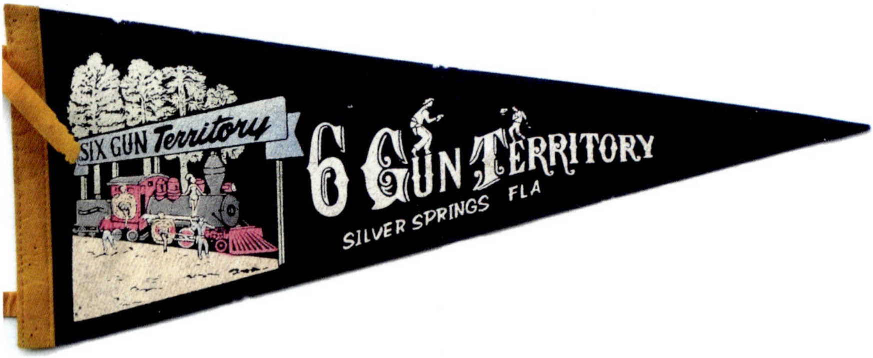

Yes, felt pennants of several different styles were sold at Six Gun over the years. This was apparently one of the earliest, as it based its artwork on the postcard view we saw at the beginning of this chapter. *Author's collection.*

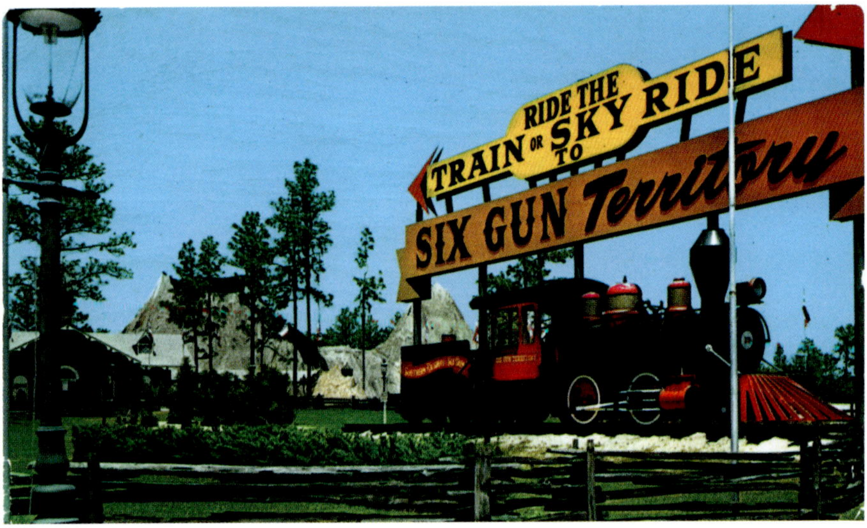

ABOVE & OPPOSITE: For Six Gun's second season in 1964, one addition made some folks feel it was getting too far away from the authentic Western theme. That new arrival was the Sky Ride, a soon-to-be-traditional amusement park feature that gave folks a choice of using the ground or the air for their journey back in time. *Author's collection.*

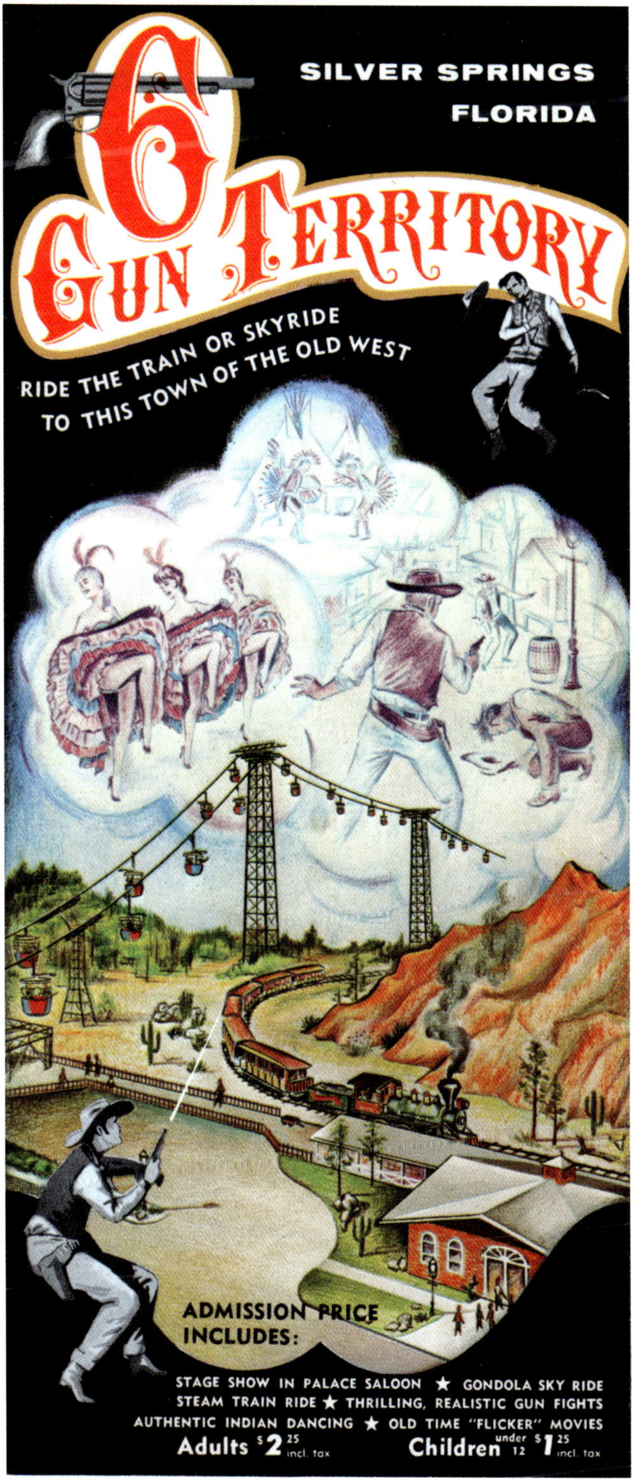
6 Gun Territory
SILVER SPRINGS
FLORIDA
RIDE THE TRAIN OR SKYRIDE
TO THIS TOWN OF THE OLD WEST
ADMISSION PRICE
INCLUDES:
STAGE SHOW IN PALACE SALOON ★ GONDOLA SKY RIDE
STEAM TRAIN RIDE ★ THRILLING, REALISTIC GUN FIGHTS
AUTHENTIC INDIAN DANCING ★ OLD TIME "FLICKER" MOVIES
Adults $2.25 incl. tax
Children under 12 $1.25 incl. tax

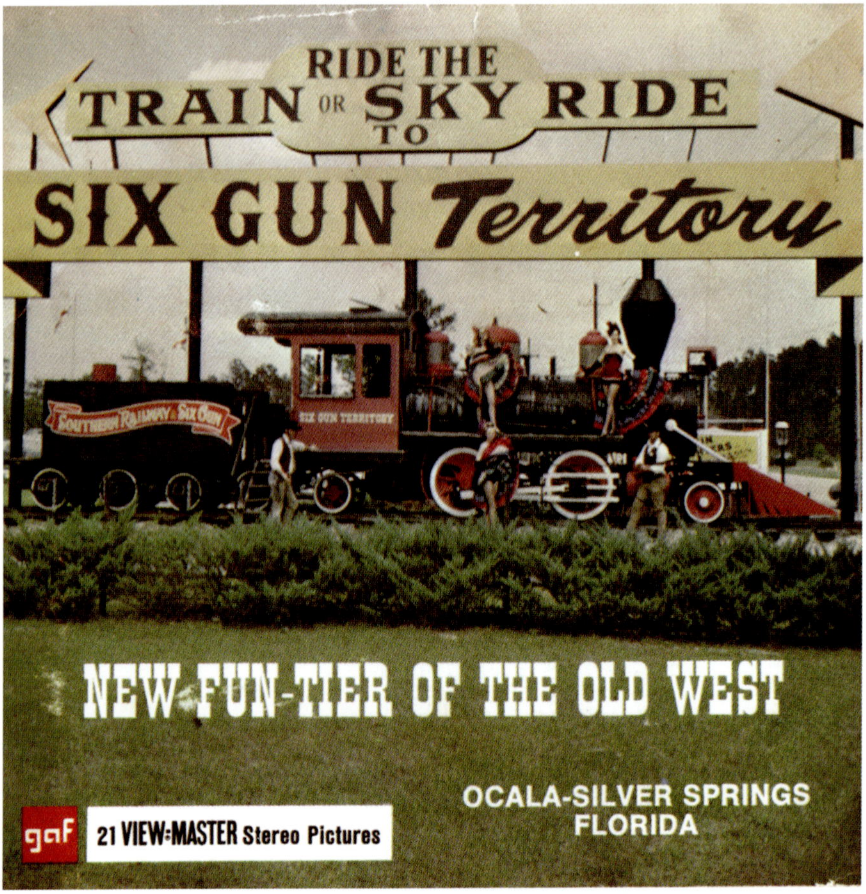
RIDE THE
TRAIN OR SKY RIDE
TO
SIX GUN Territory
SOUTHERN RAILWAY & SIX GUN
SIX GUN TERRITORY
NEW FUN-TIER OF THE OLD WEST
OCALA-SILVER SPRINGS
FLORIDA
gaf
21 VIEW-MASTER Stereo Pictures

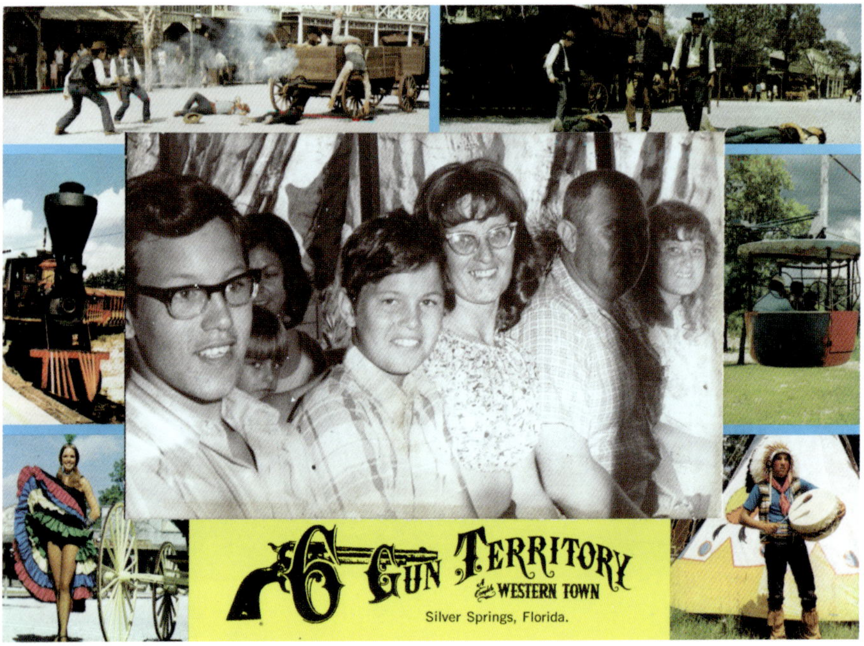
6 GUN TERRITORY
WESTERN TOWN
Silver Springs, Florida.

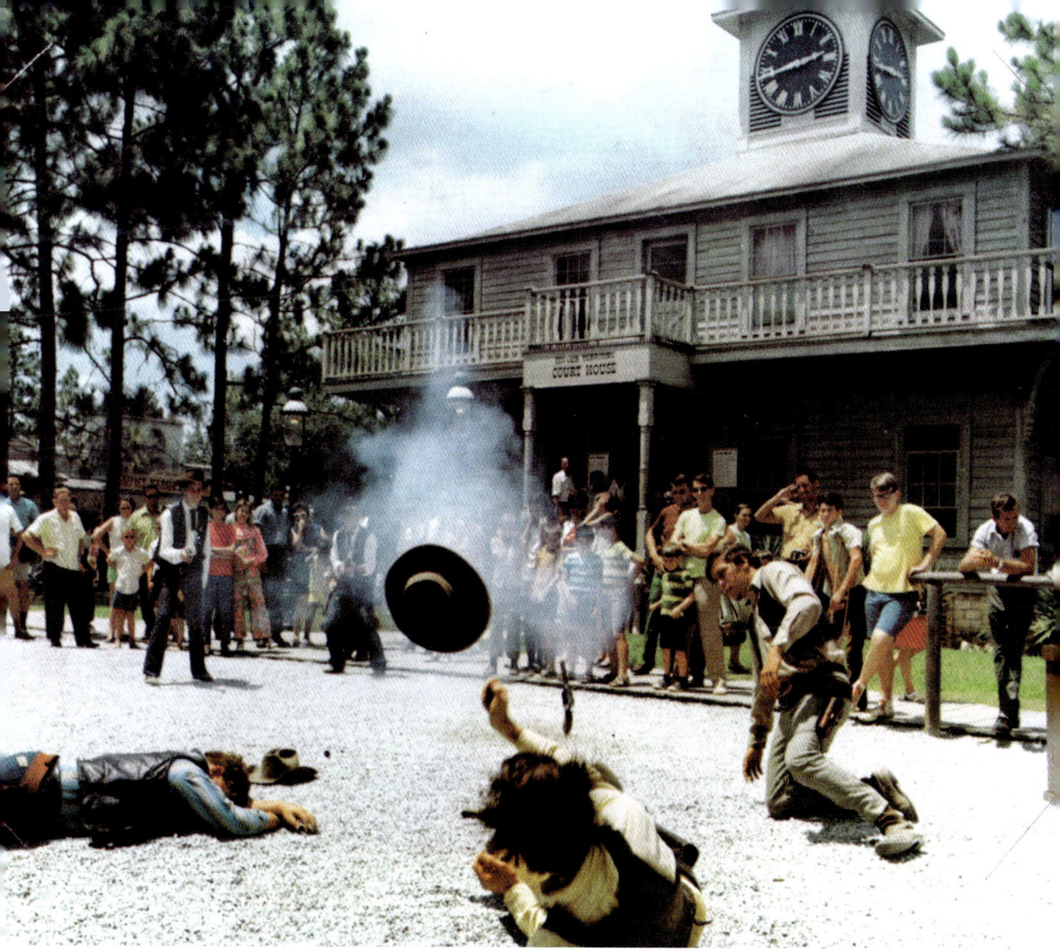

OPPOSITE, TOP: As with Silver Springs and most other attractions of any size, the Six Gun Territory View-Master packet captured twenty-one stereoviews of the park in brilliant color. For the cover, the cowboys and saloon girls again displayed their talents by the front entrance. *Author's collection.*

OPPOSITE, BOTTOM: One souvenir idea that seemed unashamedly copied from Silver Springs' glass-bottom boat photos was Six Gun's group shots that could then be sold inside a colorful cardboard frame. Unfortunately, it appears the shadow of a nearby post obliterated one member of this family. *Author's collection.*

ABOVE: The clock in the tower of the Six Gun Territory courthouse was a genuine antique, having originally been installed in the Marion County courthouse. In its new location, it presided over several daily gunfights in the street, where the good guys won and the bad guys inevitably ended up on Boot Hill. *Author's collection.*

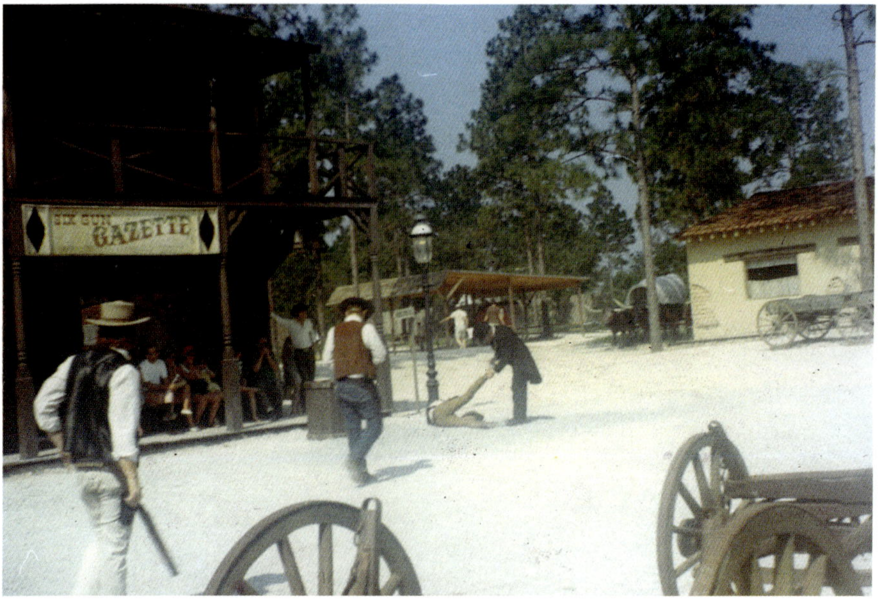

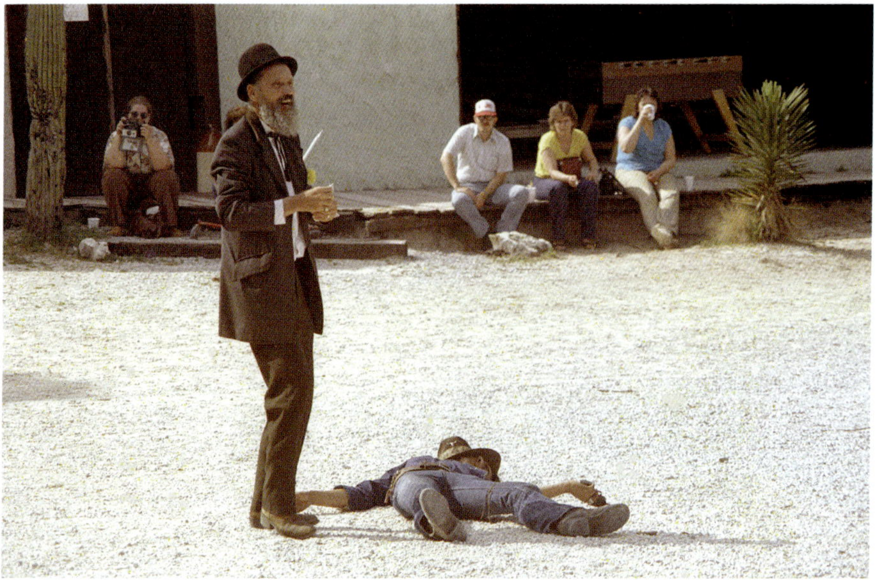

Although there was a feeling that the gunfight routines should be kept as historically accurate as possible, another train of thought said that there needed to be more comedy to offset the grim subject matter. One compromise was the character "Digger the Undertaker," who would get laughs by trying to recover valuables from the still-warm corpses littering the street after each confrontation. *Top, author's collection; bottom, Neal Frisbie collection.*

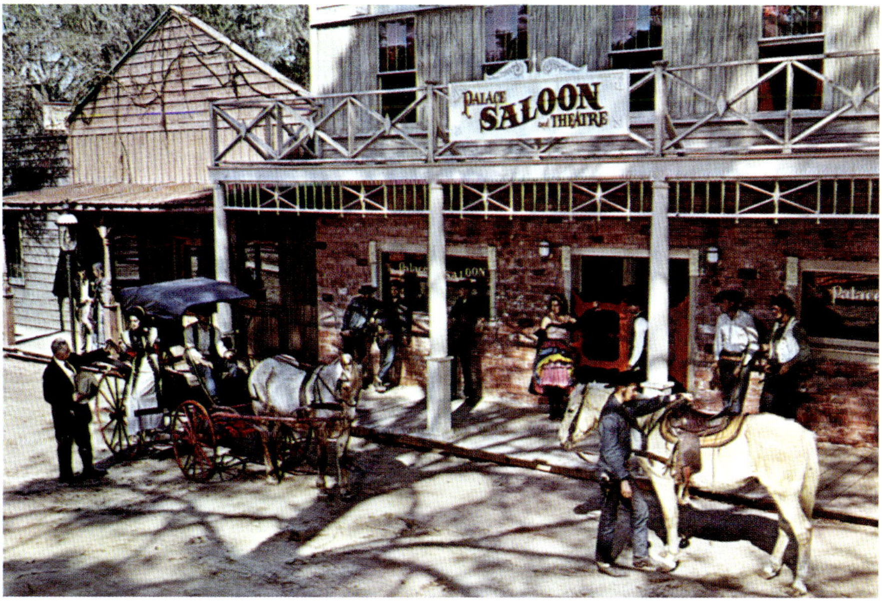

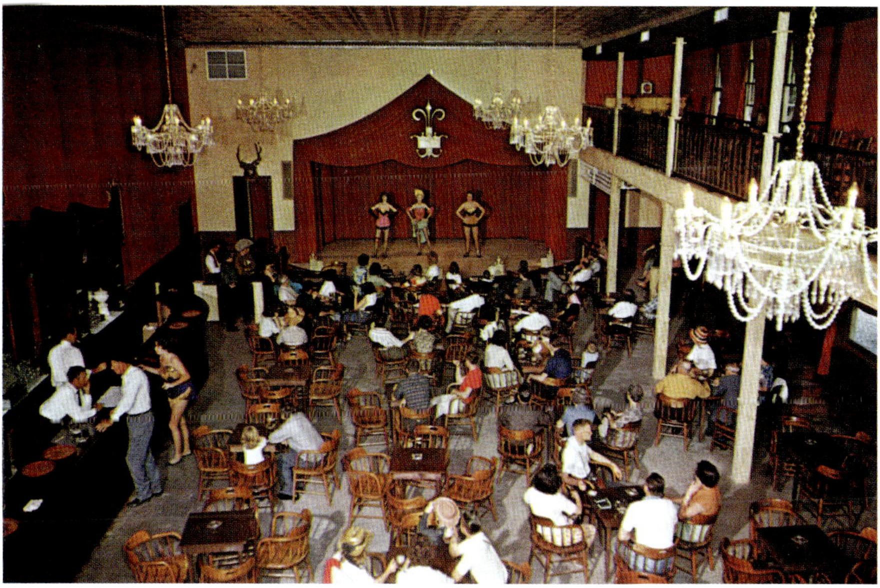

Historical accuracy was fine and all, but the Palace Saloon took that only so far. Patrons could belly up to the fifty-foot-long bar, but the only beverages served were soft drinks. Meanwhile, the red velvet curtains, the balcony, the stage show and the rinky-tink piano added a touch of atmosphere. *Top, author's collection; bottom, Delee Perry collection.*

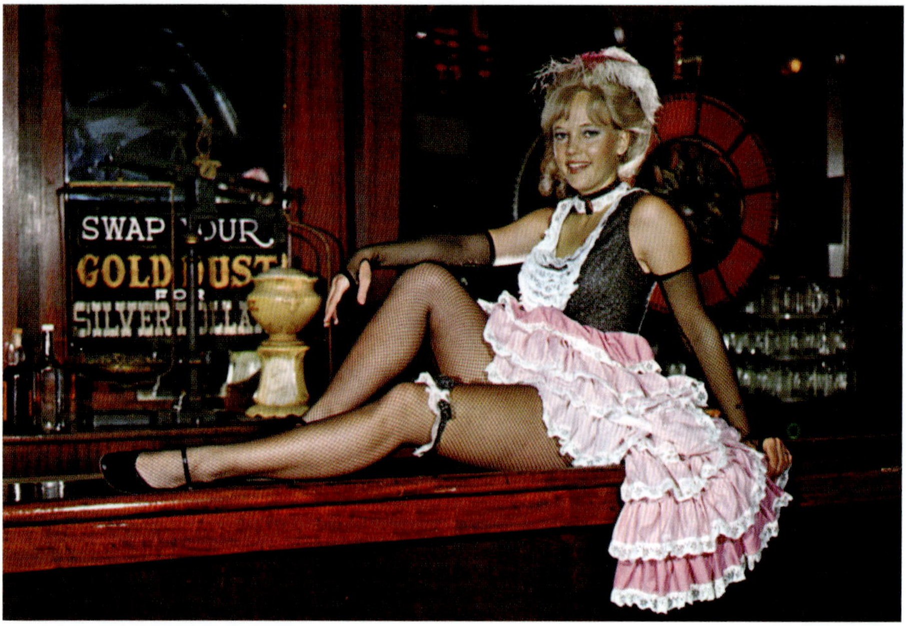

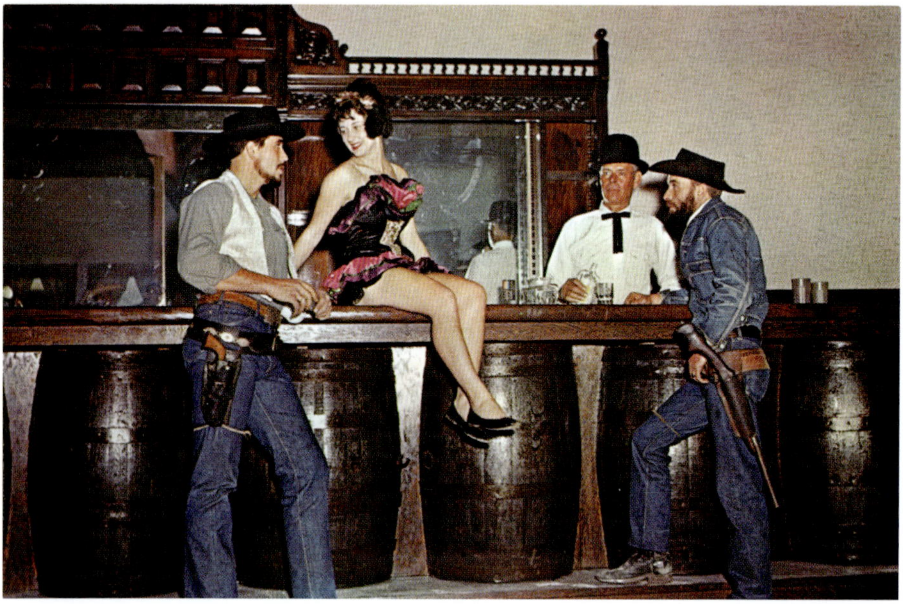

Okay, so the rotgut and redeye served at the Palace's bar might have been fake, but the pretty saloon girls were as real as possible. Among the many roles that had to be filled by both male and female performers, the majority of Ocala high school students ended up working at Six Gun in some capacity or another at some point. *Author's collection.*

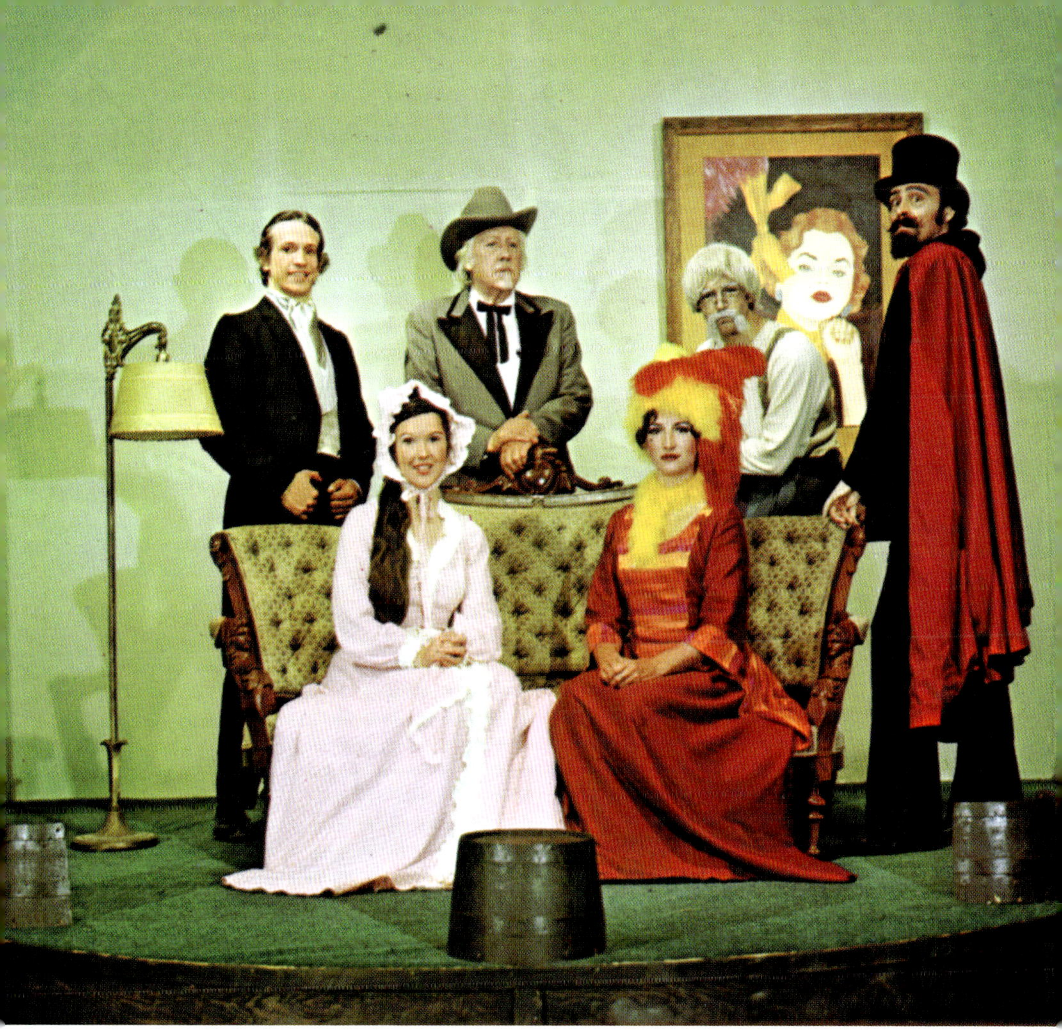

Besides the can-can dancers, the Palace Saloon stage was also used for presentations such as the legendary 1800s melodrama known as *The Drunkard*. Most people today may not realize that the creaky old play was the origin of the traditional villain in top hat, cape and sneer: "Ah, me proud beauty, I've come to collect the mortgage." *Delee Perry collection.*

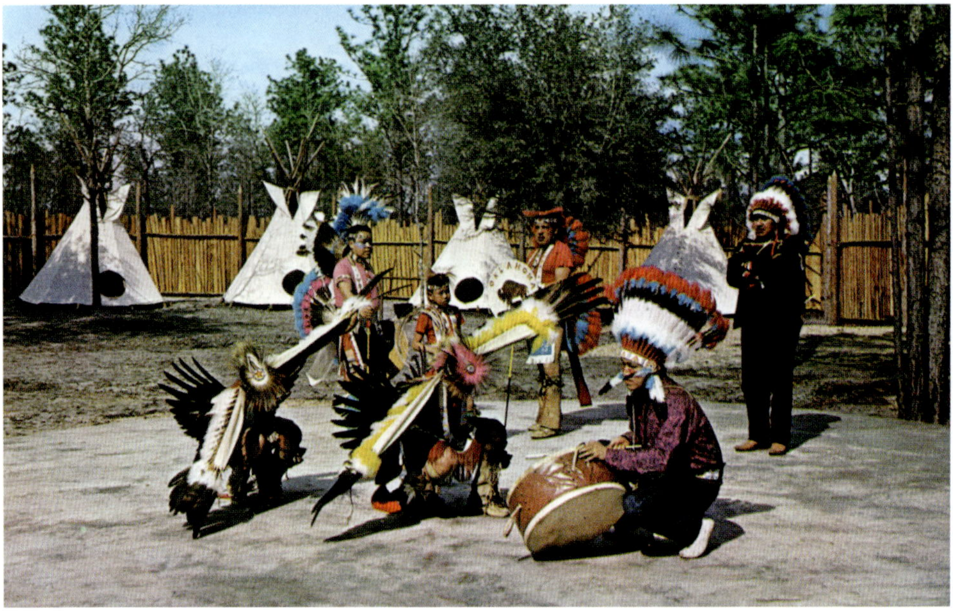

Whereas most Western theme parks had only enough room for one street, Six Gun's huge acreage meant it could incorporate other "neighborhoods" in addition to the town proper. According to the press materials, the Indian Village was home to members of five Oklahoma tribes: Osage, Sac and Fox, Pawnee, Ponca and Iowa. *Author's collection.*

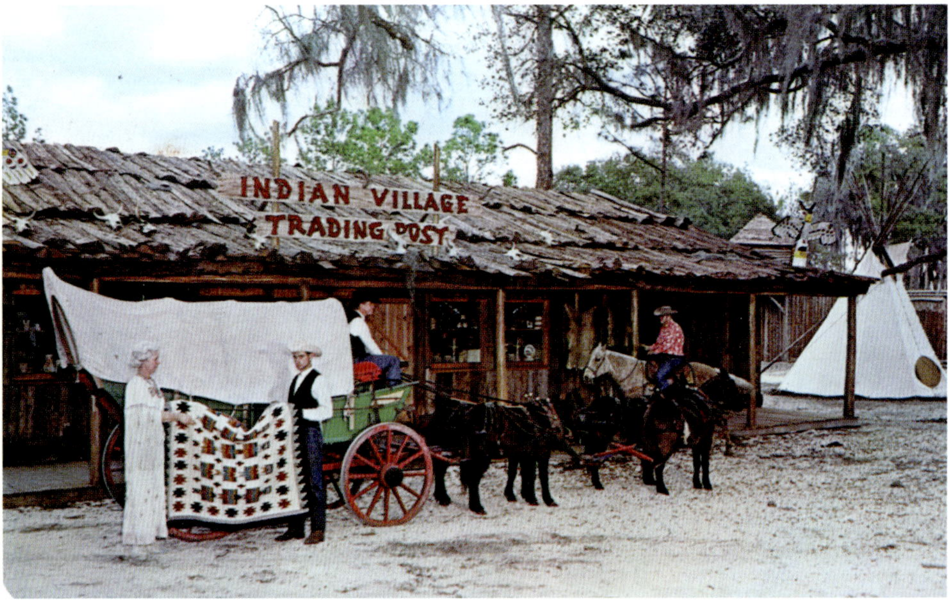

Six Gun's Indian Village might have picked up an idea or two from Ross Allen's Seminole settlement. Not only did the inhabitants live on the property, but they also sold their traditional wares in the Trading Post. At least the Plains imagery was more appropriate to the Oklahoma tribes than it was to the Cherokee community in North Carolina. *Author's collection.*

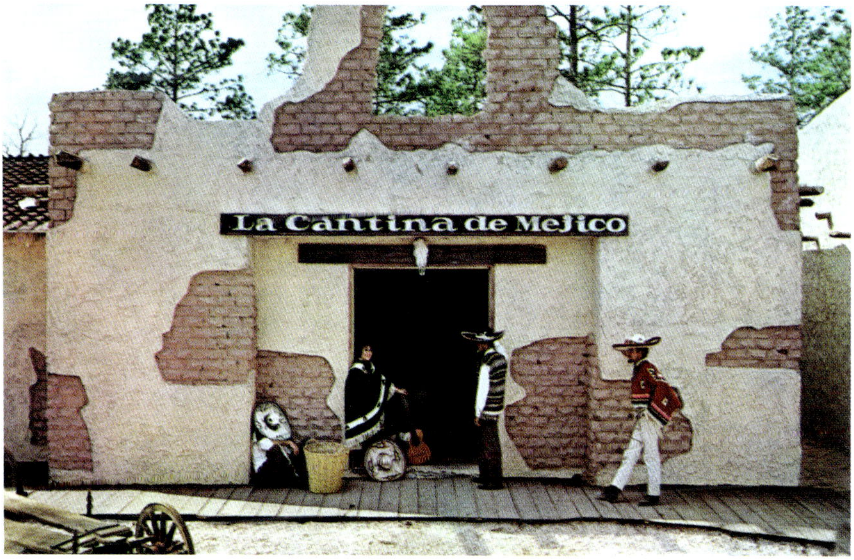

Even more unusual than the Indian Village was Six Gun's "Mexican border town," which helped blur the simulated town's geographical location. That element alone would indicate that it was not supposed to be Oklahoma or even Dodge City, but rather some mythical locale that never actually existed—even if the Mexican food was real. *Author's collection.*

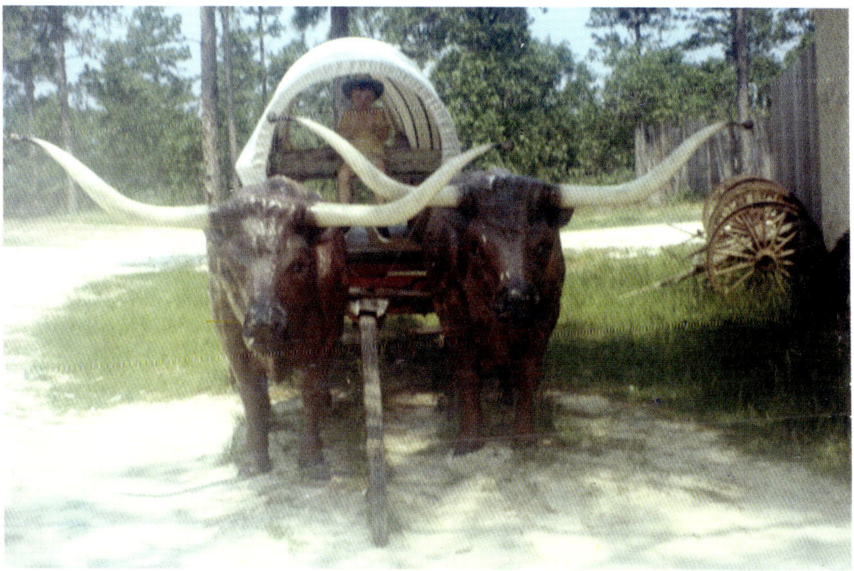

Six Gun Territory abounded in photo opportunities that had little or nothing to do with the action or business being conducted all around. Many family albums ended up showing the kids posing on this covered wagon pulled by concrete oxen. *Author's collection.*

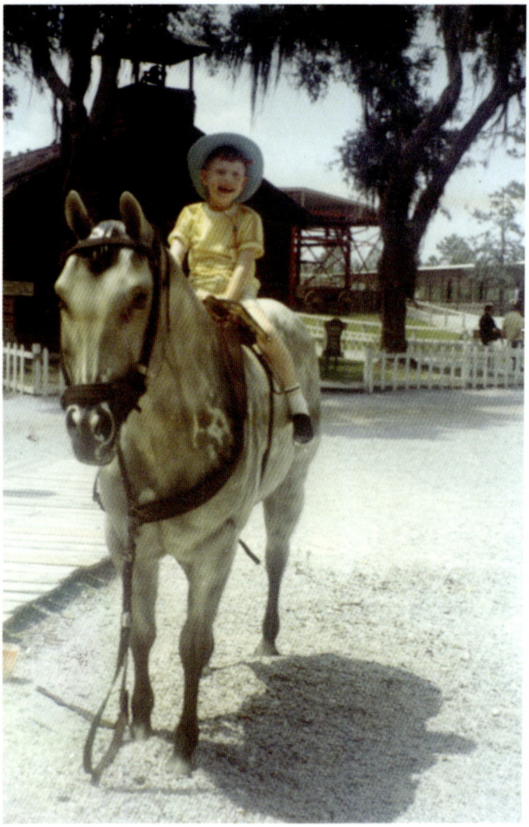

In case you did not guess it, both of these views are of the author on his 1970 visit to Six Gun Territory. As you can see, the model horses ranged in style from the majestic Silver or Trigger type to another that looked somewhat dopey and more like a hippopotamus than a horse (maybe a horseapotamus?). The author's dad was also a whiz at cutting off the tops of his photo subjects' heads. *Author's collection.*

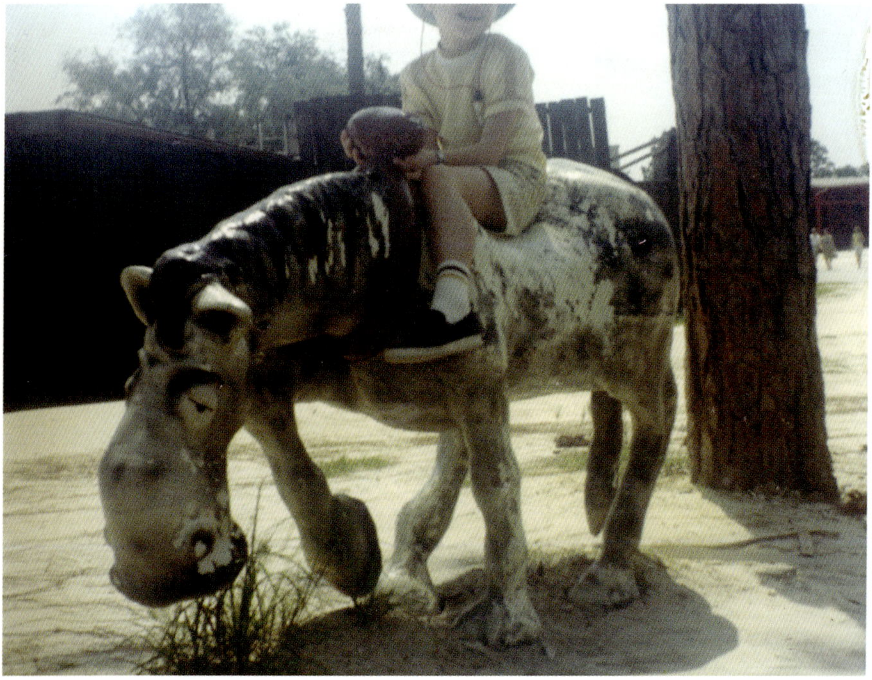

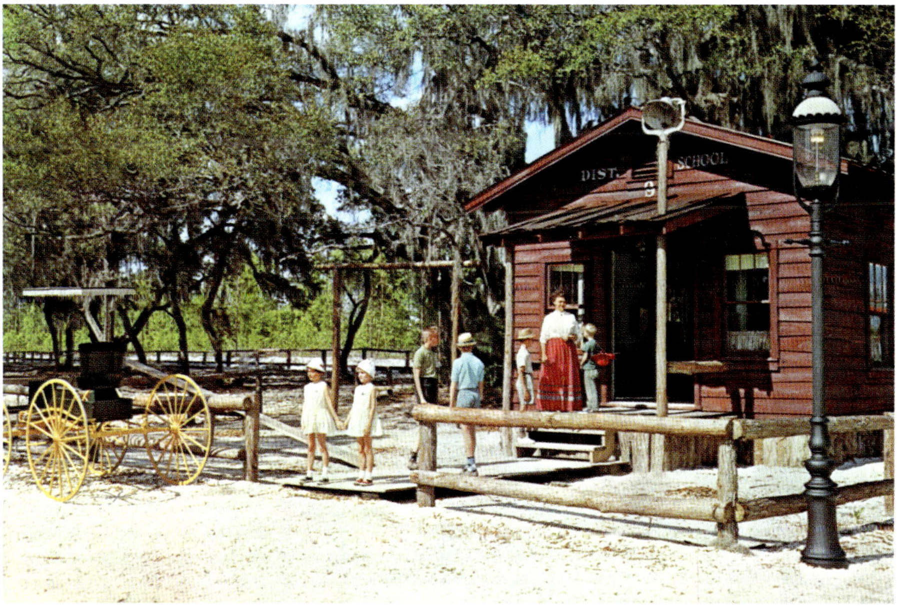

Kids visiting Six Gun Territory during summer vacation probably wanted to run as far away from a school as possible. In the interest of completeness, though, a typical little red schoolhouse was part of the scenery, giving the youngsters a chilling reminder of what they would be facing once again in just a few months. *Delee Perry collection.*

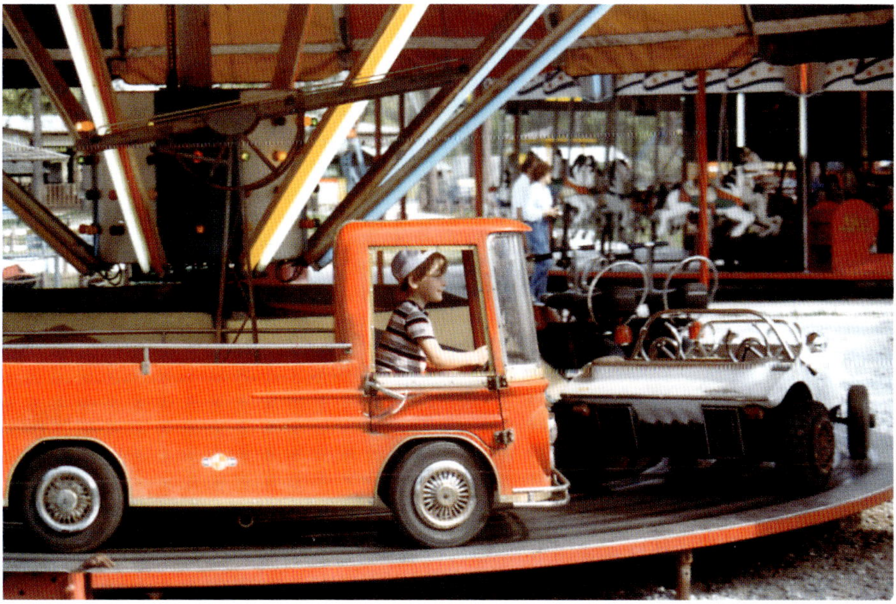

Many people felt that Six Gun's last grip on being any sort of authentic Western town was shot to pieces with the addition of Funland, a collection of traditional amusement park rides. As out of place as they might have been at the time, today, some of them are just as much historical relics as the more antique Six Gun displays. *Neal Frisbie collection.*

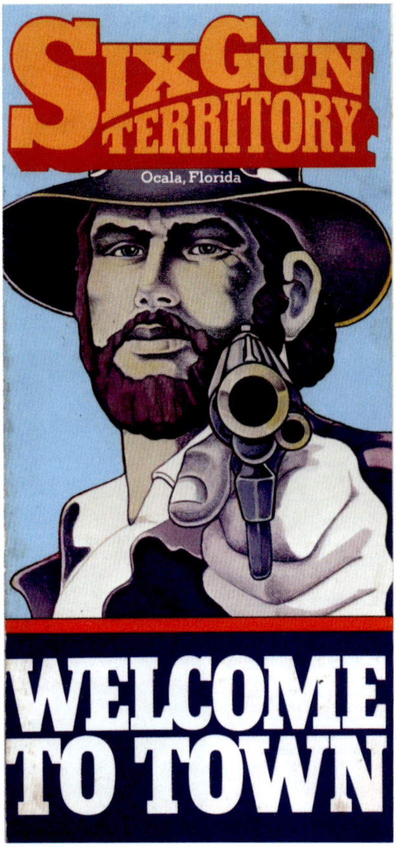

LEFT: Around 1970, R.B. Coburn sold his chain of Western theme parks to National Service Industries (NSI), but as that decade pushed onward, the popularity of TV Westerns continued to decline. This striking brochure from the late 1970s or early '80s seems to be virtually daring the tourists to skip a Six Gun visit. *Author's collection.*

BELOW: In 1978, NSI put Six Gun Territory up for sale, and the next few years were rough ones. Finally, in early 1984, the gunfighters and the saloon girls packed up their weapons of choice and retreated back into the historical past. A three-day auction during the month of April sent the closed attraction's many components into the hands of individuals and other parks from all over the country. *Author's collection.*

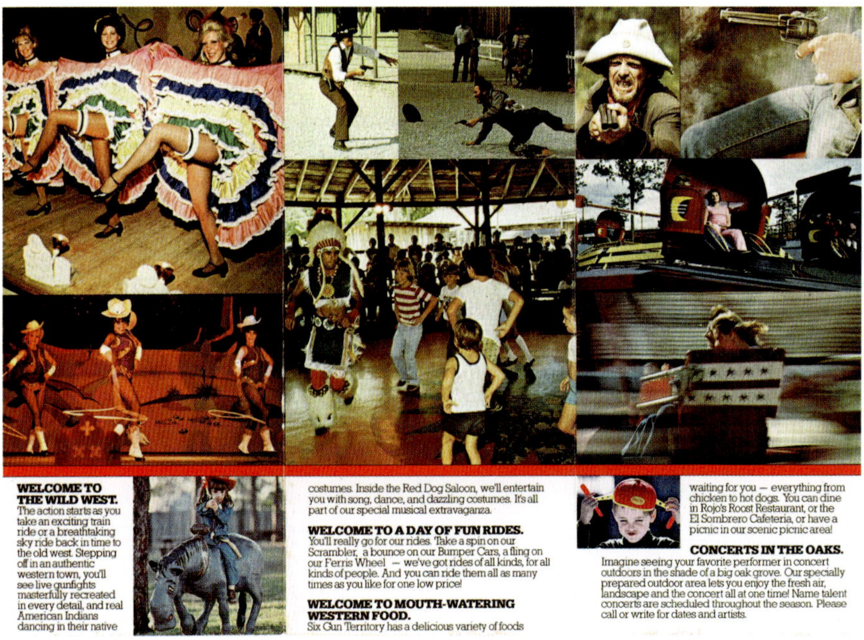

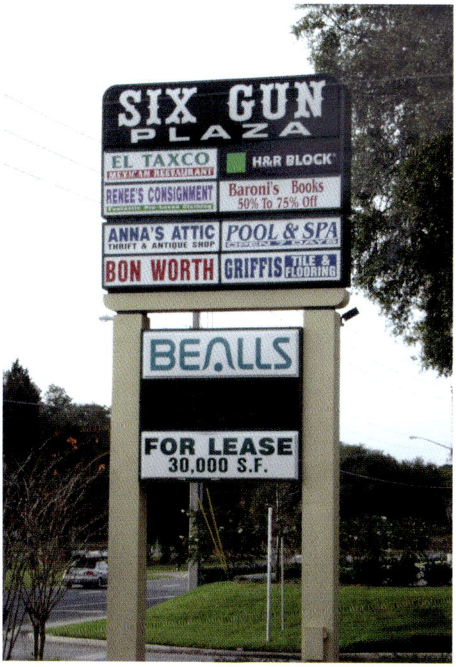

LEFT: Today, the area next to Highway 40 where Six Gun's entrance and railroad depot once stood is home to a shopping center known as Six Gun Plaza. Those who have lived in Ocala for fewer than forty years might not even realize the origin of the name. *Author's collection.*

BELOW: The site of the Six Gun frontier town sat abandoned for years after the park closed. The buildings were so solidly constructed that even bulldozers were unable to push them down; finally, in a desperate attempt to clear the property, the wooden structures were burned to the ground. This is how the former town looked in 2007; it has since been developed into a residential neighborhood. Six Gun Territory is now as much a part of history as the Old West it tried so hard to represent. *Author's collection.*

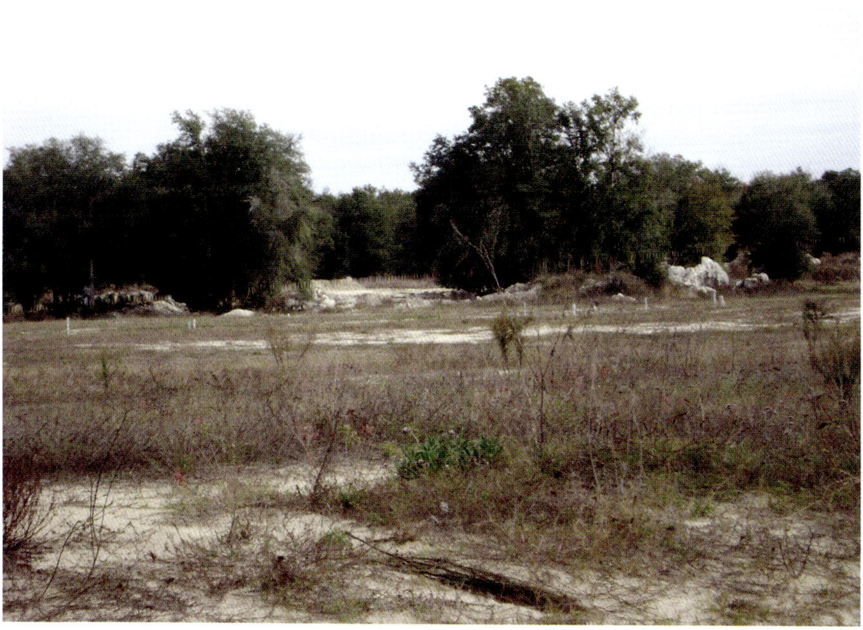

CHAPTER SEVEN

Meanwhile, in the Rest of the County

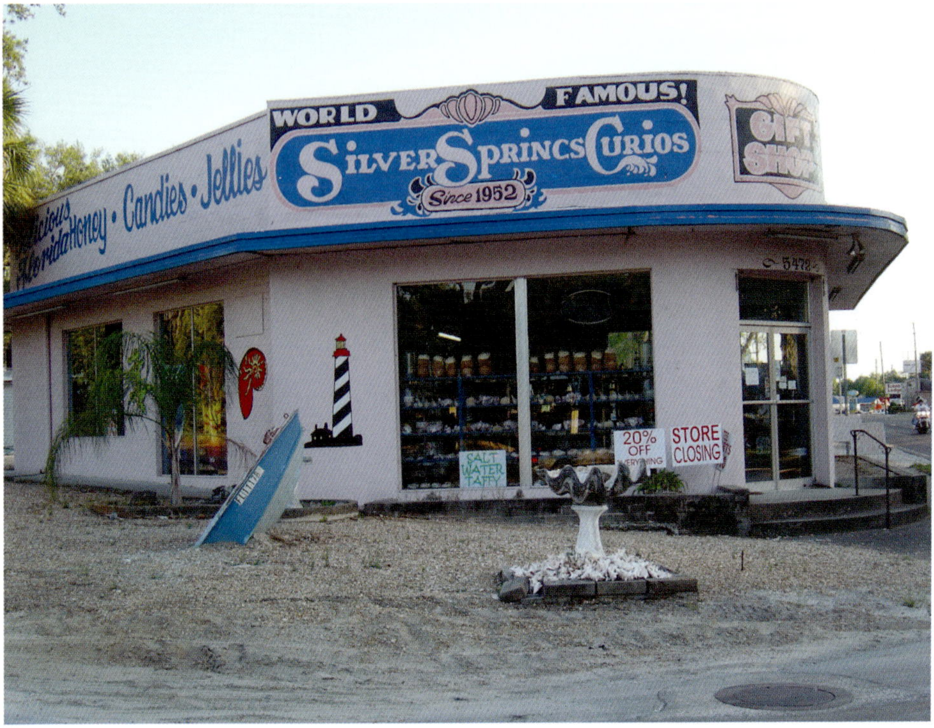
WORLD FAMOUS!
Silver Springs Curios
Since 1952
Florida Honey • Candies • Jellies
SALT WATER TAFFY
20% OFF
STORE CLOSING

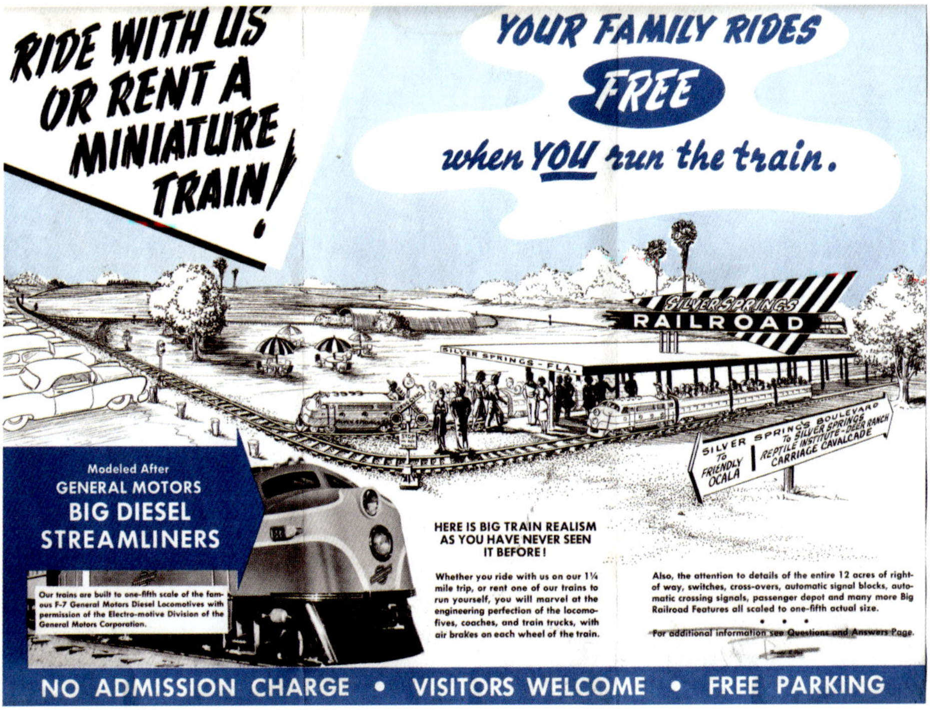
RIDE WITH US OR RENT A MINIATURE TRAIN!
YOUR FAMILY RIDES FREE when YOU run the train.
SILVER SPRINGS RAILROAD
SILVER SPRINGS FLA.
SILVER SPRINGS BOULEVARD
To FRIENDLY OCALA
To SILVER SPRINGS REPTILE INSTITUTE-DEER RANCH CARRIAGE CAVALCADE
Modeled After GENERAL MOTORS BIG DIESEL STREAMLINERS
Our trains are built to one-fifth scale of the famous F-7 General Motors Diesel Locomotives with permission of the Electro-motive Division of the General Motors Corporation.
HERE IS BIG TRAIN REALISM AS YOU HAVE NEVER SEEN IT BEFORE!
Whether you ride with us on our 1¼ mile trip, or rent one of our trains to run yourself, you will marvel at the engineering perfection of the locomofives, coaches, and train trucks, with air brakes on each wheel of the train.
Also, the attention to details of the entire 12 acres of right-of way, switches, cross-overs, automatic signal blocks, automatic crossing signals, passenger depot and many more Big Railroad Features all scaled to one-fifth actual size.
For additional information see Questions and Answers Page.
NO ADMISSION CHARGE • VISITORS WELCOME • FREE PARKING

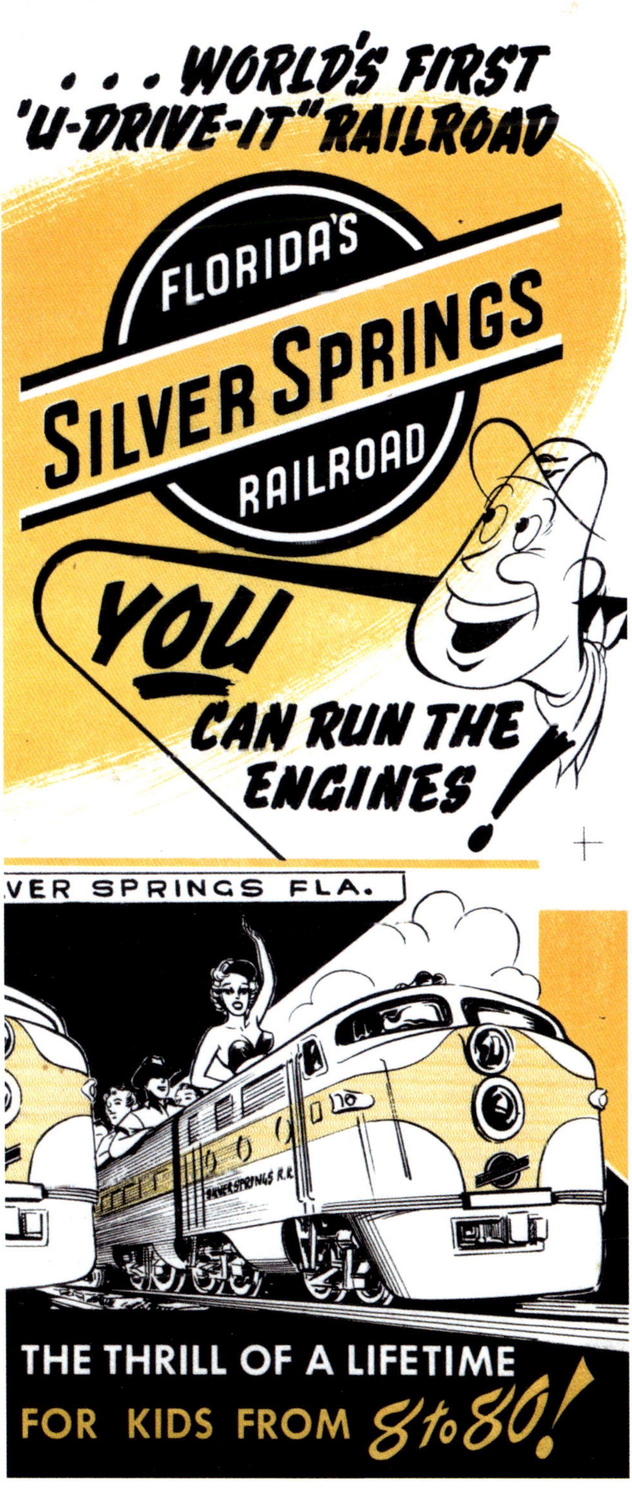

OPPOSITE, TOP: The distinctive pink-and-blue building of Silver Springs Curios shelled out its shells and other Florida souvenirs from 1952 until 2006, when this photo was taken during its going-out-of-business sale. Its property was needed for the widening of the busy intersection, and cars now zoom through its former site without even a respectful pause. *Author's collection.*

OPPOSITE, BOTTOM & THIS PAGE: Unlike Silver Springs Curios, some attractions did not remain around long enough to make a lasting impression. One of those was this miniature "U-Drive-It" railroad. The artwork on this brochure was the work of our old friend Val Valentine, which probably helps date it to around 1955 or thereabouts. *Author's collection.*

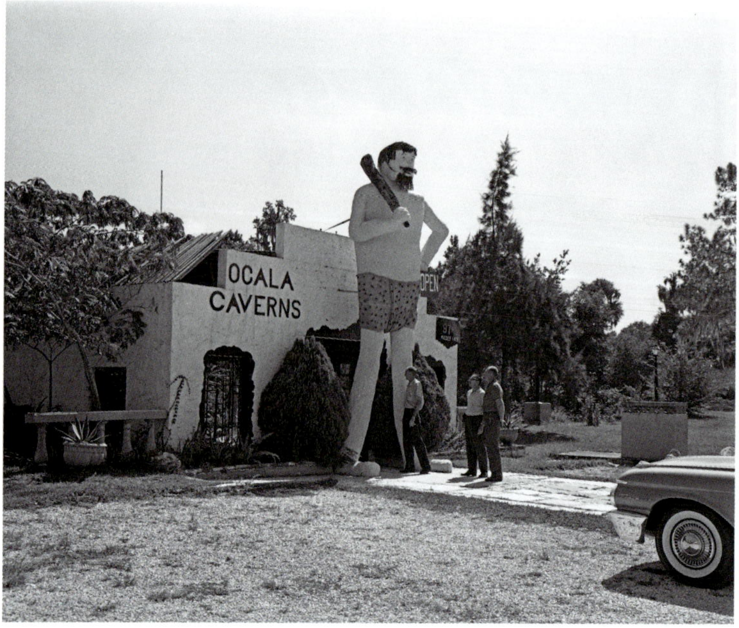
OCALA
CAVERNS
OPEN

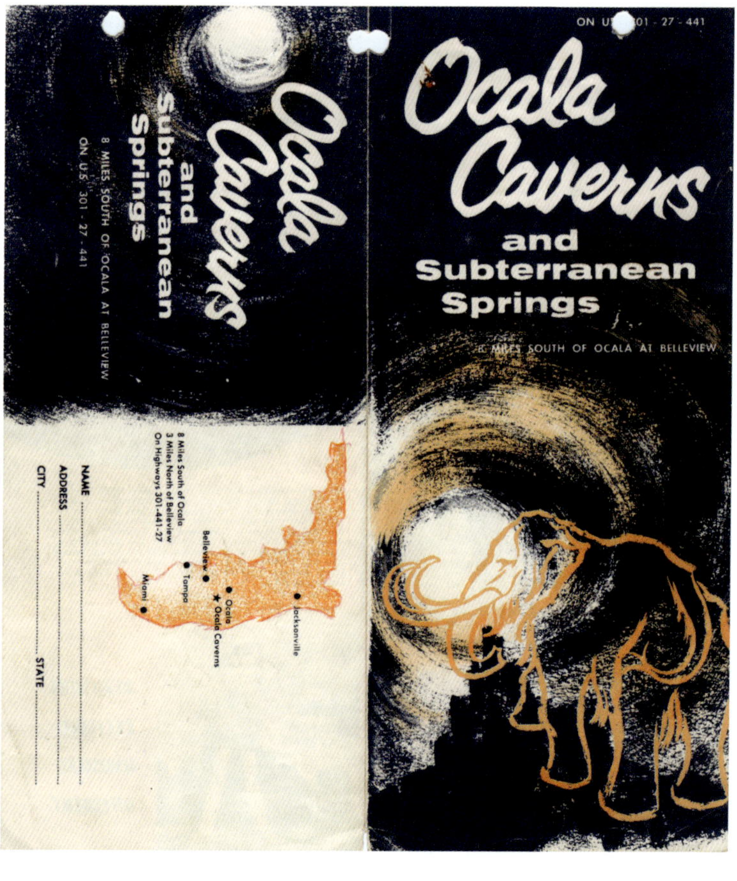
Ocala Caverns
and
Subterranean
Springs
8 MILES SOUTH OF OCALA AT BELLEVIEW
ON U.S. 301 - 27 - 441
8 Miles South of Ocala
3 Miles North of Belleview
On Highways 301-441-27
Jacksonville
Ocala
Ocala Caverns
Belleview
Tampa
Miami
NAME
ADDRESS
CITY
STATE

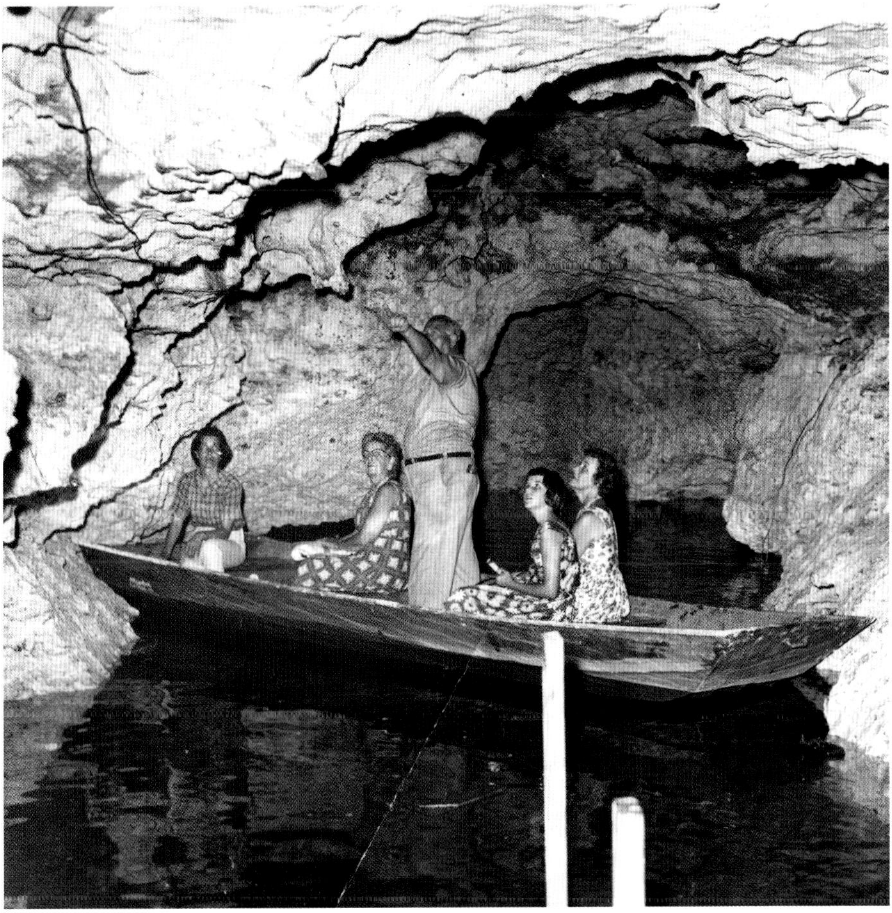

OPPOSITE, TOP: When people think of Florida attractions, the state's geography usually precludes caves as being among the top contenders. One of the relatively few commercially developed caves was located on U.S. 301 between Ocala and Belleview and usually known as Ocala Caverns—although, as we shall see, that was not its only name. *Florida State Archives collection.*

OPPOSITE, BOTTOM & ABOVE: Ocala Caverns was operated by a pair of former professional wrestlers, Jim "Man Mountain" Dean and Violet Ray. They certainly knew their way around the showmanship ring, playing up the caverns' supposed prehistoric relics and its brief boat ride through a portion of the crevasse. Somehow, at every point in its history, Ocala Caverns seemed to be an attraction in desperate search of a theme. *Rob Bradshaw collection.*

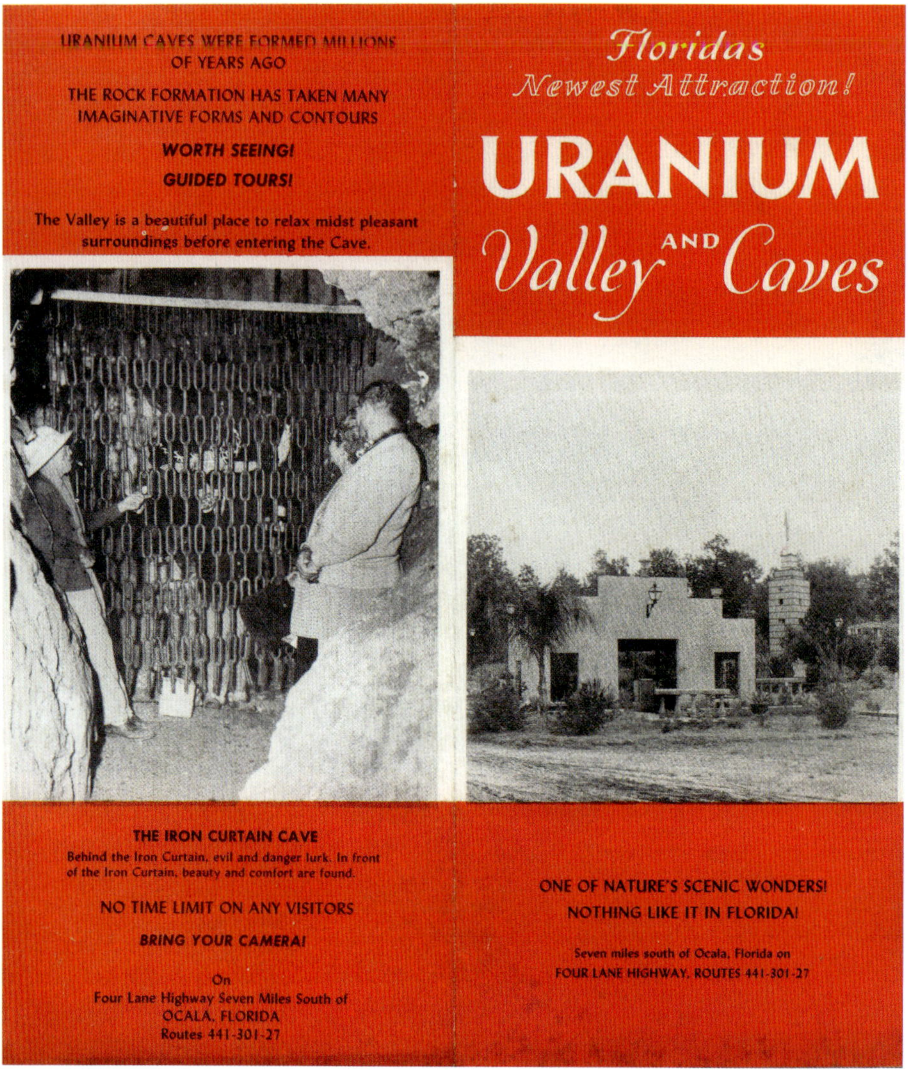

At some other point in its history—but no one seems to be certain just when—the former or future Ocala Caverns was known as Uranium Valley and Caves. This iteration included some Cold War–era propaganda, with one display dubbed the "Iron Curtain Cave." Pains were taken to point out how awful things were behind the Iron Curtain as opposed to on the viewers' side. *Brian Rucker collection.*

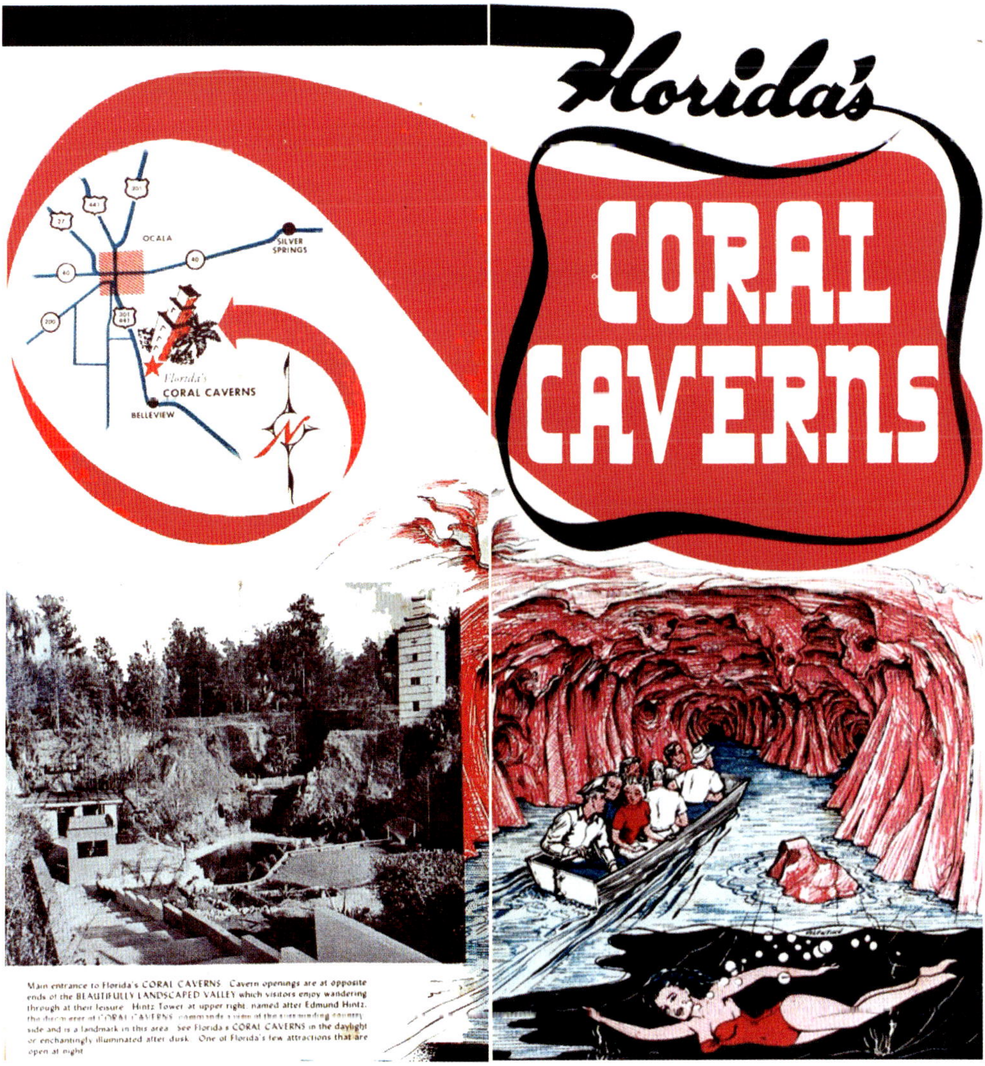

That tireless artist Val Valentine got involved with Ocala Caverns during his sojourn in the Silver Springs area; apparently during his tenure, it received the name "Coral Caverns." This appellation was based on the coral-like appearance of the cave ceiling and walls. Valentine could not resist adding one of his trademark swimsuit girls diving beneath the flat-bottomed skiff. *Author's collection.*

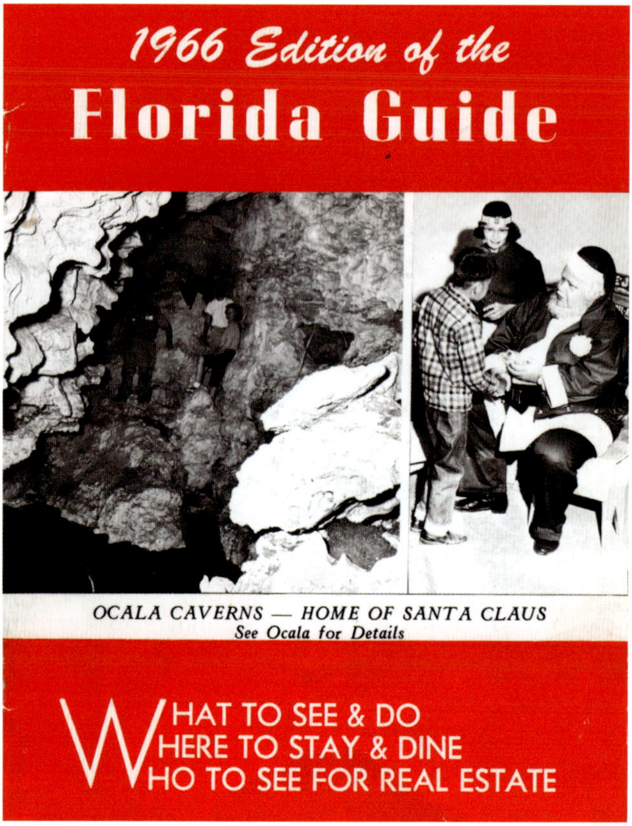

ABOVE: By the mid-1960s, the name was back to Ocala Caverns, and Jim Dean was making jolly as the attraction's year-round Santa Claus—"weighs 628 pounds and has real whiskers," to quote the publicity blurb. This must have made him the only Santa capable of body-slamming the dads of any of the kids who came to sit on his family-size lap. After Santa Dean's death in 1974, the Ocala Caverns property was allowed to revert to its pre-commercial subtropical state, and the property continues to sit undeveloped today. *Rob Bradshaw collection.*

OPPOSITE: Nearer to Silver Springs' main entrance, this wax museum operated during the 1970s and early 1980s. The owner was Herby Moore, who was otherwise quite active in the tourism world of Mammoth Cave, Kentucky. After the wax figures had come and gone, the building became a bank; today, it looks almost exactly as it did when it was an attraction. *Top, Florida State Archives collection; bottom, author's collection.*

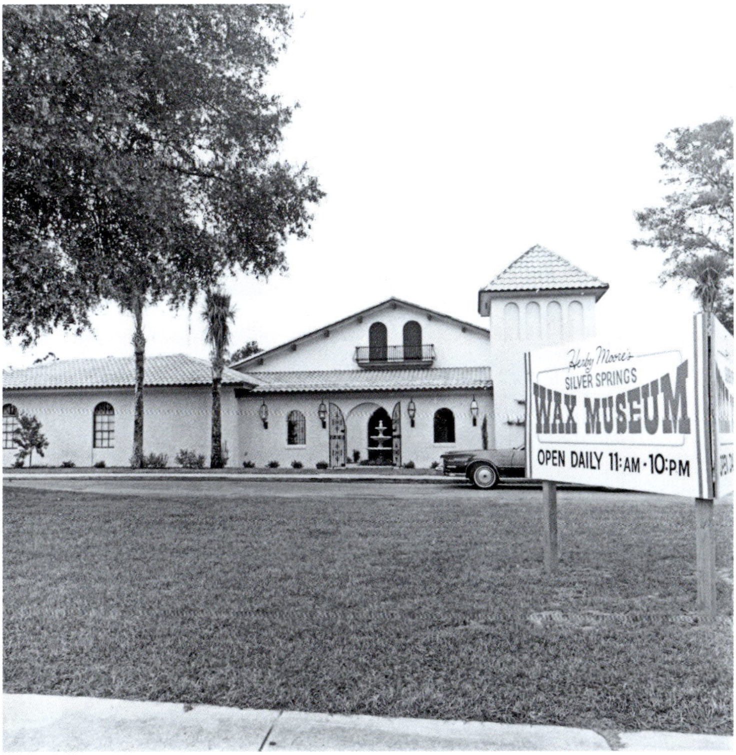
SILVER SPRINGS
WAX MUSEUM
OPEN DAILY 11:AM-10:PM

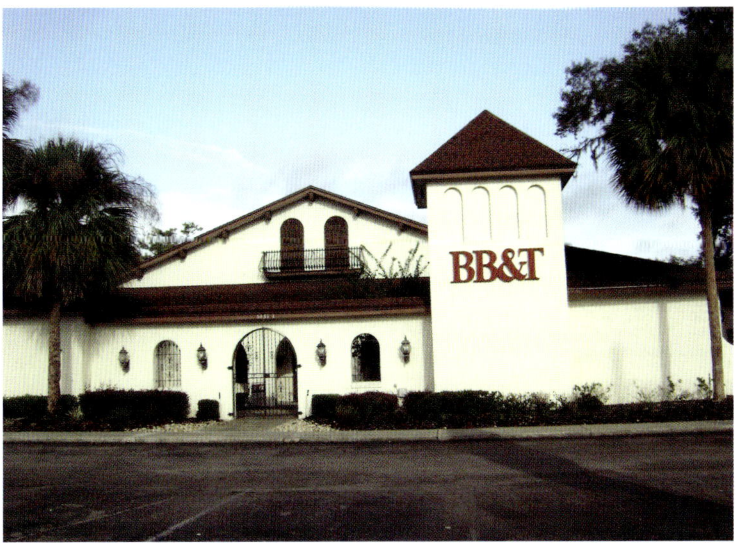
BB&T

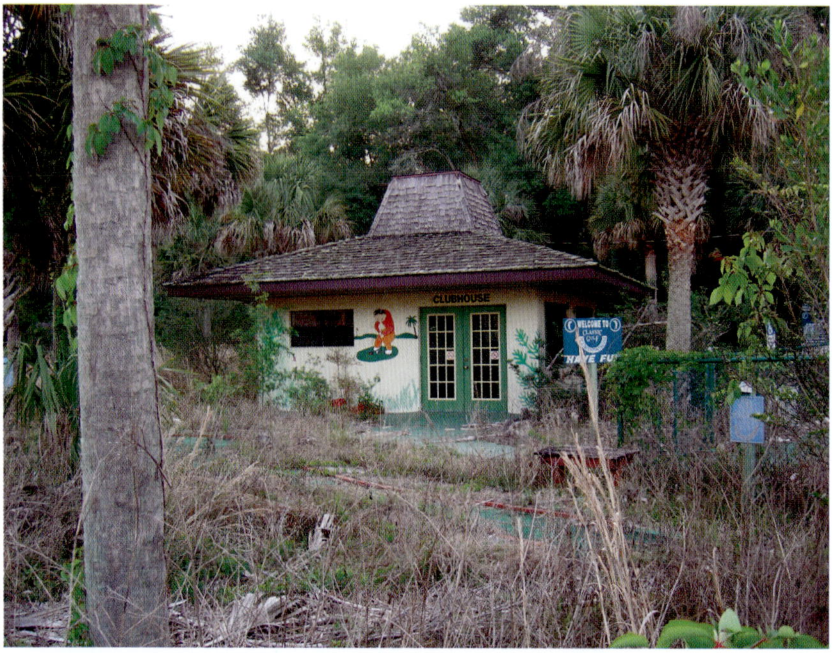

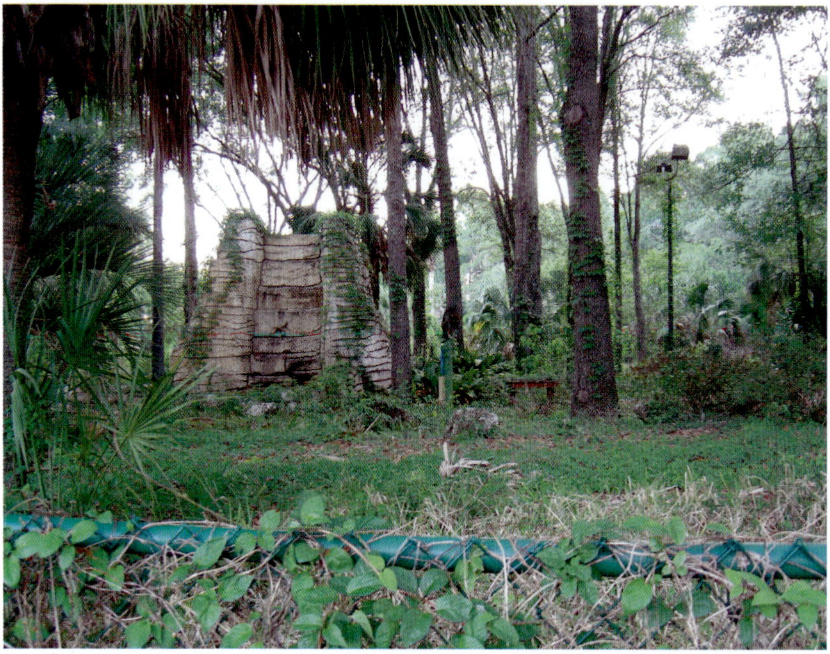

This abandoned and overgrown miniature golf course near Silver Springs is a terrific example of what happens to any property within Florida's climate that goes without maintenance for any length of time. The state was truly a jungle before human habitation, and it is always ready to reclaim any piece of land that is left to its own devices. *Author's collection.*

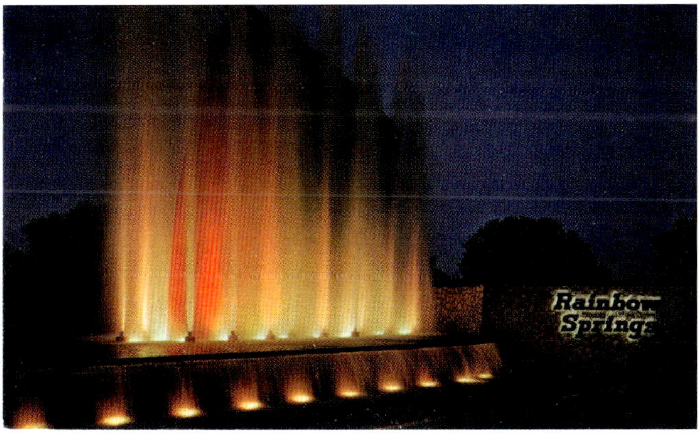

Outside of Silver Springs' immediate neighborhood, Marion County's most famous attraction was Rainbow Springs. This magnificent sight greeted tourists on US 41, in the far western reaches of the county. *Author's collection.*

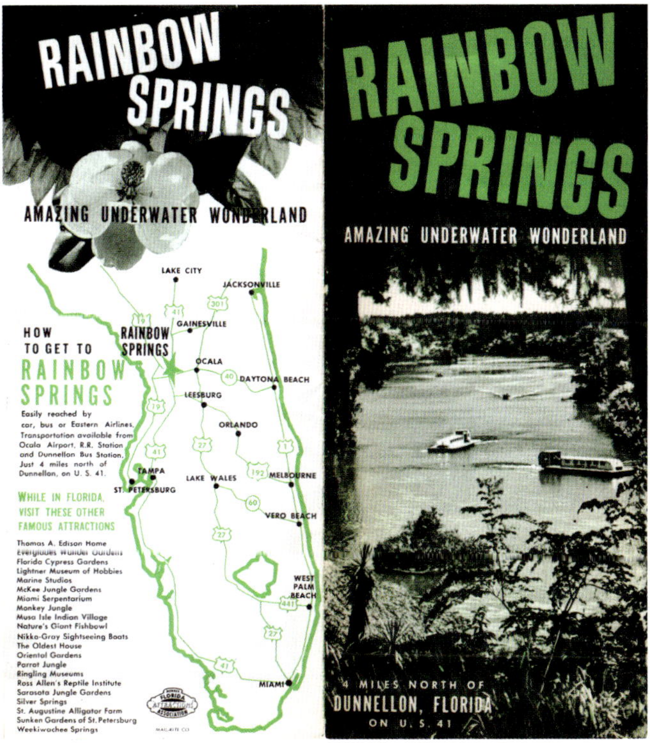

Originally known as Blue Springs, the beautiful natural spot was purchased by developers in 1937. Seeking a more colorful name, they simply added red, orange, yellow, green, indigo and violet to the existing blue, and the newly christened Rainbow Springs was born. *Delee Perry collection.*

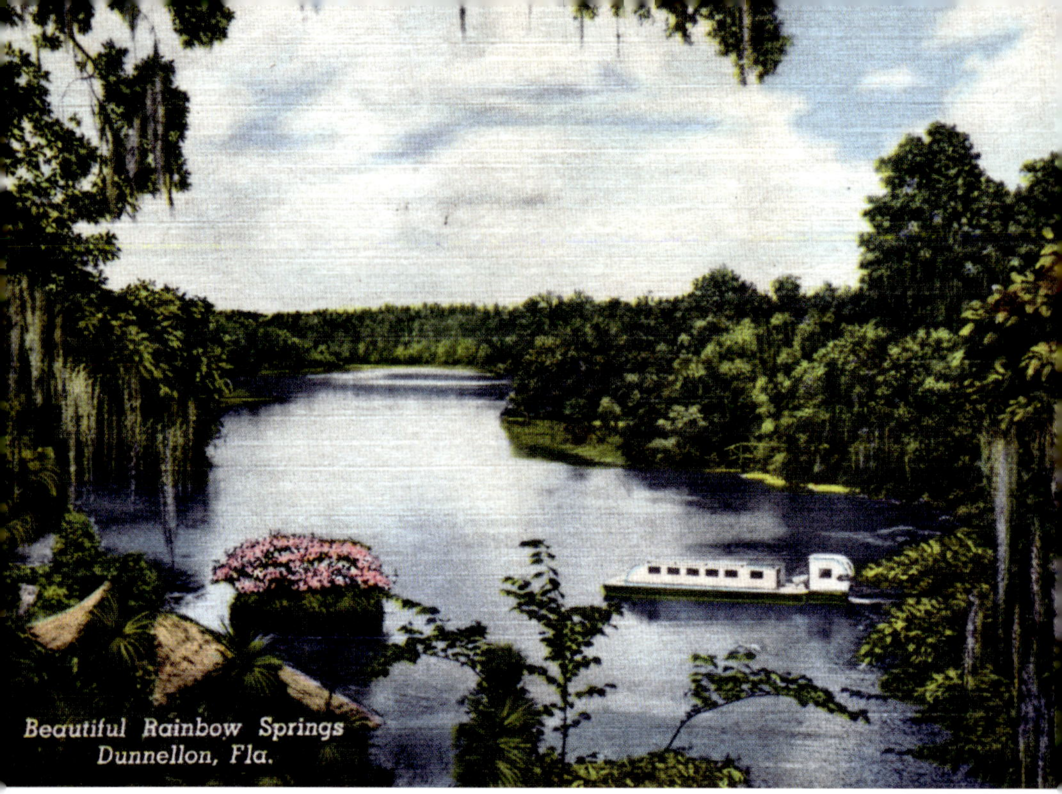

Beautiful Rainbow Springs
Dunnellon, Fla.

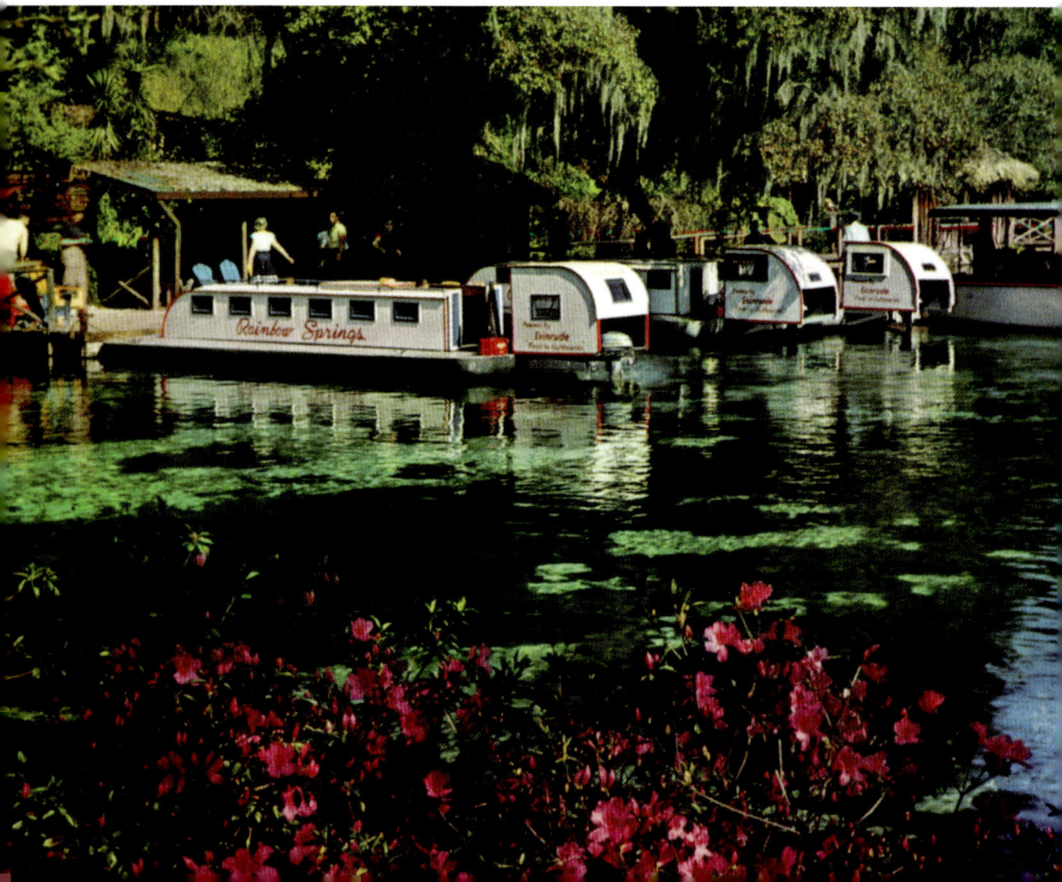

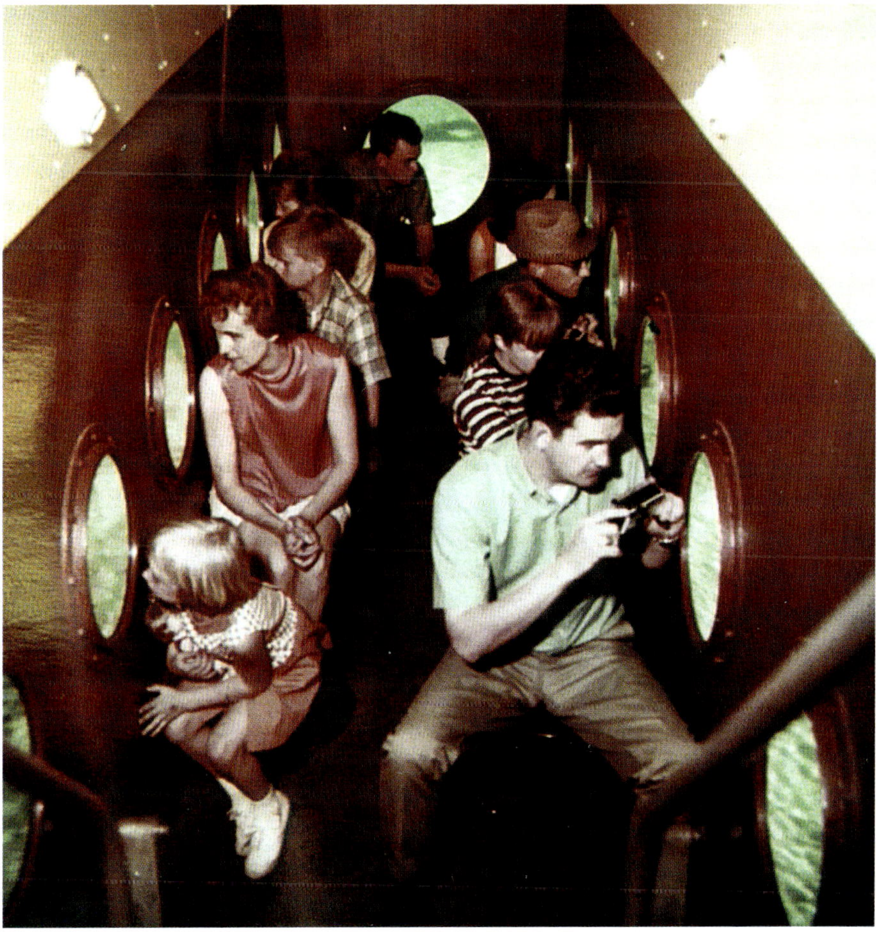

OPPOSITE, TOP: Soon after its May 1937 opening, Rainbow Springs had a variety of crafts plying the waters. Among these was a fleet of glass-bottom boats that betrayed the attraction's debt to Silver Springs. However, that could work both ways. *Delee Perry collection.*

OPPOSITE, BOTTOM & ABOVE: Earlier, we saw Silver Springs' Photo-Sub boats, with the passengers seated below the water's surface. Well, Rainbow Springs had them first, and they became the most identifiable features of the park. The boat captains sat topside and narrated the trip as tourists peered through the portholes. This same concept was later adapted for the "Submarine Lagoon" rides at both Disneyland and Walt Disney World. *Author's collection.*

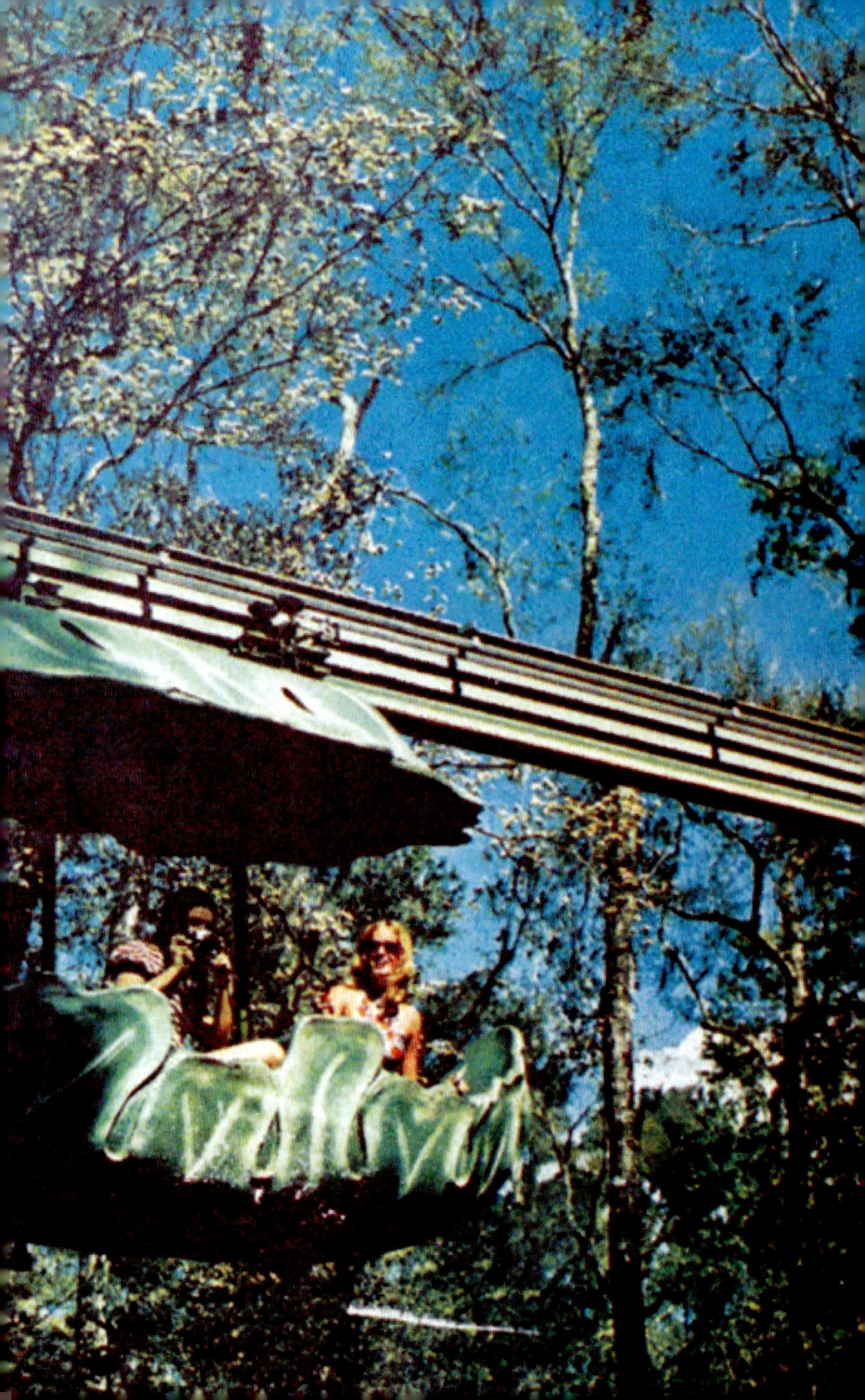

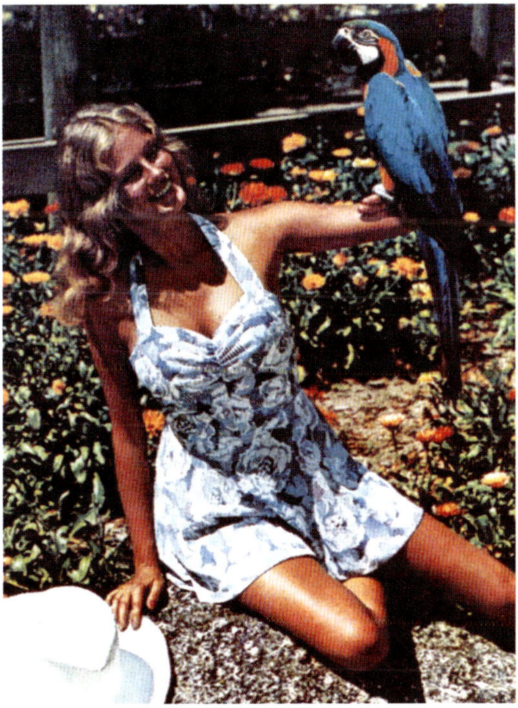

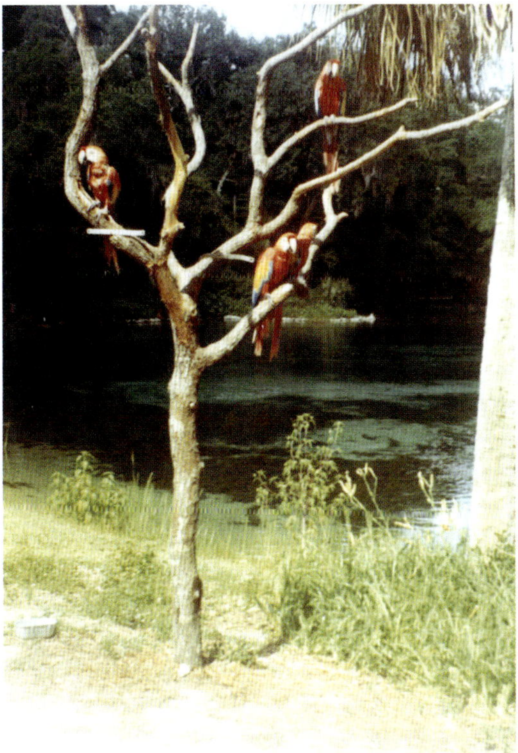

OPPOSITE: The opening of I-75 diverted most tourist traffic away from Rainbow Springs' entrance on U.S. 41, but during the late 1960s and early 1970s, it was still a much-promoted Florida attraction. One of the additions from that period was the fondly remembered Forest Flite monorail, which whisked visitors through the jungle in giant leaf-shaped gondolas. *Author's collection.*

TOP & BOTTOM: Rainbow Springs was justifiably proud of its collection of parrots and macaws; in fact, at one point, the Forest Flite ride passed directly through a large aviary. The feathered friends could also be found throughout the park, posing for photos with tourists or one of those ubiquitous sun-bronzed Florida beauties. *Author's collection.*

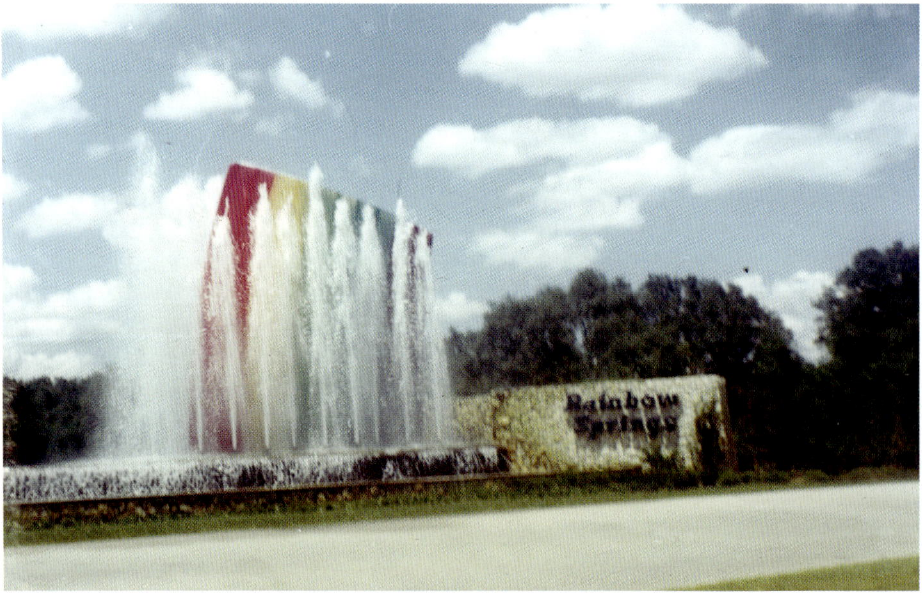

The changing traffic patterns, combined with the 1973 fuel shortage, brought an end to Rainbow Springs as an attraction in 1974. It sat abandoned and neglected for ten years, until a local garden club was allowed onto the property in 1984 to try to salvage what was left of the park. *Author's collection.*

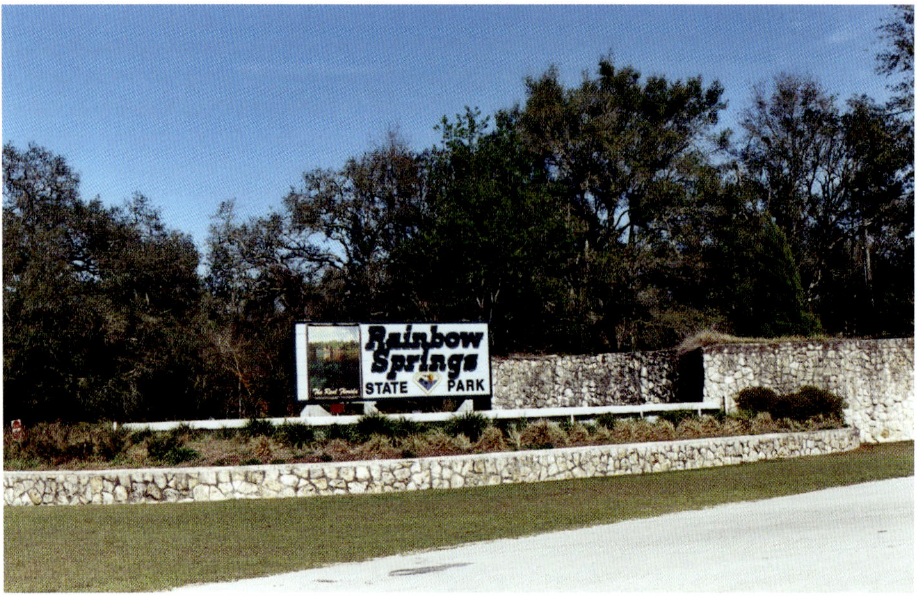

In March 1995, Rainbow Springs State Park opened to the public. The monorail and the giant rainbow fountain at the entrance are gone, but the view of the springs and the surrounding landscape remains just as beautiful as when the developers first found it in the 1930s. *Author's collection.*

CHAPTER EIGHT

And to All a Good Night

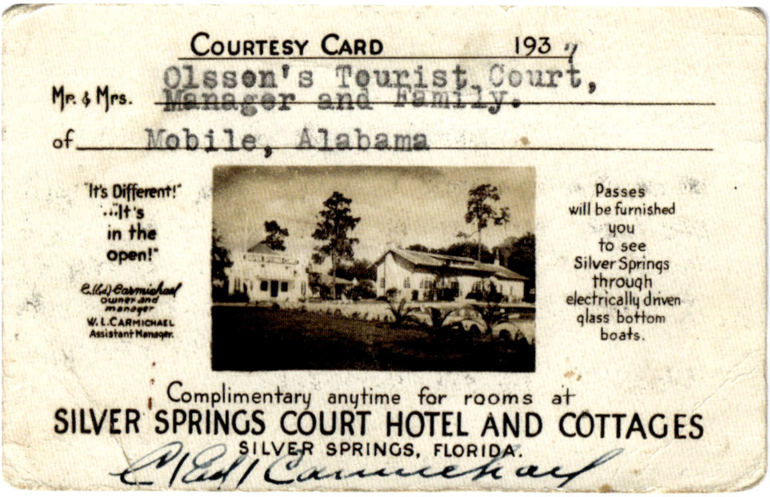
COURTESY CARD 193 7
Mr. & Mrs. Olsson's Tourist Court, Manager and Family.
of Mobile, Alabama
"It's Different!" ...It's in the open!"
C.(Ed) Carmichael owner and manager
W. L. CARMICHAEL Assistant Manager
Passes will be furnished you to see Silver Springs through electrically driven glass bottom boats.
Complimentary anytime for rooms at
SILVER SPRINGS COURT HOTEL AND COTTAGES
SILVER SPRINGS, FLORIDA.
C (Ed) Carmichael

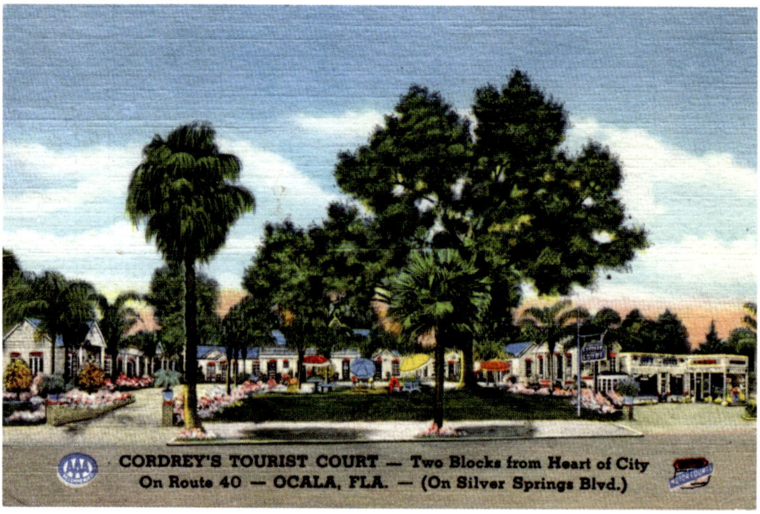
CORDREY'S TOURIST COURT — Two Blocks from Heart of City
On Route 40 — OCALA, FLA. — (On Silver Springs Blvd.)

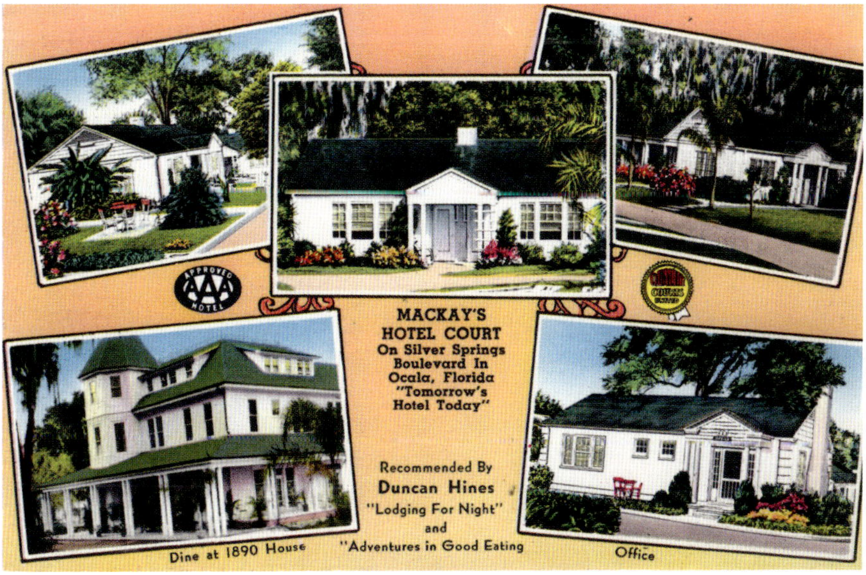

OPPOSITE, TOP: Ed Carmichael was one of the first people to see the commercial possibilities of Silver Springs. After he turned management of the attraction over to other entities in 1924, he stayed in the game by operating a tourist court across the street. In 1937, he signed this courtesy card for some fellow motel owners from Mobile, Alabama. *Author's collection.*

OPPOSITE, BOTTOM: Once Silver Springs' popularity started increasing during the 1930s, more and more tourist courts and motels began lining the entire stretch of Highway 40 east of Ocala. One of those was Cordrey's Court, which may or may not have been as colorful in real life as it was in this postcard, which was mailed in 1949. *Author's collection.*

ABOVE: Early tourist courts seemed to go out of their way to make themselves "homey." Before motels with connected rooms took over, many courts such as Mackay's situated their guests in miniature cottages surrounded by attractive landscaping. *Author's collection.*

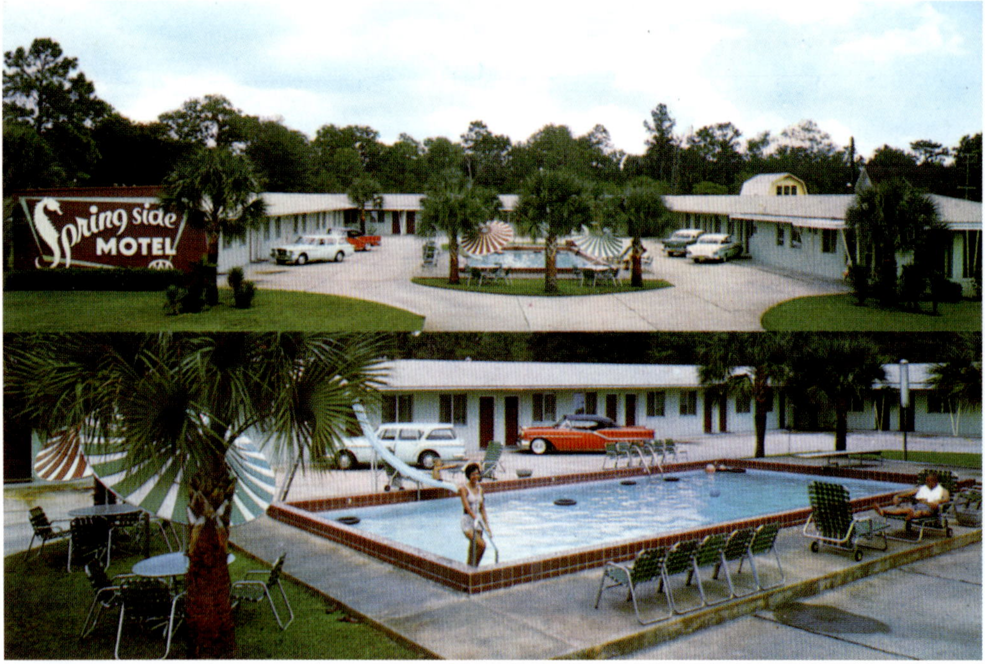

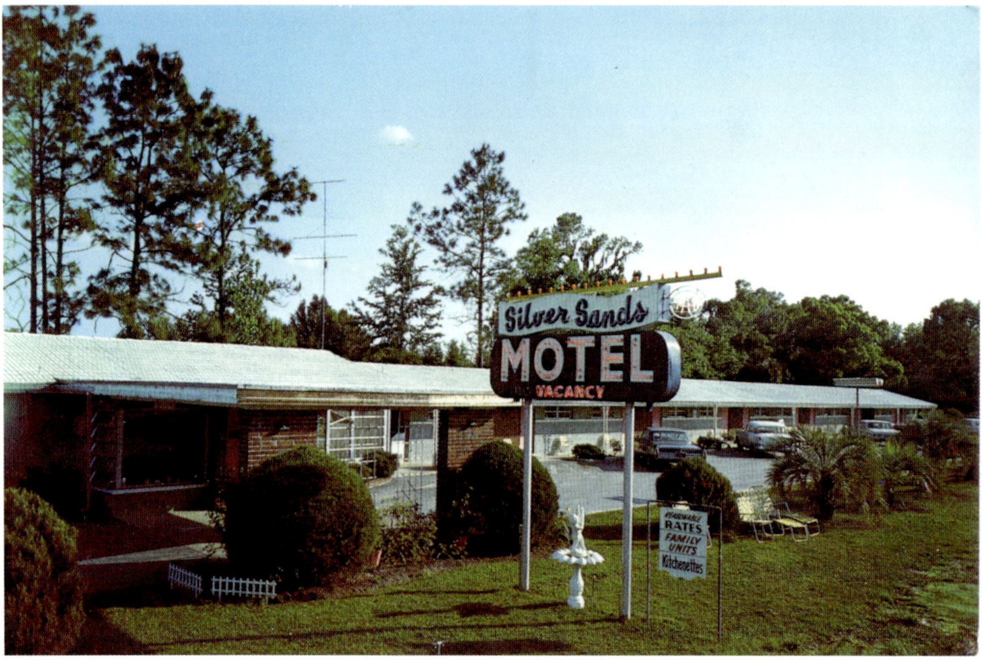

One of the many charming features about motels of the 1940s and '50s was their attempt to relate to their neighborhood. The Springside Motel, with a seahorse forming the capital S, might not have been directly beside Silver Springs, but it was close enough. The Silver Sands also traded on its proximity to the legendary park. *Author's collection.*

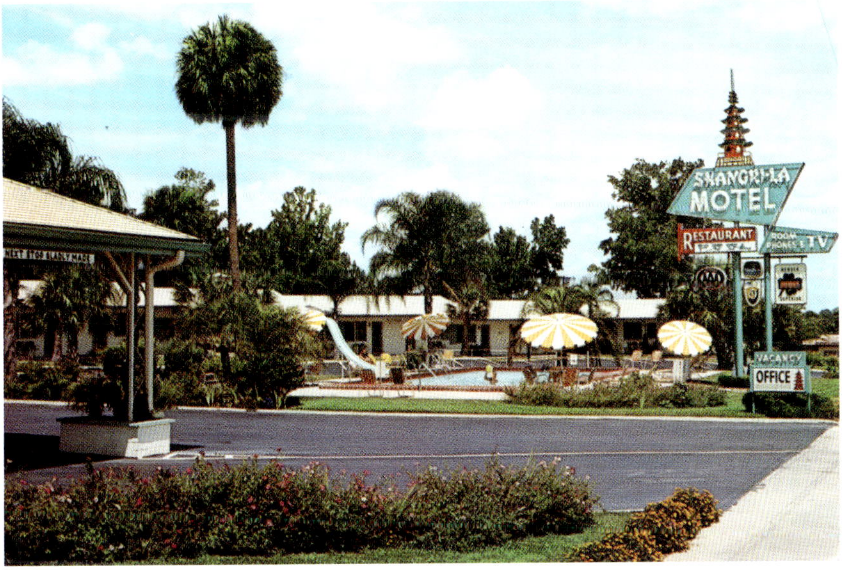

There was another feeling in the industry that said tourists who were already somewhere else needed to feel like they were somewhere else. How else to explain mismatched themes such as the Shangri-La Motel, with a miniature pagoda atop the sign? Weren't glass-bottom boats and Ross Allen's reptiles exotic enough? *Author's collection.*

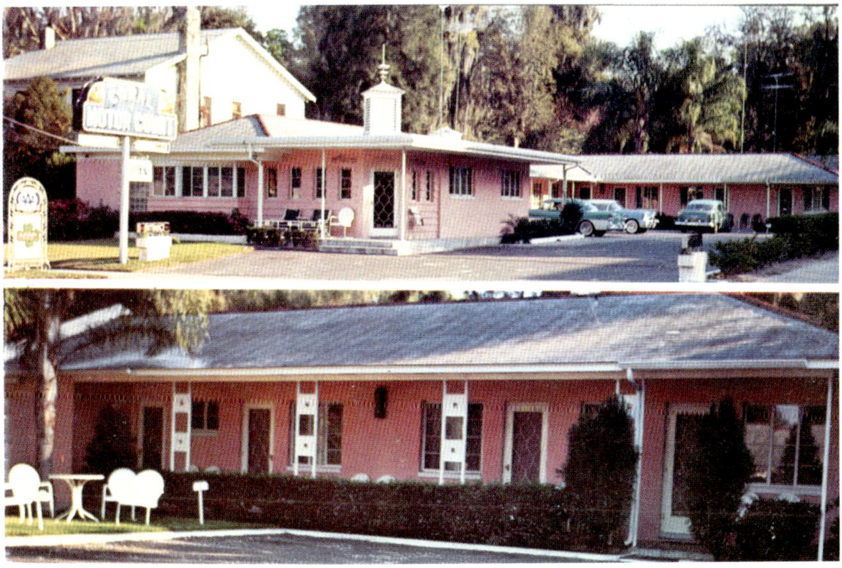

Motels along any busy tourist strip had to find ways to make themselves stand out from the rest. Often it was through their flashing signage, but sometimes, the entire building had to become a sign. The Coral Motor Court made its presence known by its Pepto-Bismol pink walls, which stubbornly refused to melt into the scenery. *Author's collection.*

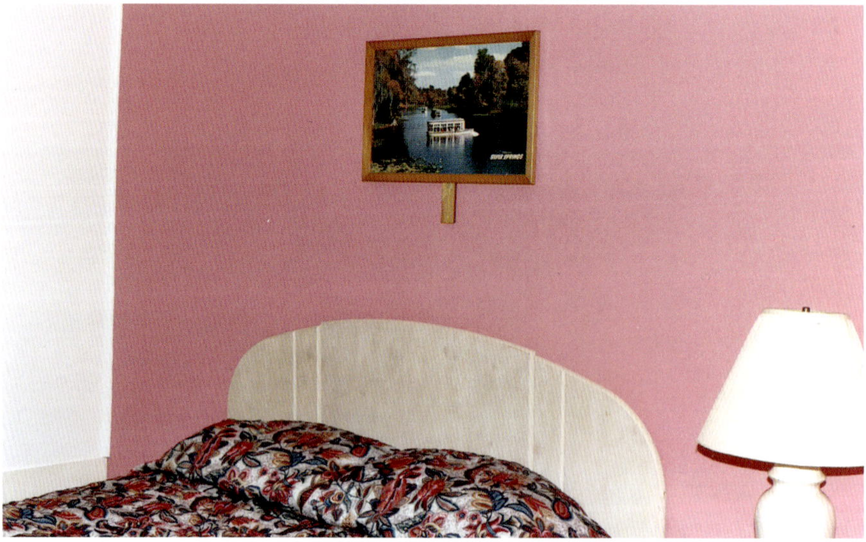

Silver Springs had a cozy relationship with mom-and-pop motels throughout Florida. Framed photos of the glass-bottom boats and other attractions could be found hanging on motel room walls from the Gulf to the Atlantic—although reports are that photos of Ross Allen's snakes were not too popular hanging above people's beds. *Author's collection.*

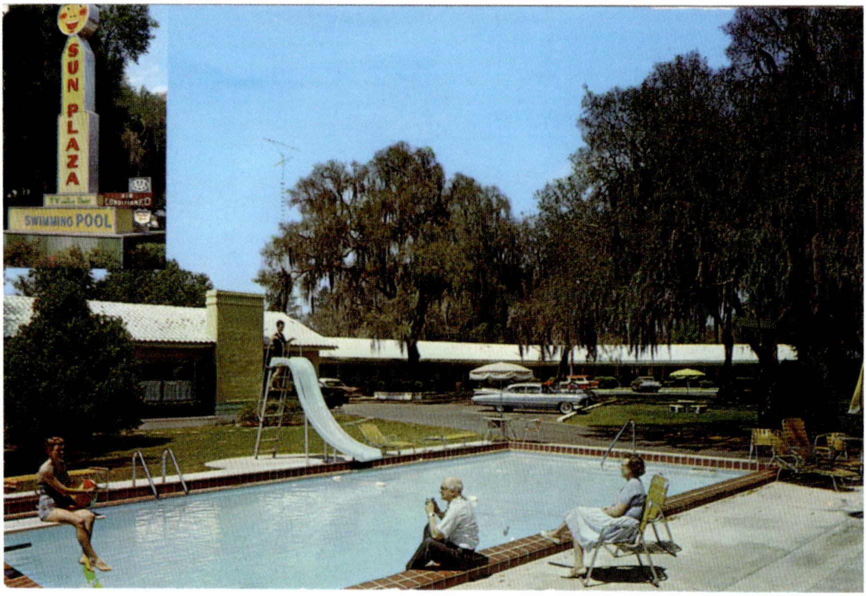

Most of the motels we are seeing in this chapter either no longer exist or changed names long ago. The Sun Plaza is still very much in business, within walking distance of Silver Springs, but this obelisk-styled sign was soon replaced by a more classic neon spectacular that can still be enjoyed. The rest of the motel looks like time has stood still since the 1950s. *Author's collection.*

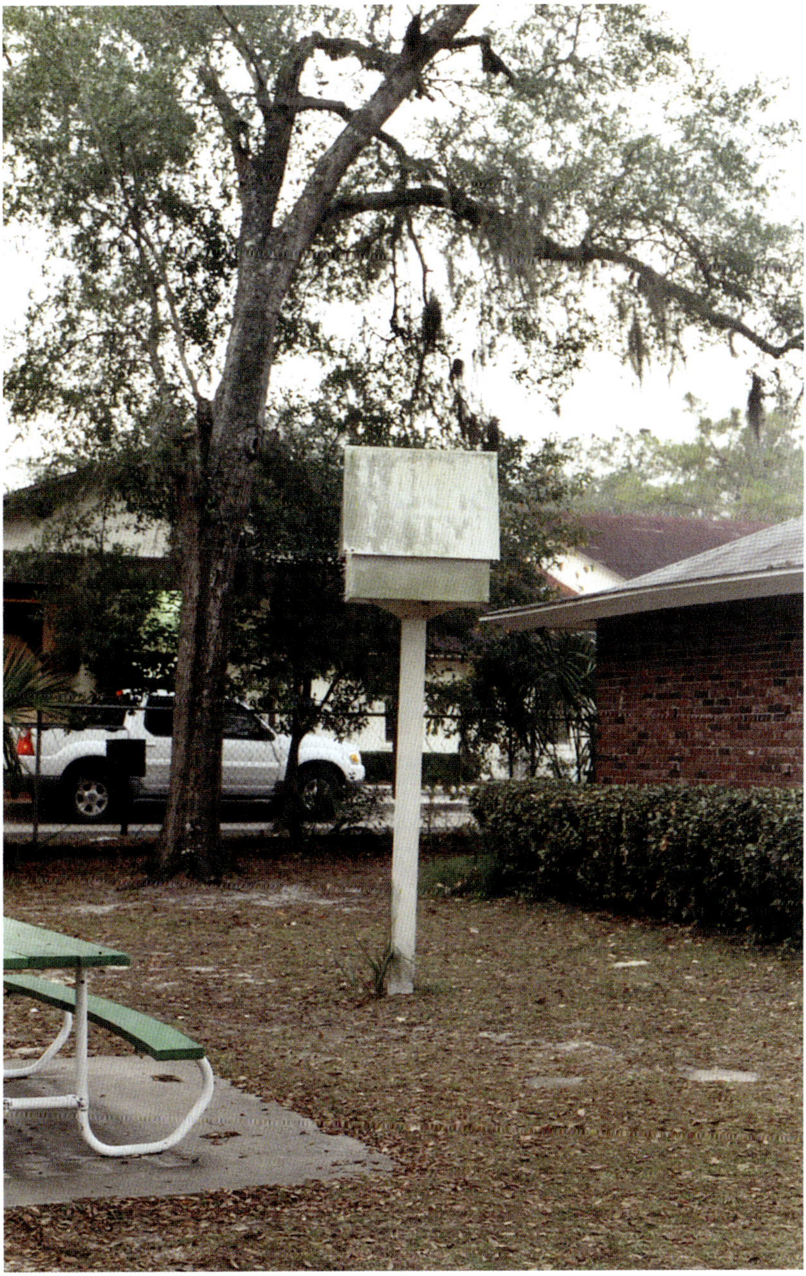

Not only is the Sun Plaza a relic of a lost tourism era, but in 2007, its lawn even featured another artifact: a painted-over birdhouse that once advertised Silver Springs' nearest rival when it came to roadside advertising, Rock City Gardens atop Lookout Mountain. *Author's collection.*

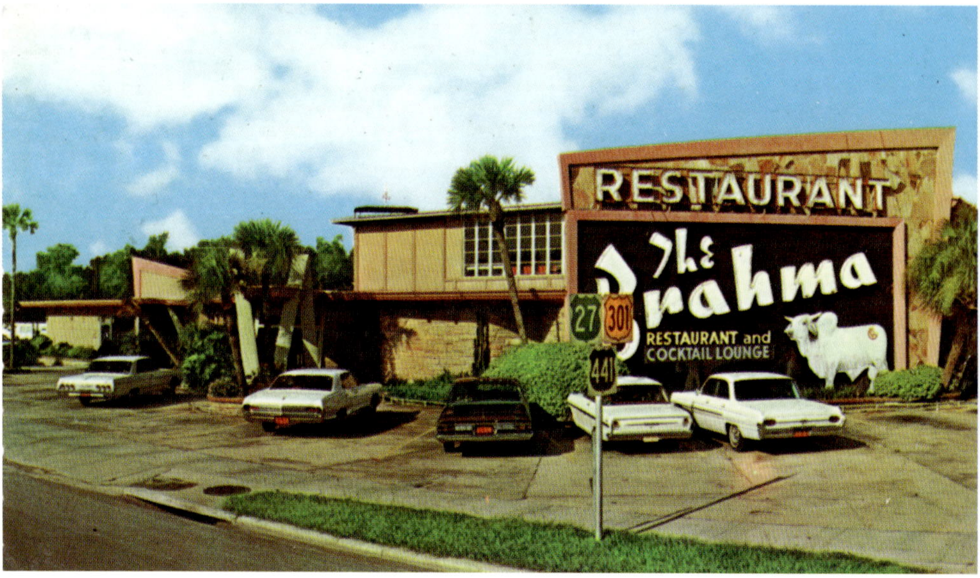

One of Ocala's most popular restaurants was the Brahma—and that's no bull. There is a lot to enjoy in this postcard view, from the classic cars to the example of Florida's unusually colorful highway number shields on the pole in the foreground. *Author's collection.*

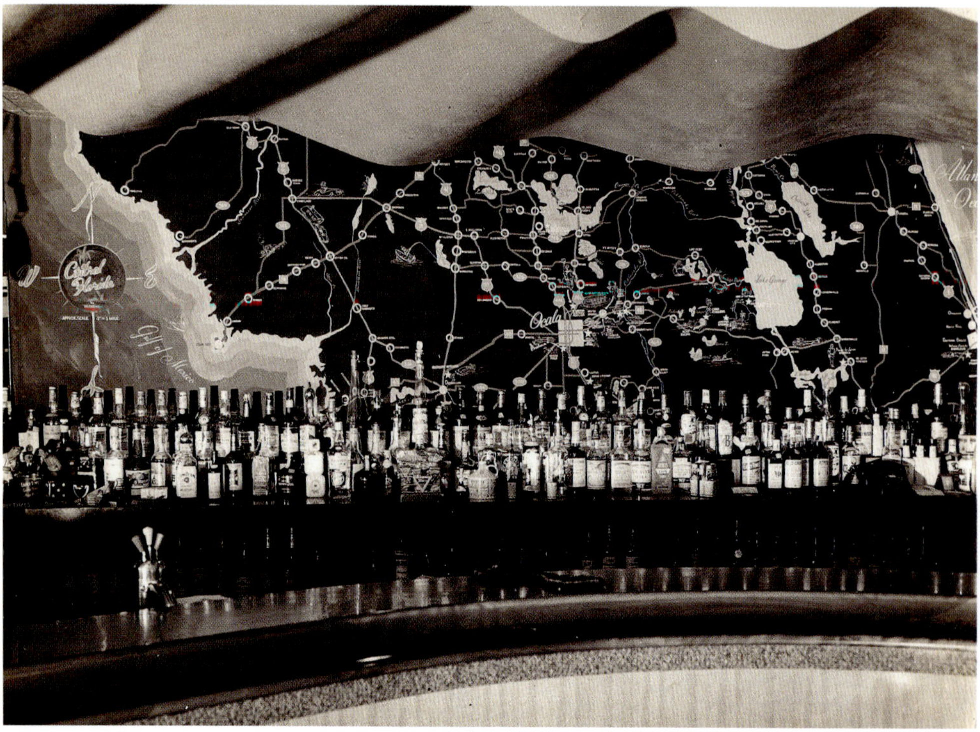

Artist Val Valentine was called into service to provide this incredible mural for the Brahma's bar. Look closely, and you will see that it illustrates the highways, towns and principal attractions of central Florida from sea to shining sea. *Author's collection.*

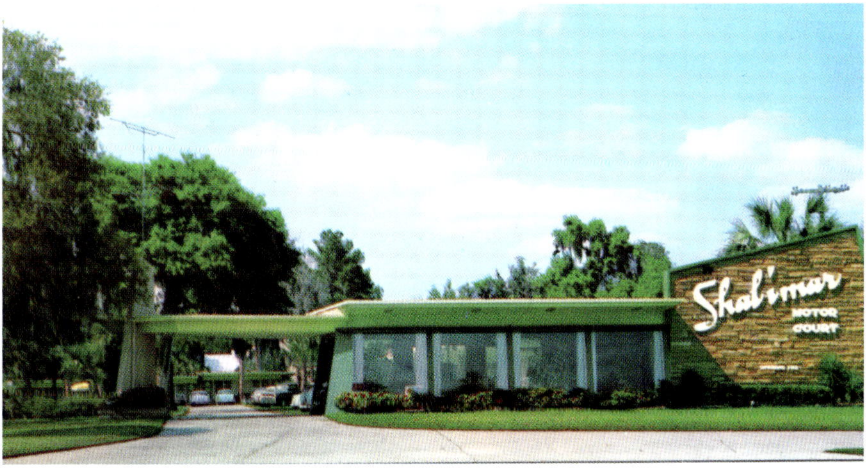

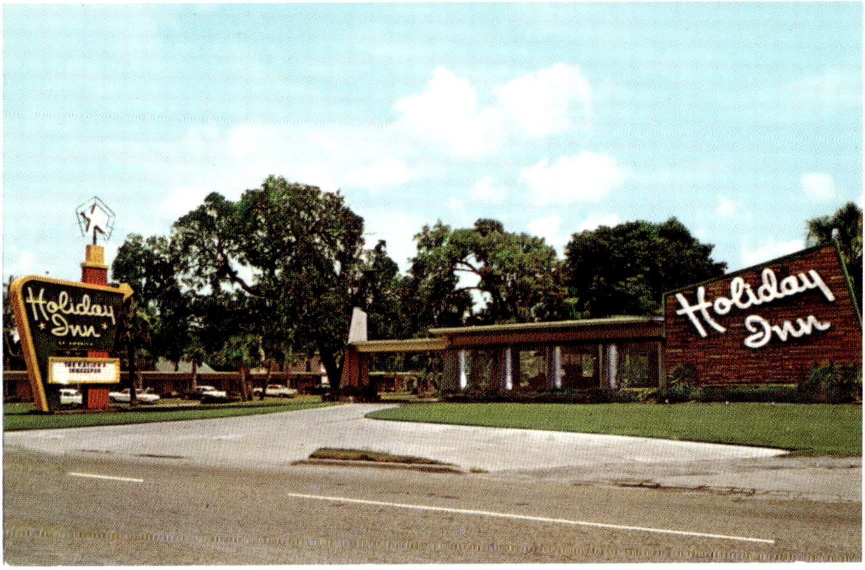

TOP: By the 1950s, Ed Carmichael's old Silver Springs Court across the street from the entrance had been replaced by the more modern facilities of the Shalimar Motor Court. *Author's collection.*

BOTTOM: The Shalimar Motor Court, in turn, became an outlet of the most famous motel chain in the world during the 1960s. It was not the first Holiday Inn in the Ocala area—there was an older one on U.S. 301—but it was certainly positioned to get plenty of those year-round Silver Springs tourists. *Author's collection.*

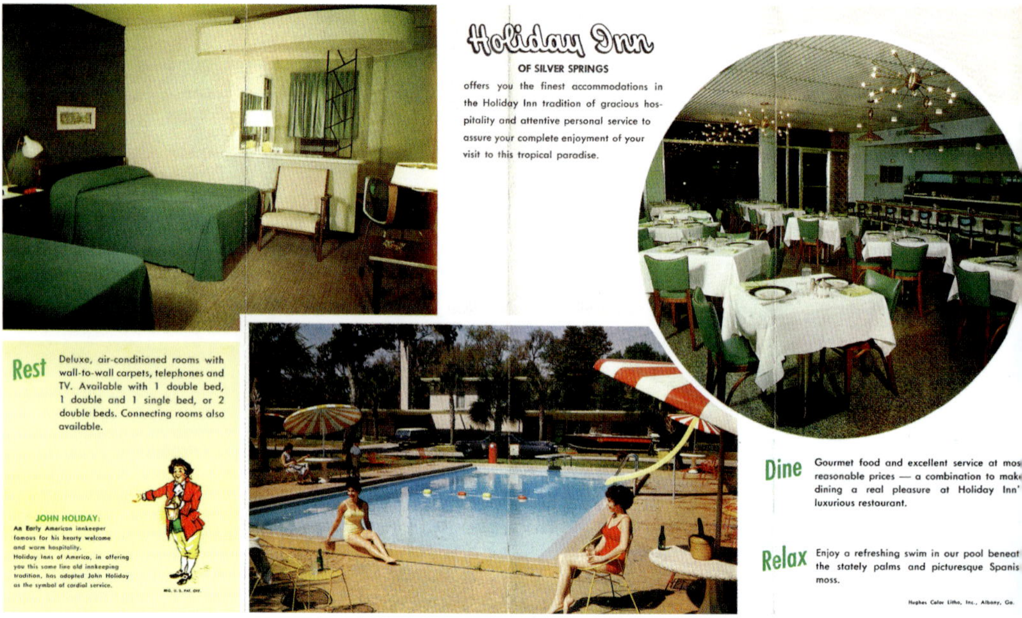
Holiday Inn
OF SILVER SPRINGS
offers you the finest accommodations in the Holiday Inn tradition of gracious hospitality and attentive personal service to assure your complete enjoyment of your visit to this tropical paradise.
Rest
Deluxe, air-conditioned rooms with wall-to-wall carpets, telephones and TV. Available with 1 double bed, 1 double and 1 single bed, or 2 double beds. Connecting rooms also available.
JOHN HOLIDAY:
An Early American innkeeper famous for his hearty welcome and warm hospitality.
Holiday Inns of America, in offering you this same fine old innkeeping tradition, has adopted John Holiday as the symbol of cordial service.
REG. U.S. PAT. OFF.
Dine
Gourmet food and excellent service at mos reasonable prices — a combination to mak dining a real pleasure at Holiday Inn' luxurious restaurant.
Relax
Enjoy a refreshing swim in our pool beneat the stately palms and picturesque Spanis moss.
Hughes Color Litho, Inc., Albany, Ga.

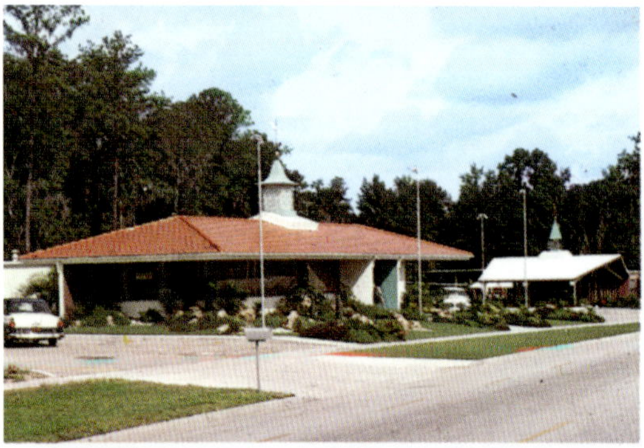

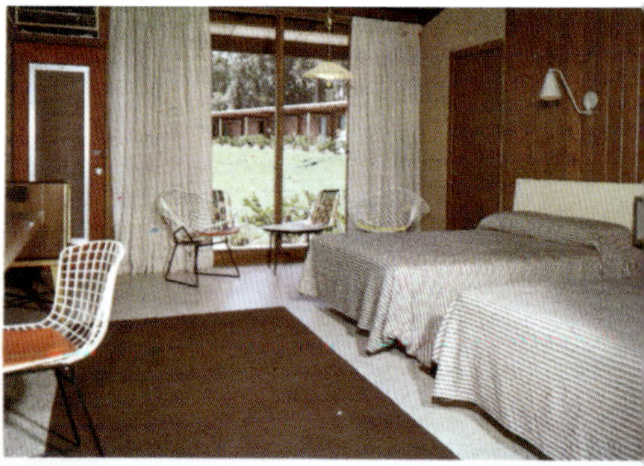

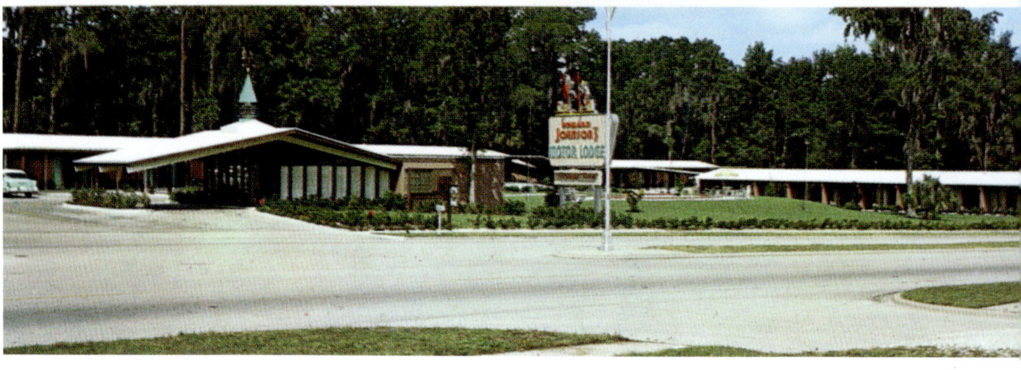

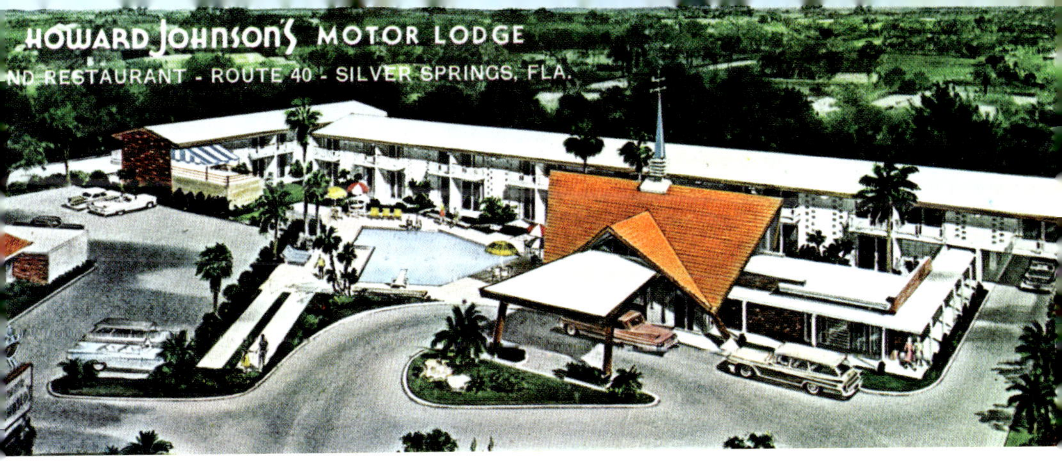

OPPOSITE, TOP: From this impressive brochure spread, we can safely assume that Holiday Inn had a natural affinity for the color green. We also get to enjoy a brief appearance by the motel chain's mascot, colonial innkeeper John Holiday. The former Shalimar/Holiday Inn complex still exists as a Days Inn and Denny's restaurant, but there is little that is recognizable from these older views. *Author's collection.*

OPPOSITE, BOTTOM: Like Holiday Inn, the chain of Howard Johnson's Motor Lodges (and their even longer-established restaurants) first set up camp on U.S. 301 south of downtown Ocala. From this postcard, it would appear that only the restaurant building featured Howard Johnson's trademark orange roof. *Author's collection.*

ABOVE: Around the same time that Holiday Inn first flashed its pulsating neon star across the street from Silver Springs, Howard Johnson's raised its orange roof and aqua spire just a few yards away. This panoramic postcard was obviously produced before anything had been constructed, using the architect's rendering instead of photos. *Author's collection.*

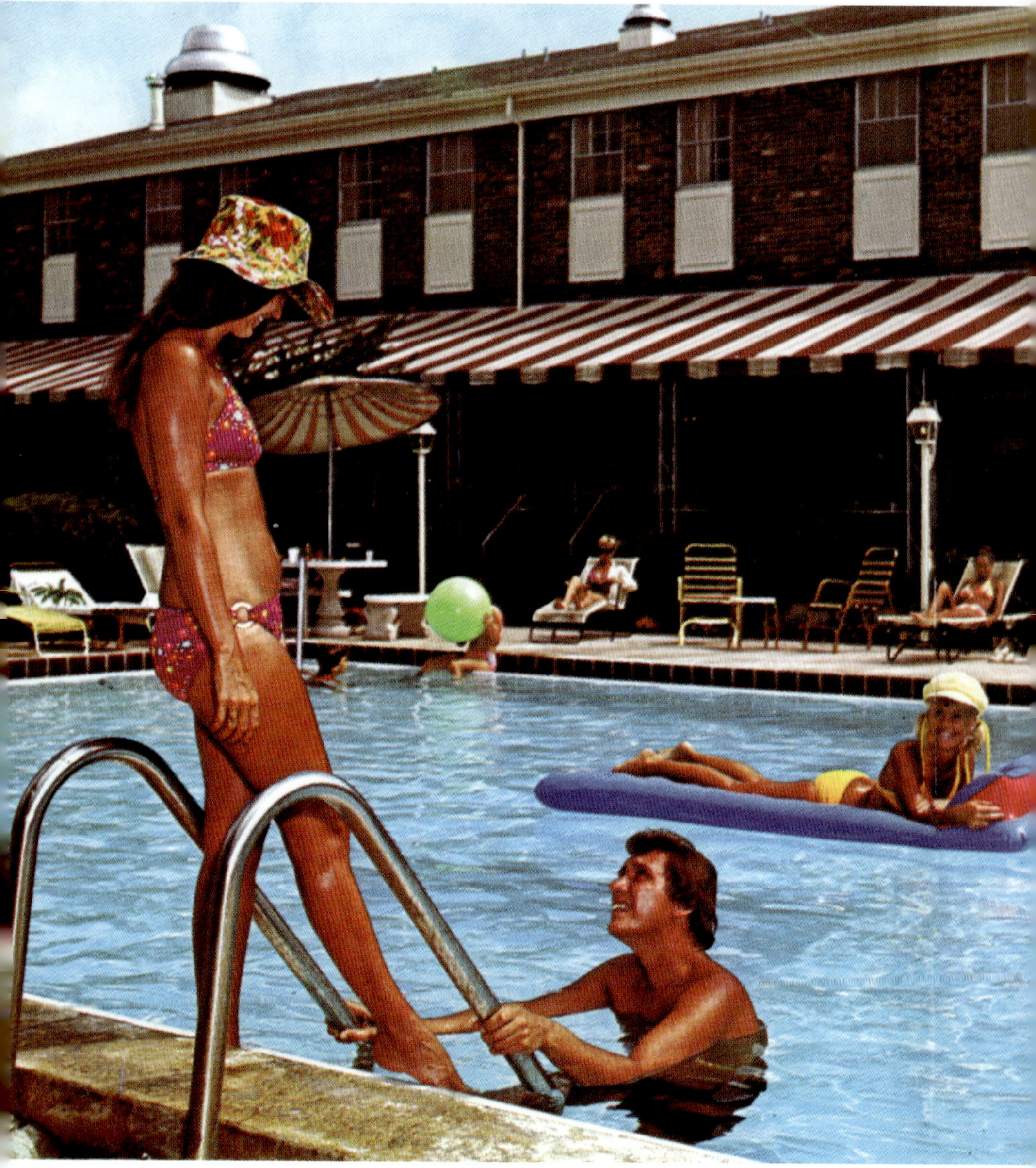

Soon, other chain motels were crowding their way into the area, especially after the opening of I-75 created several Ocala/Silver Springs exits that were prime commercial opportunities. Ramada Inn countered Holiday Inn's John Holiday with its own innkeeper character, officially known as "Uncle Ben." Those must be some of his nephews and nieces enjoying their six-pack abs in the pool. *Author's collection.*

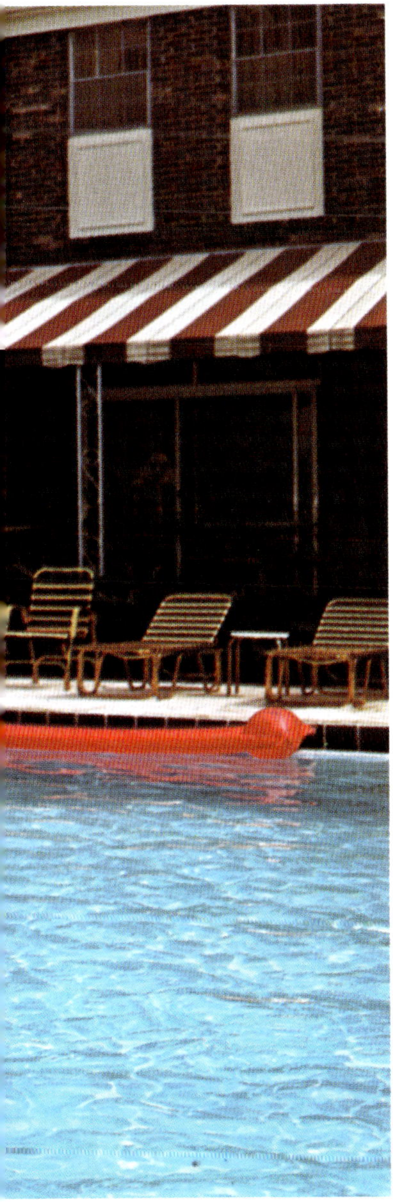

OCALA, FLORIDA

RAMADA INN®

I-75 at U.S. 27 • 3810 N.W. Blitchton Road • Ocala, Fla. 32670
(904)732-3131 • TWX 800-228-2828

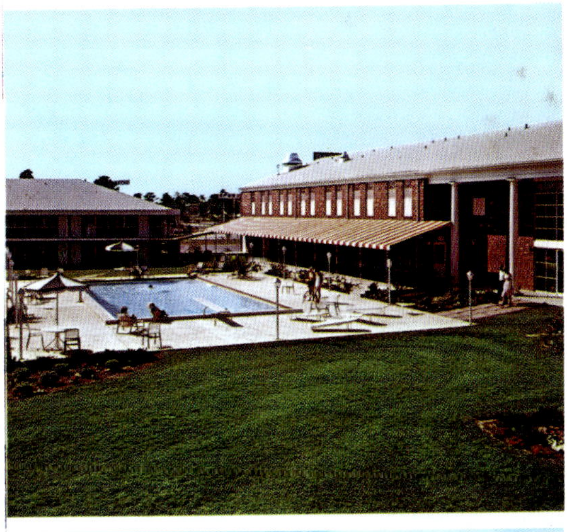

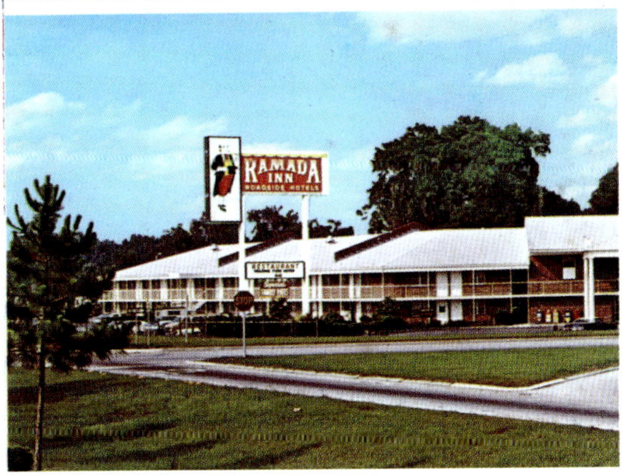

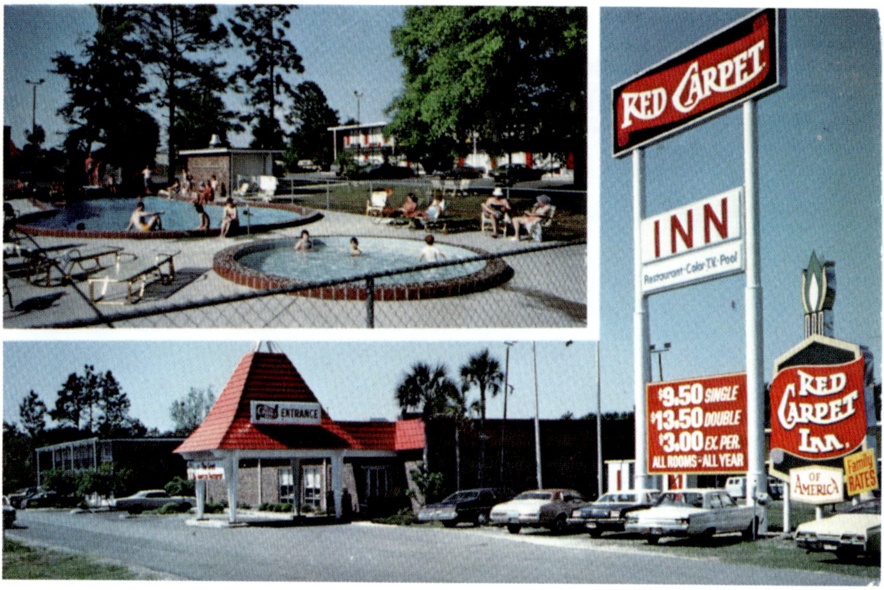
RED CARPET
INN
Restaurant-Color T.V.-Pool
$9.50 SINGLE
$13.50 DOUBLE
$3.00 EX. PER.
ALL ROOMS-ALL YEAR
RED CARPET Inn
OF AMERICA
Family RATES
ENTRANCE

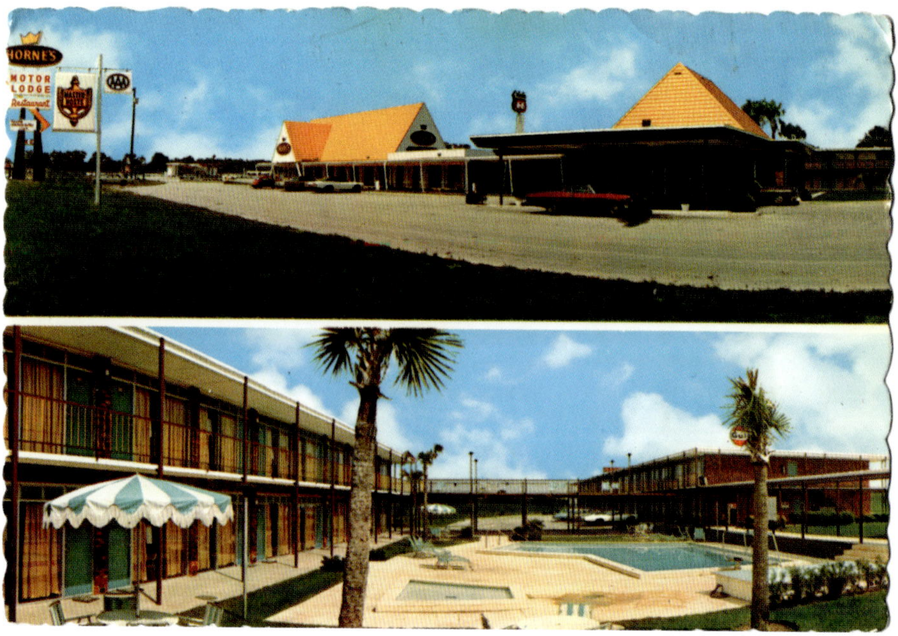
HORNE'S
MOTOR LODGE
Restaurant

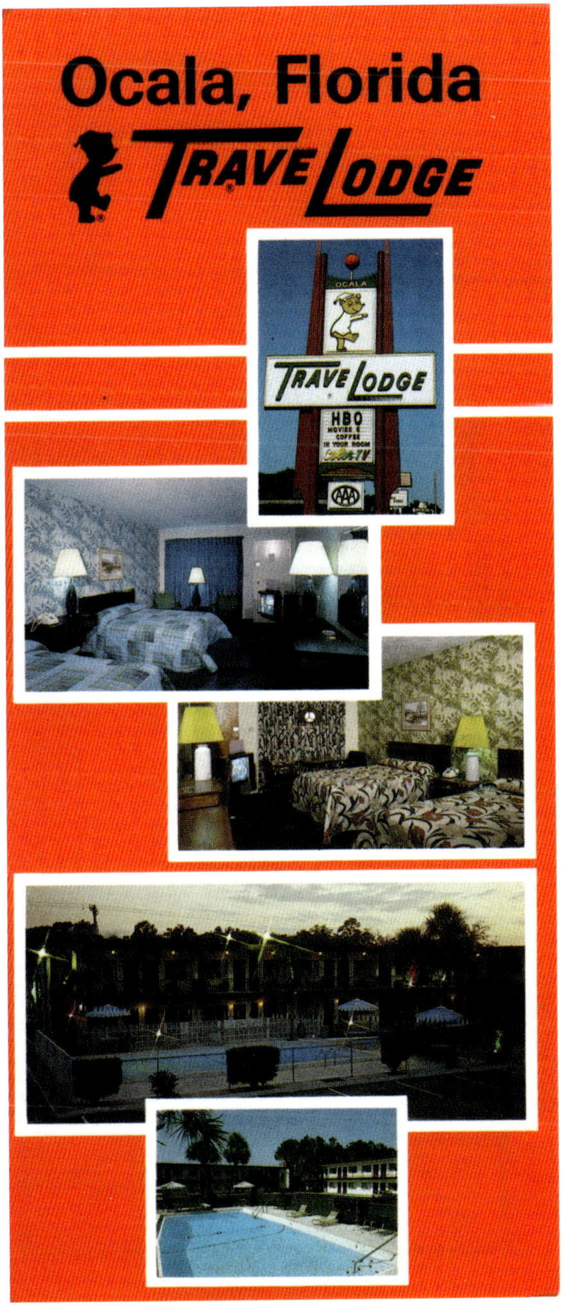

OPPOSITE, TOP: The Red Carpet Inns are less remembered than some of the other motel chains, but they had a flashing sign that was impossible to miss. Notice that the portico in front of the office bears some resemblance to the "little red schoolhouse" architecture of the KinderCare kindergarten chain. *Author's collection.*

OPPOSITE, BOTTOM: In the days when Stuckey's ruled the interstate exits with its pecan logs and seashell souvenirs, Horne's was probably its closest rival. Stuckey's made an unsuccessful venture into lodging in the early 1960s, but the Horne's Motor Lodges survived for many more years. The one on I-75 at the Highway 40 exit kept the Horne's name into the late 1990s, long after the chain had been officially dissolved. *Author's collection.*

LEFT: Okay, we will look at one final motel chain before bringing this whole parade of nostalgia to its end. Who could forget TraveLodge and its cuddly icon, the sleepwalking Sleepy Bear? TraveLodge and Sleepy are still around, but the pajama-clad bruin has been redesigned so often that he is now unrecognizable. *Author's collection.*

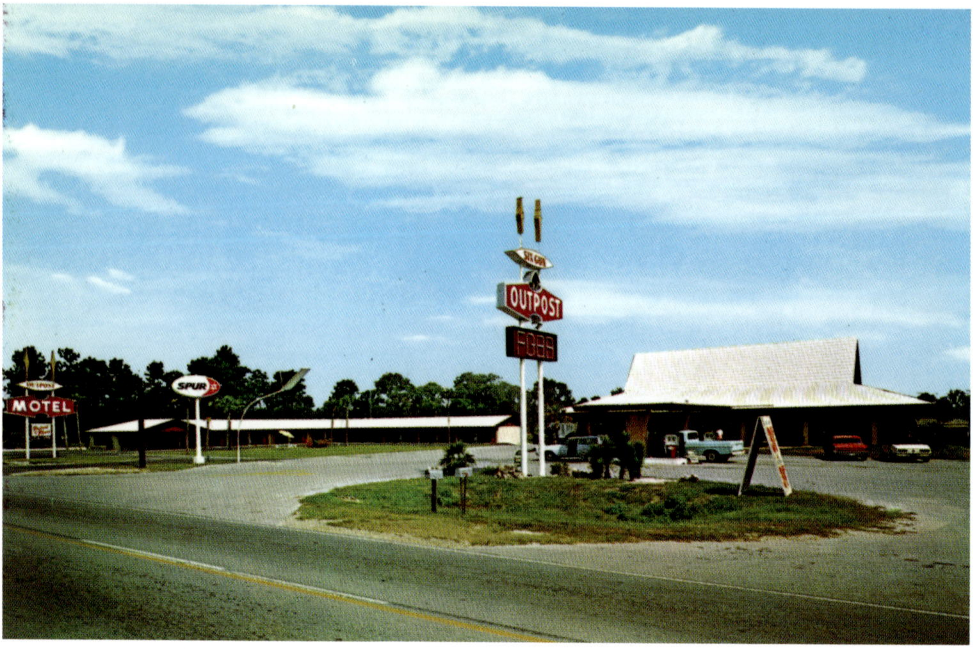

ABOVE: It was not only Silver Springs that inspired area motels and restaurants. This complex was known fittingly as the Six Gun Outpost, as it sat on I-75 several miles from that wild and woolly Western town. It seems appropriate, if perhaps coincidental, that the Six Gun Outpost sold the Spur brand of gasoline. *Author's collection.*

OPPOSITE, TOP: Within the mile or two between Six Gun Territory and Silver Springs, the Stage Stop Motel and Restaurant pulled out all the (stage) stops to capitalize on those families bringing their little buckaroos to play among the gunslingers and dance hall girls. As you can see, the motel was part of the Quality Courts chain, with its bright yellow sunburst signage. *Author's collection.*

OPPOSITE, BOTTOM: Long after Six Gun Territory had bitten the dusty street, the Stage Stop Restaurant still dished up its grub to cowpokes and city slickers alike. Until the very end, its primary breakfast platter was still listed on the menu as the "Six Gun Special." But, like the other attractions and businesses in this book, it, too, eventually hitched up its cowboy britches and moseyed off into the sunset, leaving only photos and a lifetime of memories to be preserved. *Author's collection.*

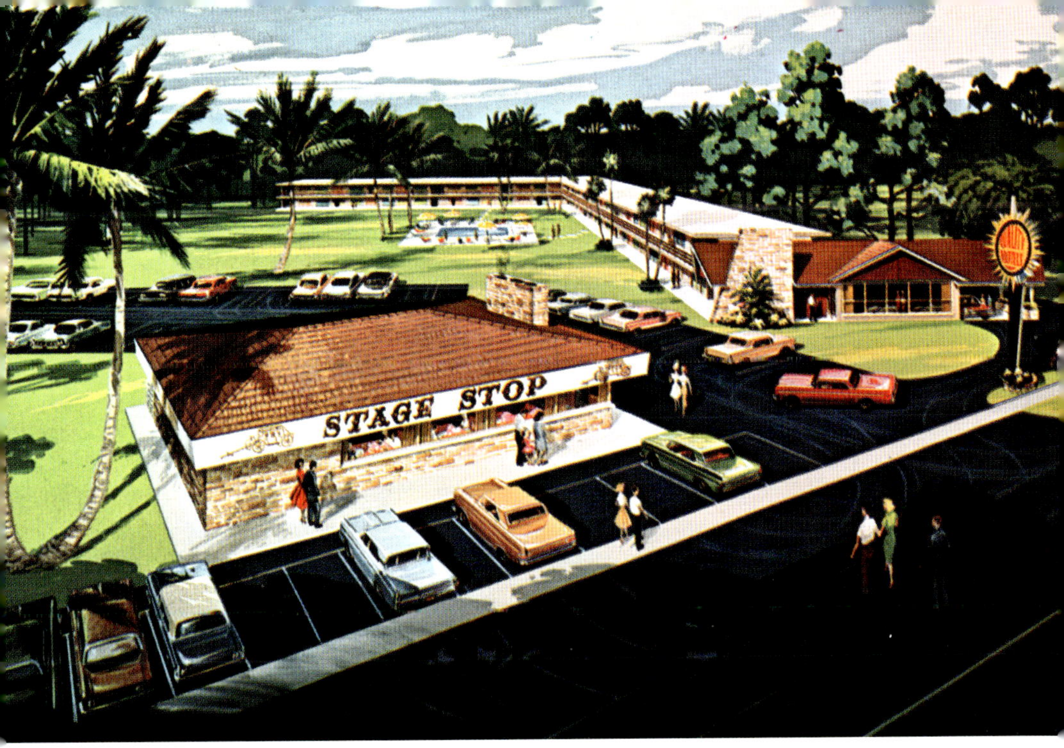
STAGE STOP

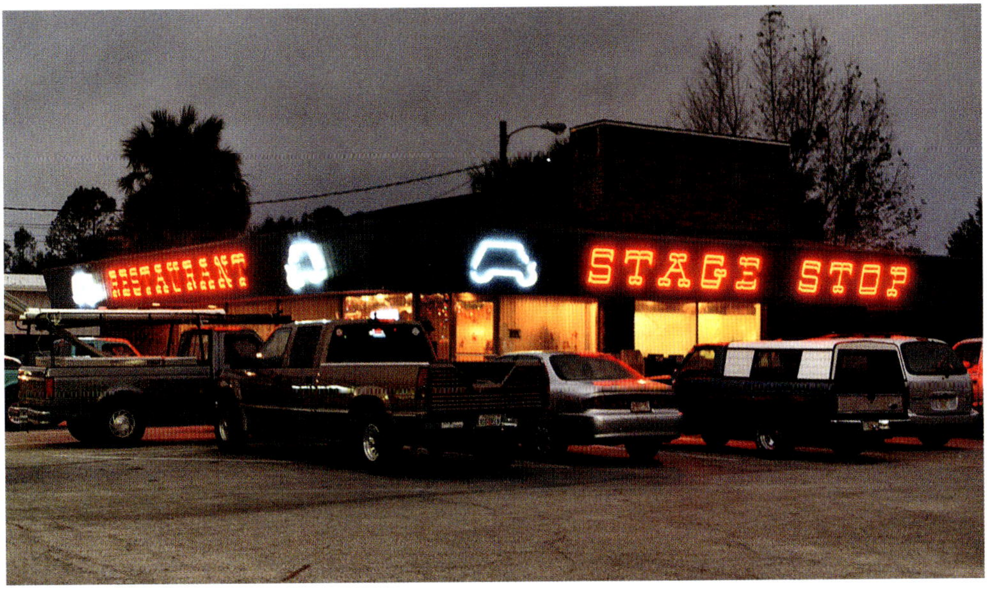
RESTAURANT
STAGE STOP

BIBLIOGRAPHY

Allen, Rick. "Remnants of Six Gun Territory Were Strewn across America." *Ocala Star-Banner*, September 8, 2015.

Belleville, Bill. "Florida's Beautiful and Exotic Springs." *Florida Trend* (July 1978).

Breslauer, Ken. *Roadside Paradise*. St. Petersburg: RetroFlorida, 2000.

Coker, William S., and Jerrell H. Shofner. *Florida from the Beginning to 1992*. Houston, TX: Pioneer Publications, 1991.

Corse, Carita Doggett. *Shrine of the Water Gods*, Silver Springs, FL: Ray and Davidson, 1947.

Dinkins, J. Lester. *Dunnellon: Boomtown of the 1890s*. St. Petersburg, FL: Great Outdoors, 1969.

Flynn, Stephen J. *Florida: Land of Fortune*. Washington, D.C.: Luce, 1962.

Genovese, Peter. *Roadside Florida: The Definitive Guide to the Kingdom of Kitsch*. Mechanicsburg, PA: Stackpole Books, 2006.

Hollis, Tim. *Dixie Before Disney: 100 Years of Roadside Fun*. Jackson: University Press of Mississippi, 1999.

———. *Glass Bottom Boats and Mermaid Tails: Florida's Tourist Springs*. Mechanicsburg, PA: Stackpole Books, 2006.

———. *Remembering Florida Springs*. Gainesville, FL: Seaside Publishing, 2016.

———. *Selling the Sunshine State: A Celebration of Florida Tourism Advertising*. Gainesville: University Press of Florida, 2008.

Martin, Richard A. *Eternal Spring*. St. Petersburg, FL: Great Outdoors, 1966.

McCarthy, Kevin, and Ernest Jernigan. *Images of America: Ocala*. Charleston, SC: Arcadia Publishing, 2001.

McDowell, Frank E., Jr. *The Story of Six Gun Territory*. Ocala, FL: Six Gun Territory, 1965.

Monroe, Gary. *Silver Springs: The Underwater Photography of Bruce Mozert*. Gainesville: University Press of Florida, 2008.

Mormino, Gary R. *Land of Sunshine, State of Dreams: A Social History of Modern Florida*. Gainesville: University Press of Florida, 2005.

O'Brien, Claudia. "The Wild, Wild West." *Ocala Style* (October 2004).

Riley, Ruth J. *Memories of Rainbow Springs*. Dunnellon, FL: Fruit Tree Press, 2000.

Rizzo, Marian. "Tourist Season." *Ocala Star-Banner*, June 18, 1999.

Roberts, Larry. *Florida's Golden Age of Souvenirs, 1890–1930*. Gainesville: University Press of Florida, 2001.

Sherer, Ed. "Plans Revealed for 'Frontier Town' Attraction on Silver Springs Blvd." *Ocala Star-Banner*, May 24, 1962.

Terrell, Bob. "R.B. Coburn: Mountaintop Disney." *Carolina Senior Citizen* (November 1991).

Vickers, Lu, and Cynthia Wilson-Graham. *Remembering Paradise Park: Tourism and Segregation at Silver Springs*. Gainesville: University Press of Florida, 2015.

ABOUT THE AUTHOR

Author Tim Hollis has written thirty previous books on pop culture history, a number of them concerning southeastern tourism. He has collected the best images from his personal archives as well as those across Florida to showcase the various attractions featured in this volume.